Records, Information and Data

Records, Information and Data

Exploring the role of record-keeping in an information culture

Geoffrey Yeo

facet
publishing

Published by Facet Publishing
7 Ridgmount Street, London WC1E 7AE
www.facetpublishing.co.uk

Facet Publishing is wholly owned by CILIP: the Library and Information Association.

British Library Cataloguing in Publication Data
A catalogue record for this book is available from the British Library.

ISBN 978-1-78330-226-0 (paperback)
ISBN 978-1-78330-227-7 (hardback)
ISBN 978-1-78330-228-4 (e-book)

First published 2018

Text printed on FSC accredited material.

Cover design by Kathryn Beecroft
Typeset from author's files in 11/14pt Palatino Linotype and Frutiger by Flagholme Publishing Services
Printed and made in Great Britain by CPI Group (UK) Ltd, Croydon, CR0 4YY.

Contents

Introduction

It is often said that we live in an information age. Our ability to deploy information creatively, we are told, makes our lives today radically different from those of our ancestors. One commentator has affirmed that we are experiencing a 'third wave' in the way that humans organise their affairs, and that new forms of society based on information are superseding the agricultural and industrial societies of the first and second waves (Toffler, 1980). Another commentator, using a different metaphor and a different approach to enumerating change, has described a 'fourth revolution' founded on information: a revolution whose achievements may alter our understandings of human existence as profoundly as the earlier 'revolutions' generated by the works of Copernicus, Darwin and Freud (Floridi, 2014). Although information was not always highly esteemed in the past, it is now widely perceived as 'the stuff of human communication', a constitutive force in society and a 'universal principle' at work in the world (Balnaves and Willson, 2011, 4–6, 31).

Claims such as these need not be accepted uncritically, but cannot be ignored; our contemporary environment is undoubtedly one in which information is accorded a leading role. In the sub-title of this book, I refer to this phenomenon as an 'information culture'. Other writers have sometimes understood 'information culture' as the range of attitudes towards information shown by the staff of a particular organization; from this perspective, 'an organization has a mature information culture when it . . . easily . . . uses information in its everyday activities' (Svärd, 2017, xi). Writers who adopt this view tend to assume that information belongs in an organizational context and that the main issue to be addressed is the extent to which an organization's employees acknowledge the value of information and the benefits of using it. This book, however, challenges some of these assumptions. It suggests that notions of information as a beneficial commodity cannot simply be taken for granted, and it places 'information culture' at societal rather than primarily organizational level, using the term in a broadly similar way to writers such as Steven Lubar (1999) and Luke Tredinnick (2008), to refer to a contemporary culture in which leading figures in governments, universities, the computer industry and the popular media promote information as a commodity of central importance.

Concepts of information, data and records

Information – and its close companion, *data* – are topics discussed in the literature of many disciplines, including business management, public policy, computing, mathematics and philosophy, as well as the discipline of information science, which has its roots in librarianship. They are also topics increasingly mentioned, although not always analysed in depth, in writings by – or intended for – records managers and archivists. In this book, I set out to investigate relationships between information and records, and to examine the place of record-making and record-keeping in today's information culture. I discuss different ways of interpreting concepts of 'records', 'information' and 'data', and ask whether the principles and practices of archives and records management can still make distinctive contributions in what is said to be a world of digital information.

In recent years, records have often been *defined* in terms of information. For example, a much-cited definition appears in the international standard for records management, where records are defined as '*information* created, received and maintained as evidence and as an asset by an organization or person, in pursuance of legal obligations or in the transaction of business' (ISO 15489-1: 2016, clause 3.14; my italics). Information, however, is not defined in this standard. Some commentators suggest that debates about 'the nature of information' have been considered tangential to record-keeping concerns (Furner and Gilliland, 2017, 589), but it seems equally likely that the authors of the international standard simply assumed that information is an unproblematic concept, needing little or no further explanation.

Certainly, when A asks B 'Can you give me any information about yesterday's meeting?', B may reply 'yes', or 'no', or 'I'm not sure; let me think . . .', but B is unlikely to say 'I do not understand what you mean by *information'*. Indeed, much the same seems to apply to 'records'; if A decides to ask 'Do you have any records of yesterday's meeting?', many responses seem possible, but it is unlikely that B will reply 'I'm sorry, I have no idea what you mean by *records'*. Not everyone is readily able to produce a definition of 'information' or 'records', but most people think they know what is meant when they hear the words used.

Nevertheless, the concept of 'information' is notoriously difficult to pin down. In the literature of information science, as we will see in later chapters, information is often defined in relation to data; it is frequently described as data that have been concentrated, organised, processed or improved. But data in their turn have often been defined as 'the raw material of information' (Brotby, 2009, 7), thus introducing a circularity that renders attempts at definition questionable, if not pointless. As I endeavour to show in this book, both 'information' and 'data' are contested terms, capable of bearing multiple meanings.

Definitions are written with the aim of reducing or eliminating ambiguity and dissent, but our understandings of concepts are rarely unambiguous and are inevitably influenced by our social and professional backgrounds and the mental baggage we carry when we look at the world. All too often, attempts at achieving consensus lead to one group of 'opinion formers' seeking to impose their view on others who do not share it. Critics have noted that definitions of records – of which there are many – are not exempt from these weaknesses (Gilliland, 2017, 53–4; Yeo, 2008, 125–6). In general, I prefer to follow the advice of philosopher John Searle, whose work we will meet again later in the book. Searle wrote that philosophers have learned:

> to be very cautious about asking questions of the form, 'What is . . .?', as in, for example, 'What is truth?', 'What is a number?', 'What is justice?' . . . The best way to approach such problems is to sneak up on them. Do not ask, 'What is truth?', but ask, 'Under what conditions do we say of a proposition that it is true?' Do not ask, 'What is a number?', but ask, 'How do numerical expressions function in actual mathematical practice?'
> (Searle, 2005, 2)

Perhaps, then, we should not ask 'what is a record?', but should ask what kinds of entities people choose to identify or recognise as records in particular contexts. Towards the end of the book, I offer what I hope is a reasonably inclusive characterisation of records, but in the opening chapters I have sought to 'sneak up on the problem' by looking at the ways in which people have viewed record-making and record-keeping, in the past as well as in our own times.

Some commentators affirm that records are ubiquitous in contemporary society; for Australian records consultant Barbara Reed (2005, 101), 'every day . . . we are enmeshed in records to the point where they become . . . a . . . background to the conduct of our lives'. For others, however, records now seem to be a disappearing species, and the future lies with information. According to Reed's Australian colleague David Moldrich, for example, records management professionals 'must . . . understand that our new mandate is to manage information processes, architecture and frameworks' (Moldrich, 2017, 12). In the USA, Kenneth Megill (2005, 62) wrote that 'the transformation of the records manager . . . to an information manager is well under way'. Even among those who maintain a more traditional view of records and archives, ideas about wider information environments are increasingly commonplace; for archival scholars Luciana Duranti and Giovanni Michetti (2017, 77), the proximity of archivists to the profession of information science demands a redefinition of the archival discipline 'to position it correctly in the broad information field'. This book seeks to analyse and reassess these views. In exploring the implications of new emphases on information for the work of archivists and records managers, it asks whether claims that they must now become information managers, or that their discipline must be reinvented for an age of information, can be justified.

Background to the book

Records, Information and Data is a much-revised and expanded version of a Jenkinson Lecture, entitled 'Records and Archives in the Age of Information', which I presented at University College London in March 2015. Later versions of several chapters have been presented at conferences and workshops at a number of other venues in Europe, Australia and South America, and the evolution of the book benefited from discussions with practitioners and scholars during and after these events. It also benefited from informal conversations and e-mail exchanges about records and information with a number of archivists and records managers, chiefly in English-speaking countries, between 2014 and 2017. Although I cannot claim to have undertaken a scientifically rigorous survey of professional opinion, these discussions and conversations provided insights on many of the topics that the book examines.

The individuals with whom I was in contact put forward a wide variety of views. Many of them welcomed attempts to open a debate on the concepts of records and information, affirming that the relationship between these concepts was a crucial issue for records managers and archivists in the 21st century. Several expressed anxiety that ideas connecting records with information had been introduced into the discourse of record-keeping without sufficient discussion or contemplation.

Others, however, felt that the matter was already settled. Some took the view that a distinction between records and information was well established: that records are fixed, while information is fluid and unstable; or that records are concerned with risk, while information is concerned with value. But some expressed contrary views, arguing that records, too, can be fluid – at least in the digital world – or that records and information can both offer value and can both be associated with risk and its management.

Consensus was also lacking among those who contended that records and information were inseparable or that their differences were less important than their similarities. Some who saw strong connections between records and information affirmed that records *contain* information. Others argued that records are a *class* of information, designated for or demanding special treatment; that 'information objects' become records when someone decides to preserve them or capture them in a record-keeping system; or that information is deemed to be a record when it is usable for evidentiary purposes. Those who put forward these views often expressed a belief that distinctions between records and information were of diminishing significance or were more apparent to custodians than to users. While assumptions about the close relationship of records and information were commonplace, opinions on the precise nature of their relationship were very varied.

The diversity of views expounded by those with whom I spoke did not surprise me; nor will it surprise others who have worked in the record-keeping field or studied its recent professional literature. Much more surprising, to me at least, was the extent to which many people thought that discussion of relations between records and information would be superfluous and that their particular view of this topic would be universally acceptable. A common reaction to my proposal for further work on this question was 'But everyone knows what the right answer is'. Despite the considerable variation in the 'answers' suggested, the conviction that a single answer is 'obvious' was widespread; many individuals voiced strong opinions about the relative standing of records and information, and on more than one occasion I was bluntly told that other views were 'outdated' or simply 'wrong'. Although the place of record-keeping in an information culture remains a contentious topic, some believe that no contention is necessary.

One of the aims of this book is to demonstrate that relationships between records and information are more complex than has often been thought. I hope that the book will be of interest to readers who see close connections between the two concepts as well as those who perceive them as largely distinct, and to readers who believe that the place of record-keeping in an information culture has largely been resolved as well as those who view it as a matter for continuing debate. *Records, Information and Data* focuses on concepts rather than methods of working, but is intended to appeal to reflective practitioners as well as students and academic scholars. Although written primarily for records managers and archivists, it may also interest information specialists in other disciplines. While its main emphasis is on records and information, it also considers understandings of data and relations between records and data – another topic, incidentally, on which opinions are both varied and strongly held.

Structure and content

The first two chapters of the book explore the concept of 'records' and set today's record-keeping ideas and practices in a historical context. In Chapter 1, I consider how record-making and record-keeping practices originated, how they have developed and how people have understood needs for, and uses of, records in the past. This chapter does not attempt to offer a complete history of the records discipline (which would be impossible in a few short pages), but centres on aspects of relevance to the questions raised in later chapters; it also examines distinctions, real or supposed, between records and 'archives' and between the work of records managers and archivists. In Chapter 2, I consider how traditional ways of understanding records and archives have been, and might continue to be, challenged and adapted in the context of the transition to a more fluid digital environment. I also review the four 'archival paradigms' proposed by Canadian archivist Terry Cook, and suggest that 'information' could, and perhaps should, be seen as a fifth paradigm.

Chapters 3 and 4 look in more depth at information and its increasing prominence in contemporary thinking and practice. In Chapter 3, I examine the information culture of the late 20th and 21st centuries and how records managers and archivists have responded to it. I discuss changing perceptions of records management and archival work, including notions of information governance and disciplinary convergence. In Chapter 4, starting with Peter Morville's dictum that 'when we try to define information, we become lost in a hall of mirrors', I consider different understandings of the concept of 'information' and their applicability to the field of archives and records management.

Chapter 5 looks at the world of data science and data administration, and asks whether and how far recent work in this area can enhance our knowledge of how records and archives function. It investigates a range of seemingly conflicting views about the character of data, about relationships between data and information and about their supposed connection with truth and matters of fact.

Chapter 6 puts forward what are probably the densest arguments in the book. In this chapter, I suggest that concepts derived from information science and data science are not sufficient for understanding record-making and record-keeping. Building on work I have published previously, I discuss the concept of representation and use ideas from speech act philosophy to argue that records are not merely a variety of information, or a container of information, but have distinct roles in the performance of action and the construction of our social world. Records can be seen as a source of information, but they offer many other affordances to those who create and use them.

In contemporary records management literature, even when

distinctions are drawn between records and information, records management is often presented as a subset or component of information management (Kahn and Blair, 2009, 23; McLeod and Hare, 2006, 11). In Chapter 7, I investigate conceptions and practices of information management and ask how they relate to record-keeping concerns. I affirm that the making and keeping of records cannot simply be subsumed into information management; there are many points of contact between the work of records managers and archivists and that of information managers, but there are also crucial differences, which oblige records managers and archivists to maintain their distinctive priorities.

The final chapter offers a brief examination of some of the practical implications of the ideas put forward in the book. What issues can records managers and archivists be expected to face, today and in the future, in working in a world of digital profusion, where information – rather than records – is placed at the centre of business practice and societal concern?

The topics addressed in this book are multifaceted, and discussion of them necessarily involves a discussion of other concepts often associated with records or information, including evidence, accountability, knowledge and memory. It also requires consideration of the qualities that can be demanded of records, such as authenticity and integrity. In the chapters that follow, some of these concepts and qualities are examined at greater length than others, but every one of them would ideally have merited fuller treatment than I have been able to provide in a book of this size. However, the book supplies plentiful references to other relevant literature, which I hope will allow and encourage readers interested in these subjects to investigate them more thoroughly. There is ample scope for further research into many of the questions this book explores.

Acknowledgements

While very many people have contributed, directly or indirectly, to the genesis of this book, I am particularly grateful to Terry Eastwood, Eric Ketelaar, Vicki Lemieux, James Lowry, John McDonald, Julie McLeod, Laura Millar, Rod Stone, David Thomas, Anne Thurston and Geir Magnus Walderhaug, all of whom have offered helpful suggestions, stimulating ideas or judicious messages of encouragement. Some of them have also generously found time to read and comment on drafts of my text. They do not all agree with the book's more radical arguments, but they have all made invaluable contributions to its development. Responsibility for any remaining errors, of course, is entirely mine.

References

Balnaves, M. and Willson, M. (2011) *A New Theory of Information & the Internet*, Peter Lang.

Brotby, K. (2009) *Information Security Governance*, John Wiley & Sons.

Duranti, L. and Michetti, G. (2017) The Archival Method. In Gilliland, A. J., McKemmish, S. and Lau, A. J. (eds), *Research in the Archival Multiverse*, Monash University.

Floridi, L. (2014) *The Fourth Revolution: how the infosphere is reshaping human reality*, Oxford University Press.

Furner, J. and Gilliland, A. J. (2017) Archival IR: applying and adapting information retrieval approaches in archives and recordkeeping research. In Gilliland, A. J., McKemmish, S. and Lau, A. J. (eds), *Research in the Archival Multiverse*, Monash University.

Gilliland, A. J. (2017) Archival and Recordkeeping Traditions in the Multiverse and Their Importance for Researching Situations and Situating Research. In Gilliland, A. J., McKemmish, S. and Lau, A. J. (eds), *Research in the Archival Multiverse*, Monash University.

ISO 15489-1: 2016, *Information and Documentation – Records Management. Part 1: concepts and principles*, International Organization for Standardization.

Kahn, R. A. and Blair, B. T. (2009) *Information Nation: seven keys to information management compliance*, 2nd edn, Wiley Publishing.

Lubar, S. (1999) Information Culture and the Archival Record, *American Archivist*, **62** (1), 10–22.

McLeod, J. and Hare, C. (2006) *How to Manage Records in the e-Environment*, Routledge.

Megill, K. A. (2005) *Corporate Memory: records and information management in the knowledge age*, K. G. Saur.

Moldrich, D. (2017) Records Management and the Governance of Things, *IRMS Bulletin*, **199**, 10–12.

Reed, B. (2005) Records. In McKemmish, S., Piggott, M., Reed, B. and

Upward, F. (eds), *Archives: recordkeeping in society*, Charles Sturt University.

Searle, J. R. (2005) What Is an Institution? *Journal of Institutional Economics*, **1** (1), 1–22.

Svärd, P. (2017) *Enterprise Content Management, Records Management and Information Culture Amidst e-Government Development*, Chandos.

Toffler, A. (1980) *The Third Wave*, William Morrow.

Tredinnick, L. (2008) *Digital Information Culture: the individual and society in the digital age*, Chandos.

Yeo, G. (2008) Concepts of Record (2): prototypes and boundary objects, *American Archivist*, **71** (1), 118–43.

CHAPTER 1

The making and keeping of records: a brief historical overview

Written down so as not to forget.

> Mesopotamian clay tablet, about 3200 years ago (Postgate, 2013, 198)

Things that we are unable to hold in our weak and fragile memories are conserved by writing.

> Burgundian charter, about 850 years ago (Fentress and Wickham, 1992, 8)

'I shall never, never forget!' [said the White King]. 'You will, though,' the Queen said, 'if you don't make a memorandum of it'.

> *Through the Looking Glass, and What Alice Found There* (Carroll, 1872)

Introduction

The making and keeping of records appear to be among the oldest human activities. As far as we can tell, they are distinctively *human* activities; no other species has developed them in the same way. As well as being dependent on changing technologies, they are deeply entwined in social conventions and have been undertaken very differently at different times and in different places. Records have often been associated with literacy and the use of written texts, but the first records were undoubtedly made long before writing was invented. As record-making and record-keeping practices matured, they came to underpin governments, institutions and commercial businesses in formal public realms; they have sometimes – although not always – been less responsive to the needs of individuals, informal communities or minority groups. This chapter looks at some of the key aspects of their historical development. It aims to set a context for the record-making and record-keeping practices of our own era, by examining some of the ways in which records have been perceived, used, valued and protected in the past.

Record-making and record-keeping over 10,000 years

In today's western societies, we can use an extensive range of tools and artefacts to assist us when we need to recall what was said or done at earlier moments. We often take such tools for granted, but we also know that people in earlier eras were not always able to call on them. In prehistoric times, spoken language enabled our distant ancestors to communicate and share memories with others, but the long-term survival of memories must have depended on mental recollection and perhaps on ceremonies, recitations or rituals that may have helped to protect them from oblivion. With the passage of time, however, our ancestors also began to use tangible material aids to supplement mental recollection of the actions they performed and the world in which they performed them. Although it is often claimed that oral cultures support individual memories or communal memory systems – *milieux de mémoire*, or environments of memory, as French historian Pierre Nora (1989, 7) called them – more powerful than those in contemporary western societies, there are always limits to what any individual or group of individuals can expect to remember, and it seems almost certain that for more than 10,000 years people have employed material aids alongside older oral methods to help them retain and share their memories.

The first such aids were probably marks on rock surfaces, bones or wooden sticks, or piles of pebbles used in counting. At an early stage in their use, people will have become aware that an elementary counting mechanism can also provide a trace of the completed count. If I have forgotten the total, I can revisit the pile of pebbles or the marks on the stick to see how many sacks of grain I had, or how many sheep I surrendered to the person who demanded them. Moreover, if I need evidence in a dispute, I can point to the marks or the pile of pebbles and say: 'this is how many marks I made, or how many pebbles I counted'. In societies that have developed methods of arbitration, an arbitrator or judge can say: 'this is the number of marks X made, which provides evidence of the number of sheep that X handed over to Y'. Importantly, too, a judge may be able to identify the marks as evidence even if X and Y are unable to testify in person. The pile of pebbles or the set of marks on the stick constitutes a record, albeit a record that seems very rudimentary to modern eyes.

The use of natural objects as counting tools and as records was commonplace in many parts of the world until recent times. Basic record-keeping using pebbles, shells or pieces of wood has been observed in Africa and Asia (Herskovits, 1932; Lagercrantz, 1968, 123–4; Oppenheim, 1959, 123). The use of tallies (marks or notches made on an object) to record quantities counted is widely attested in Europe, Africa, the Pacific region and elsewhere, and notched bones over 10,000 years old found in various parts of the world are thought to have been used as tallying devices in much the same way (Chrisomalis, 2009, 60; Lagercrantz, 1973; Menninger, 1969, 226–40). Quantitative records have also been kept in non-literate societies by tying knots in stalks of grass or in cords or strings, and knot records were extensively used in Africa, North and South America and south-east Asia (Birket-Smith, 1966–7; Lagercrantz, 1968). Two and a half millennia ago, there was already a tradition in China that knotted cords had been employed in the past 'for the administration of affairs', and the making of knot records is believed to be considerably older than this (Jacobsen, 1983, 57–8).

These simple techniques can be effective when records are kept for short periods of time and when records are used only by their makers or by people who know the circumstances of their making. But records of this kind do not easily retain meaning over longer periods; sooner or later, questions arise as to what the marks or notches were meant to signify. The invention of writing, in Mesopotamia and Egypt about 5000 years ago, opened the way to more sophisticated methods of recording and allowed records to be read and interpreted with much greater confidence. At a functional level, however, the earliest written records were made for much the same purposes as their unwritten predecessors. They served to account for the administration of resources (chiefly crops, animals and animal products) in a redistributive economy (Englund, 1998, 26–7). Writing removed much of the ambiguity inherent in the older systems – it allowed the maker of the record to specify whether the counted goods were sheep or sacks of grain, who gave what to whom and in what circumstances – but the reasons for making and keeping records do not seem to have changed very greatly: records were intended to help circumvent human forgetfulness or absence and perhaps to supply verification if disputes arose about what had happened in the past. In societies that became increasingly bureaucratic, they also enabled officials to monitor and assess the work of their subordinates (Hudson and Wunsch, 2004, 19, 180; Nissen, Damerow and Englund, 1993, 6).

As writing became more widespread, human ingenuity devised a wider range of record types. First, record-keeping expanded beyond accounting and administration into the sphere of what jurists see as legal acts, particularly the recording of conveyances of property. About 400 years after the earliest written accounting records, wealthy private individuals in Mesopotamia and Egypt adopted writing to make records of land purchases and sales and began to preserve these records as a means of supporting claims to ownership (Gelb, Steinkeller and Whiting, 1991). Writing systems also opened up new possibilities for sending messages by methods other than word of mouth. Letter-writing began shortly after the appearance of the first records of property transactions, and it was soon discovered that a written letter could serve a dual purpose, preserving a message across time as well as communicating it across space. Some early letter writers asked recipients to keep letters; even if a writer did not suggest it, a recipient could choose to retain a letter, and many did so. In Mesopotamian temples and palaces and in the private houses of the rich, rooms were set aside for record-keeping, and letters were often stored alongside other records (Benati and Lecompte, 2016, 24; Eidem, 2011, 13; Tanret, 2011, 271). Other types of record that came into use at this period included labour duty rosters, debt notes, wills, marriage settlements and records of lawsuits. Over time, the practice of keeping written records was adopted by other individuals besides the wealthy and the governing elite (Larsen, 1989, 139; Postgate, 2013, 61–3), although record-making and record-keeping in ancient societies almost certainly never reached the very poorest.

From Mesopotamia and Egypt, the use of written records spread to other parts of the Near East and the eastern Mediterranean. In Greece, about 4000 years ago, the people of Minoan Crete began to adopt Mesopotamian-style recording practices (Schoep, 1999), and a little later written record-keeping reached the Hittite empire in what is now Turkey, where Mesopotamian influence was even more apparent (Charpin, 2010, 69; Van Den Hout, 2011). Elsewhere, the use of records developed largely or wholly independently. In China, there is little sign of outside influence on early written record-keeping, although the surviving evidence is very scanty (Boltz, 2000–1). In central and south America before the 16th-century Spanish conquest, record-keeping techniques owed nothing to the prior developments in Mesopotamia, Egypt, China and Europe, yet attained a level of considerable sophistication (Boone and Urton, 2011).

In Inka Peru, records were kept using knotted cords joined in complex branchlike patterns. These records were known as *khipu* (or, in Spanish, *quipu*). Each *khipu* had numerous pendant cords of cotton or wool attached to a primary cord, which could be several metres long (Chrisomalis, 2010, 310; Urton, 2010, 55). The system is no longer fully understood, but is known to have used various kinds of knot, the location of the knots on the cords and the colour and material construction of the cords to indicate different aspects of the matters recorded. Some *khipu* may have served as 'cues' or prompts – points of departure for oral recitations of narrative traditions about Inka royal history – but most had the rather different function of recording the presence or movement of specific quantities of goods, people or livestock. Numbers were encoded in the knots, and other features of the *khipu* supplied 'non-numerical qualifiers that provided context for . . . the numbers' (Topic, 2016, 135). *Khipu* recorded population censuses and assessments of tribute, and were also used to control herds of llama and alpaca and to account for goods entering or leaving storehouses (Urton, 2010; Urton and Brezine, 2011, 344). *Khipu* were much more intricate than the knot records used in other parts of the world; Europeans who encountered them in 16th-century Peru were often surprised – and impressed – by their detailed and wide-ranging recording capabilities and the effectiveness of the protection they offered against fraud.

Different media were used for record-making at different times and on different occasions. In China, the earliest surviving written records are inscribed on ox bones or turtle shells, but there were – or are thought to have been – other early records written on more perishable materials such as bamboo. In Mesopotamia and Egypt, various media – including wooden boards and broken pieces of pottery – were used for making records, but in each society one medium predominated: tablets of clay dried in the sun in Mesopotamia and papyrus in Egypt. The remarkable durability of clay has allowed large numbers of Mesopotamian clay tablet records to survive to the present day. Wood and papyrus were also used for record-making in Greece, and later in Rome. Although few records written on wood have survived from ancient times, the use of wood for creating records is known to have been widespread in the Roman empire; besides plain wooden boards, the Romans used larger tablets of wood with a wax writing surface, particularly for records of a more formal nature.

In the literature of archival studies, record-keeping in the Roman world is often presented mainly in terms of the measures that were taken to safeguard records of legal significance and those of the imperial government. The fortuitous survival of large parts of the *Tabularium*, the central repository where the records of the Roman Senate and state officials were kept, and the reliance placed on Roman law codes by medieval and later jurists, have lent support to this picture of Roman record-keeping (Duranti, 1996; Lodolini, 2013, 53–7). The corpus of legal writings commissioned and promulgated by the 6th-century emperor Justinian includes a number of affirmations of the role of records as legal evidence or proof, which later jurists and diplomatists in Italy and elsewhere adopted as the basis for their view that the essence of a record is to be found in its legal standing; scholars sympathetic to this view have often tended to assume that the Romans also perceived records primarily in legal terms and have sometimes projected this view back to the earliest years of the Roman state. Particularly in the later years of their empire, the Romans often gave weight to records in legal disputes and stressed the importance of secure archival custody, but a legalistic view of Roman record-keeping does not tell the whole story. Records in Roman times were widely used for a variety of non-legal and private purposes. Affluent families kept household account books (Wolf, 2004, 87), merchants and bankers kept records of their business (Horsfall, 1991, 68; Wolf, 2015, 68–71) and courts of law recorded their administrative procedures as well as legal judgements (Meyer, 2015, 92–3). Record-making proliferated in the Roman army. Although few records of the army (indeed, few records of any institution of ancient Rome) remain in existence today, enough survive to enable scholars to make a rough calculation of the total numbers of records that the Roman army must have created; taking soldiers' pay records alone, it has been estimated that at least 225 million such records were produced over a 300-year period (Fink, 1971, 242). The functioning of the machinery of empire depended on records, and the Romans made and kept them in quantities unparalleled until modern times.

In the centuries following the end of the Roman empire, literacy levels fell and administrative record-keeping declined. In the early Middle Ages, while vestiges of Roman custom survived, the use of writing to create records became something of a rarity in most of the lands within the former Roman sphere of influence. Written accounting records persisted in the Islamic territories of the Near East (Zaid, 2004), but in England, and almost certainly in many other parts of Europe, the use of writing in connection with accounting disappeared, and accounting records reverted to wooden tally sticks (Jones, 2009, 273–4); the making of written records became largely restricted to grants of legal rights, privileges or properties at the upper levels of society. Kings and potentates issued charters, which typically recorded that they had transferred the ownership of a property to another party, but most people and most aspects of life were largely untouched by formal records. Even in the Frankish kingdoms of west-central Europe, where the making of records was apparently more widespread than in England, most written records related in one way or another to property ownership; other types of record seem to have been relatively rare (Geary, 1999; McKitterick, 1989; Rio, 2009). Issuances of charters were often occasions for high ceremonial, with the charter being read aloud before a large audience or placed on the altar of a church in an elaborate liturgical setting.

Later in the Middle Ages, as acceptance of written documentation revived in England and elsewhere, larger numbers of records were made. Surveys (including the remarkable 11th-century national survey of England known as Domesday Book) recorded holdings, extents and values of lands. Written accounting records reappeared in many parts of Europe from the 12th century onwards (Arlinghaus, 2006; Jones, 2009). In England, written records of pleas made in the central courts of law were first kept in 1194, and enrolled copies of royal charters began to be kept in 1199 or a little earlier; by the 1220s, some English bishops had started keeping registers of their official acts (Baker, 1989,

15–16; Clanchy, 2013, 70–7, 98–9; Vincent, 2009, xvi–xviii, 1–4). Medieval royal governments, ecclesiastical institutions and (sometimes) individuals preserved records to safeguard their interests and protect their entitlements.

The word 'record' is derived from Latin *recordari* (to remember). Its English usage has its origins in the common law of medieval England, where 'record' was originally a formal oral recollection of judicial business. When oral methods of recalling proceedings in courts of law were superseded by writing, the term 'record' was applied to their written successors. By the 17th century, it had come to be used more broadly to refer to the writings of English church and state institutions. More recently, it has been generally acknowledged that concepts of record-making and record-keeping are not confined to institutional writings, but extend to all the artefacts that bear relations to human activities and events in the ways described in this chapter.

In ancient Mesopotamia, the artefacts that we now call 'records' were usually known simply as 'tablets'. Later societies employed a variety of terms, including 'instruments', 'parchments', 'documents', 'evidences' and 'muniments', but over time most of these became obsolete. By the beginning of the 20th century, in Great Britain, 'records' had become the most usual term. Today, the word 'record' remains characteristic of English-language discourse and of countries whose legal and administrative systems have English origins, but it has increasingly been recognised and adopted in other parts of the world.

Records, memory and evidence

Perceived needs for memory and evidence long remained at the forefront of record-keeping concerns. In the Roman era, jurists spoke of written records that functioned as *perpetua memoria* or *testimonium publicum*; the 2nd-century lawyer Gaius observed that the use of writing allowed easier proof of transactions (Brendecke, 2010, 279; Duranti, 1997, 1; Salazar Revuelta, 1998, 516). A millennium later, a similar perspective was apparent in the medieval English legal textbook attributed to Henry de Bracton, which noted that a record of a gift of land or other rights may be made in the form of a charter 'for perpetual remembrance, because the life of man is but brief, and in order that the gift may be more easily proved' (Thorne, 1968, 108). In an age of faith, some saw the evidential role of records in more emotional terms; the writers of an 11th-century charter affirmed that it was common practice to make records of gifts to churches, because committing them to writing 'is the strongest rampart against the cruel lances of madmen and . . . to keep the folly of pseudo-Christians from plundering what true Christians have given to God' (Morelle, 2000, 199).

Public acceptance of the evidential value of written records was doubtless gradual (Clanchy, 1980–1, 118–19), but awareness of their evidential potential was not restricted to legal contexts or property transactions. In 12th-century England, royal accountants were able to use records as evidence of the sums of money that were due to the king (Vincent, 2004, 23–5). In France in the later Middle Ages, heads of monasteries auditing revenue collection employed surveys and financial records to hold their agents accountable for the actions they had taken (Berkhofer, 2004, 147–53). In 15th-century Italy, Cosimo de' Medici maintained control over the numerous distant branches of his Florentine banking business by insisting that each branch should send its records to Florence every year for his inspection (Soll, 2014, 37–8).

In legal circles, there was ongoing debate about whether records or human witnesses should prevail in the resolution of disputes. In the 4th century, the Roman emperor Constantine had proclaimed that written records should have the same evidential weight as witnesses (Schwind, 1950, 134), but many medieval lawyers believed that greater credence should be given to witness testimony, a view that was endorsed by Pope Innocent III at the beginning of the 13th century (Bedos-Rezak, 2003, 153). In practice, however, human witnesses – then, as now – were liable to forget what they had witnessed, to die or simply to be untraceable when they were wanted, and in these circumstances records usually had the field to themselves. In early medieval Italy, written records were often employed as evidence in legal cases and sometimes proved decisive in determining the outcome; if witnesses, or the scribe or notary who had drafted a record, could be found they would be called on to testify to the record's validity, but if they were unavailable the courts could accept a record on its own merits (Wickham, 1986, 114–15). Doubtless, records could also fulfil a memorial role, by reminding witnesses of the details of what they had seen or heard in the past. The existence of formularies – texts that provided models for drafters of records to follow – in the Middle Ages suggests the importance that was attached to the 'correct' wording of records that might need to be used in legal disputes; in France, and almost certainly elsewhere, legal cases could be lost if records were incorrectly formulated (Davies and Fouracre, 1986, 212).

Of course, notions of evidence and memory look to the passage of time; records were, and are, valued because of their ability to reinforce knowledge of the past and to help people view events from a retrospective standpoint. But besides their roles in supplying evidence or underwriting memory of the past, records also play active roles at the moment of their creation. Very often, in creating a record, people make a statement or narrate a story about the world and about how they believe things are, were or will be. On other occasions, people create records in order to perform or participate in transactions, or to generate or assign rights and responsibilities. The discovery that written records could be used to transact business and to generate rights, duties, commitments and agreements was perhaps first made in the ancient world and was given renewed vitality in later times (MacNeil, 2006; Tiersma, 2008).

Records also continue to function in practical ways after – sometimes long after – their creation. Just as enactments of the law are often regarded as 'always speaking' (Crabbe, 1994, 213), records can continue to speak over extended periods of time. Statements may be made and stories told by creating records at a particular moment, but the records can enable the voices of their creators to be heard by many audiences on many occasions. Another sense in which records continue to speak is in communicating and sustaining the rights and responsibilities that they generate. Agreements and transfers of rights are made at fleeting moments, but they can remain in force for many years, and records may attest to their continuing existence. In Britain and elsewhere, long-established institutions often operate under the terms of charters or ordinances issued many centuries ago. Almost all institutions and individuals are subject to contracts or commitments that they have made at various times in the past. Records serve institutions and individuals alike, by enabling rights and liabilities to be enforced and their extent and duration to be acknowledged.

Alongside their practical functions, records sometimes fulfil largely symbolic roles. Ironically, perhaps, their symbolic aspect may be illustrated most vividly by episodes in history when records have been publicly destroyed. In ancient Greece, when the Spartan king Agis IV announced a cancellation of debts, he publicly burnt the writings in which the debts had been recorded. Records were also openly destroyed in connection with debt cancellations by several Roman emperors, who recognised the public-relations value of a spectacular elimination of the records that symbolised the debts with which their peoples had been burdened (Cartledge, 2009, 116–17; Harris, 1989, 211). On other occasions, records that were believed to embody taxes or obligations were burnt by rebels during popular uprisings. Insurgents burnt records in Jerusalem under the Roman emperor Nero, in Constantinople in 532 and in England during the so-called 'Peasants' Revolt' against King Richard II in 1381 (Adler, 2012, 922; Mauntel, 2015, 96–101; Sarris, 2013, 19). In each case, we may infer that the rebels barely saw the records in legal or evidential terms; they were seen as symbols of hated obligations, debts or taxes that a rebellion might shake off, and their burning symbolised the new freedoms that the rebels sought to embrace.

Repositories and their curators

More generally, of course, the challenges that people have faced over the centuries have been in preserving records rather than seeking to destroy them. Since ancient times, it has often been felt advantageous to store records in dedicated repositories, where records could be protected against intrusion, loss or uncontrolled destruction, and where – ideally – they could be organised in ways that facilitated retrieving them when they were wanted. The repositories of ancient Greece and Rome were known by a variety of labels, including *chreophylakia, grammato-phylakia* and *archeia* in Greek, and *archiva* in Latin; the last of these has given us the English word 'archives' and its equivalents (*archief, archivo,* etc.) in other European languages. After the end of the Roman empire, the archival repositories of the ancient world ceased to function, and the lack of stable centres of government meant that, in most of Europe, only churches and monasteries could offer secure storage for the smaller numbers of written records that were then being made. But as records again began to proliferate in the later Middle Ages, many new archives were established. In Italy, jurists emphasised the inviolability of archives and affirmed that records preserved in them could be endowed with a privileged evidential status (Lodolini, 2013, 54–7, 103–4). The term 'archives' was often formally confined to official repositories or those that held records in support of legal rights and entitlements.

Until relatively recent times, in most European countries – and in other parts of the world to which European practices were exported – archival repositories were not centralised. Each town, guild, bishopric or landed estate kept its own records. Even at governmental level, provision was fragmented; typically, each agency of government made its own arrangements for record-keeping. Storage needs increased as records again came to be widely used for administrative as well as legal purposes. In France, in 1770, there were said to be more than 5000 separate *dépôts d'archives* (Duchein, 1993, 33; Panitch, 1996, 38). But in Spain a central repository, the *Archivo de Simancas* near Valladolid, was created in the 16th century; following royal orders of 1567 and 1568, all the records of the courts, councils and other agencies of the Castilian monarchy were concentrated there (Bautier, 1968, 141–2; Martínez García, 1999, 82–93).

In all these archives, records were kept for the use of the authorities that created them, not for the public at large or for purposes of scholarship or research. Insofar as there was public demand for access to archives, most of it was driven by needs or desires to find records that would offer support in legal quarrels. Despite a growing awareness that records had potential value for historical study, this was not an acknowledged motive for their preservation. Indeed, many archives were largely or wholly inaccessible to outsiders. The French historiographer Estienne Médicis, who died in 1565, complained of more than a dozen civil and ecclesiastical archives to which he had been refused entry (Reinburg, 2016, 177). In the 1580s, the official duties of the guardian of the *Archivo de Simancas* had included the writing of a work of history, but none of the holdings of the archive were formally opened to the public until 1844 (Martínez García, 1999, 78, 113). Even in the 16th and 17th centuries, antiquarians and historians were sometimes able to gain entrance to archives; Italian archives often allowed access for historical as well as legal purposes, and a register of 'students' visiting an archive in the late 16th century survives at Siena (Casanova, 1928, 356; Lodolini, 2013, 100–1). In England, many government records could be made available to scholars who were sufficiently tenacious, and even Domesday Book could be consulted for antiquarian purposes, although only after the researcher had obtained a formal introduction to its custodians (Hallam, 1986, 114–15). However, high fees for access or copying were commonplace; in the 16th century, copies from Domesday Book were charged at the then exorbitant rate of fourpence per line. Elsewhere, access was often granted only with extreme reluctance or refused altogether, a state of affairs that frequently continued into the 19th century. In 1803, J. P. Malcolm was the first scholar since the late 1600s to be allowed to consult the records of St Paul's Cathedral, London, but he found that 'through the exceeding care of the clerks to whom the records of St Paul's are entrusted, and their dread of trouble' he was denied sight of many of the items he had hoped to examine (Yeo, 1986, 40). In most countries, access to records was always a privilege, never a right.

Change, however, was in the air. The establishment of the *Archives Nationales* in Paris, at the start of the French Revolution in 1789, is generally thought to mark the beginning of a new era in the history of record-keeping. It rapidly became a central repository for the records of government, and in 1794 its holdings were declared open to all French citizens (Posner, 1940, 161–2). Later scholars have sometimes debated how far these developments were truly innovative (Ketelaar, 2007, 352), but they undoubtedly formed a significant landmark. Over the next 200 years, this model was followed by other nation states, and public-facing archival institutions were founded by national and local authorities in countries around the world. As a former employee of the *Archives Nationales* noted, although records of recent date often remained inaccessible to the public 'the notion that research in archives was a civic right was increasingly recognized' (Duchein, 1992, 17).

In Britain, the Public Record Office was established following an Act of Parliament in 1838, to accommodate and provide access to legal and court records; a central repository was built in the 1850s and its remit was extended to administrative records from government departments (Hallam and Roper, 1978, 78–9). The name 'Record Office' was chosen in line with British tradition, but in most other countries the new institutions were known as 'Archives'.[1] The use of the word 'archive' or 'archives' to refer to repositories was long-established in many countries, but increasingly the holdings of repositories or institutions also came to be labelled as 'archives'. In an unfortunate terminological confusion, archives were seen as places that preserve and give access to archives. In Britain, and sometimes in other parts of the world, the words 'records' and 'archives' came to be considered synonymous (Jenkinson, 1948, 2).

The growth of archival institutions was paralleled by the growth of an incipient archival profession. In the early 19th century, schools for the training and education of archivists were opened in Italy, Germany and France, and the graduates of these schools often sought employment in the new archival institutions. There had been archivists almost as long as there had been records, but their work had usually been perceived as administrative, and often as mundane; however, the new archivists generally perceived themselves as scholars, not as administrators, and 19th-century archival education focused on the study of legal and institutional history and on the sciences of palaeography and diplomatic, with particular emphasis on the records that had survived from the medieval period. The institutions where the new archivists worked, such as the French *Archives Nationales*, had often been established by political leaders who saw access to records as a means for citizens to corroborate their legal rights, but public use of these institutions during the course of the 19th century was increasingly associated with historical research. In the late 20th century, these changes were succinctly described by British/Canadian archivist Hugh Taylor:

> The creation of the *Archives Nationales* sundered the ancient records
> from their roots, placed them in common archives, and, in effect,
> labelled them 'historical'. The modern archivist was born and the
> historical archives emerged, essentially as a repository of raw material
> for the historian. . . . Across Europe, . . . the old record keepers were
> caught up in a vast 'historical shunt' during which the best curatorial
> minds and intellects were devoted to scholarship and the historian.
>
> (Taylor, 1984, 26–7)

Taylor's choice of the word 'shunt', with its apparent connotations of side-lining or relegating record-keeping to a marginal status, has sometimes been criticised, but the account that he provided seems generally correct. If archivists in the late 19th and early 20th centuries were not historians, they were almost always closer in temperament to a historian than to the relatively unskilled practitioners who had preceded them or to the cadres of officials who had come to form the staff of government departments. Record-keeping had become detached from record-making, and archivists had little or no contact with the administrative processes in which records were employed. Archival institutions largely supplied a resting place for records whose operational use was thought to be at an end, and offered a service that was increasingly directed to scholars and members of the public who sought to use the records for historical research.

When other organizations such as universities – and, in the 20th century, a small number of commercial companies – began to establish dedicated archival services of their own, these services almost always had broadly cultural, scholarly or historical objectives. Although archival institutions were traditionally associated with records of governments and organizations, many archivists began to take an interest in the records and papers of individuals and families (previously considered largely as the domain of scholarly libraries) and of less formal social groups. During the course of the 20th century, the range of archival institutions expanded to encompass those that seek to collect and acquire records from a variety of persons, organizations and informal communities, as well as those whose remit is only to maintain and make available the historic records of their parent body.

Today, it is open to question whether archival work has been fully professionalised, but archivists have moved far in this direction. The archival discipline now has a growing professional literature that addresses matters of theory as well as practice. This literature is generally said to have begun in the closing years of the 19th century, when three Dutch archivists (Muller, Feith and Fruin, 1898) published a *Manual for the Arrangement and Description of Archives*; their seminal work was followed at first by a trickle and later by a torrent of writing, now including several scholarly journals as well as less formal publication media in print and online. In the late 20th and early 21st centuries, the discipline has acquired its own professional associations, standards and codes of ethics. Archivists now generally aspire to managerial competence and a sensitivity to the needs of a wider society, as well as an appropriate level of scholarly and historical knowledge. As we will see in the concluding part of this chapter, assumptions that the role of archivists and archival institutions is primarily cultural have been challenged in recent years, but they have rarely been displaced. Archival institutions now exist in almost every country around the world, and many – perhaps most – remain historically focused; a professional archivist is usually considered to be an individual whose work centres on preserving records for cultural use.

Archivists and the emergence of records management

Especially in the early days of the archival institutions established in Europe after the French Revolution, archivists' historical interests often led them to assign particular importance to the oldest records in their care. Throughout the 19th century, archival institutions tended to give priority to the curation of government records that had survived from the medieval period; they devoted few of their resources to records from later periods of history, and generally showed even less concern for the handling of the most recent records, which remained in the custody of the officials who had created them. In Britain, as a former head of the Public Record Office observed, the research value of the earlier materials was evident, but 'it was still not clear what part modern records might play in serious academic inquiry' (Martin, 1990, 45). The records of commercial organizations were thought to be a private matter of no relevance to an outsider; in the 19th century, their potential use for scholarly research was barely recognised and they remained outside the remit of any archival institution. In commercial and governmental organizations alike, day-to-day control of operational records was largely left in the hands of junior managers and clerical staff, whose work was guided chiefly by tradition and by the organization's own notions of administrative convenience, augmented from about 1900 by advice proffered by vendors of filing equipment and authors of elementary textbooks on filing procedures.

Within governments, records that appeared to be of little further administrative use were sometimes transferred to an archival institution, but such transfers were rarely made on a regular basis, and 19th-century archival institutions generally paid less attention to the arrival of new materials from government departments than to the conservation and description of their existing holdings. However, the renewed growth of record-making in the later 19th century and a further expansion in the quantities of records in the early 20th century encouraged some archivists to turn their attention to the transfer of records from government departments, and to see the systematisation of transfer procedures as part of the mission of an archival institution. During the 20th century, the growing bulk of records led most archivists to reject notions that every organizational record could be preserved indefinitely, and archivists began to look for appraisal criteria that could be used to select records of particular merit for transfer to – and long-term preservation in – archival institutions.

American practitioners in the middle years of the 20th century developed and modelled ideas about a 'life-cycle' of records. A widely used version of the records life-cycle model (Norton, 1975, 18; Pérotin, 1966) suggested that records move through three phases: a 'current' or 'active' phase, when they are in frequent use in a business context, followed by a 'semi-current' or 'semi-active' phase, when they are less often required for business purposes, and a 'non-current' or 'inactive' phase, in which their business use is deemed to be at an end and a decision is made either to destroy them or to maintain them indefinitely for historical or cultural reasons. Proponents of this model generally assumed that records take the form of paper files, which are initially stored in or near their place of origin and are moved to a dedicated 'records centre' when they later reach 'semi-current' status. It was argued that most records would then be destroyed after an agreed period of time, but a small proportion would be selected for long-term preservation. In the USA, records were often said to 'become' archives at the moment when they were selected for transfer to an archival institution (Schellenberg, 1956, 13–16). Archivists in French-speaking countries developed a distinction between *archives courantes* kept for business purposes and *archives historiques* kept for cultural reasons, but many archivists in the USA (and increasingly in a number of other English-speaking countries) denied that records maintained for business use were 'archives'; following an example set in Germany (Brenneke, 1953), they sought to confine the term 'archives' to records that had undergone a selection process and been designated for preservation in an archival institution. Advocates of this latter view have generally perceived archives as a subset of a wider universe of records: a subset picked for long-term retention because of its presumed societal value and its contribution to cultural heritage.

The American life-cycle model was developed in parallel with, and was often used to explain, the use of the term 'records management' to denote the control of records within the organizations where they

The first records centre is said to have been established near Washington in the USA in 1941, to house records of the US Navy. Records centres are 'intermediate records depositories, which receive, store, service, process, and provide security for records that are not sufficiently active to be retained in . . . operating space but are too active to be retired' (Angel, 1968, 5–6). From the USA, the term 'records centre' spread to other parts of the world; it is still in use, although most organizations now outsource the storage of 'semi-current' paper records to commercial providers, which sometimes prefer to use other names for their depositories. Records sent to a records centre or outsourced storage facility are (or should be) assigned a disposal date; if the records are perceived to have only short-term utility, this will be the date when they are expected to be destroyed.

Although records centres are usually said to be an invention of the 20th century, many records storage facilities in the ancient world operated in much the same way, housing records that were retained for a fixed period of time and then destroyed. It is evident that, in the palaces and cities of ancient civilisations, decisions had been made that accounting records should be routinely destroyed when their immediate utility had expired; destruction often took place within a year of the records being created (Eidem, 2011, 13; Palaima, 2003). Although the repositories of ancient Mesopotamia, Egypt, Greece and Rome (like their successors in medieval Europe) have been generally referred to as 'archives', the records that they housed were held for legal purposes or administrative business, and their roles were often closer to those of 20th- and early-21st-century records management than to the research-focused archival institutions of our own era.

were created. This term was first used in the USA in the 1940s and was gradually adopted in other countries from the late 1950s or 1960s onwards. The initial focus of records management was on helping organizations to reduce the quantities of records that they kept and the periods of time for which they kept them. Its practitioners became known as records managers, and their attention was centred on the methodical storage and disposal of records that were considered to be in the 'semi-current' phase of their life. In government settings, records managers worked more or less closely both with the officials responsible for current organizational records and with the archivists who took charge of the smaller numbers of records designated for long-term preservation. Records management practices also expanded in the corporate business sector, but this sector generally attached less importance to long-term preservation, and records managers employed in the commercial world were often little inclined to see close links between their work and the work of archivists. Although a number of practitioners kept a foot in both camps, most records managers in the late 20th century came to see records management as a separate discipline; it acquired its own literature and professional bodies and codes of ethics that were distinct from those of archivists. At the same time, it expanded its scope to embrace issues of legal and regulatory compliance, and it began to address the management of records that – from the perspective of the life-cycle model – were seen as 'current', as well as those considered 'semi-current'.

While some practitioners saw these developments as beneficial, others did not wholly welcome them. Both in Britain and in North America, voices were raised in objection to the idea that the term 'archives' should be limited to 'historical' materials held in, or designated for, archival institutions (Jenkinson, 1957; Norton, 1975, 13). Despite what often seemed to be a growing *de facto* separation between records managers and archivists, some commentators continued to maintain that the field is 'whole and indivisible' and that a record is 'of the same texture and form from beginning to end' (Radoff, 1956, 5, 7). Similar ideas underlay the 'records continuum' model developed in Australia in the 1990s and early 2000s, which rejected notions of a linear progression and a rigid boundary between records and archives (Upward, 1996; 2005). Proponents of the continuum model have perceived 'records' as a comprehensive term, and have increasingly sought to argue that records have a variety of social uses that extend beyond organizational business and historical research. Repudiating life-cycle models, they have advocated a unified approach to records 'whether [they] are kept for a split second or a millennium' (Upward, 1996, 276).

The continuum model has often been associated with what may broadly be called the 'post-custodial' view that the characteristics of records are independent of any arrangements that may have been made for their storage and custody. From this perspective, if archives are to be differentiated from other records, they are viewed, not as records that have been placed in an archival repository for purposes of historical research or cultural heritage, but simply as records that are believed to have continuing value (AS 4390.1-1996, clause 4.5; Hofman, 2005, 135), particularly in terms of their plural uses in wider social contexts. As we have seen, the word 'archives', which had originally referred only to repositories, had already shifted its range of meaning when it came to be used for the material holdings of repositories; post-custodial thinking implied that its usage had undergone a further shift, and that 'archives' now connoted records of value irrespective of where they were held. More controversially, perhaps, some advocates of pluralised and inclusive archives at the beginning of the 21st century have sought not only to deprecate institutional custody but also to de-emphasise the making and keeping of records; from this perspective, 'archives' are reconceptualised as

The records continuum model, developed by Australian scholar Frank Upward, suggests that records are disembedded from their immediate contexts of creation and recursively embedded into new contexts as they are carried through time and space. Upward borrowed from British sociologist Anthony Giddens's ideas about four regions of spacetime distancing and proposed four dimensions for analysing the making and keeping of records. In the first dimension, records are created as people engage in activities; in the second, they are captured into a local framework; in the third, they are organised in ways that build, recall and disseminate corporate or individual memory; and in the fourth, in the further reaches of spacetime, they are pluralised as collective memory. Although 'no separate parts of the continuum are readily discernible and its elements pass into each other' (Upward, 1996, 277), the model is usually represented in a diagram (Upward, 2005, 203) that associates a particular set of terms (such as 'actor' and 'transaction'; 'unit' and 'activity'; 'organization' and 'function'; 'institution' and 'purpose') with each of the four dimensions. Movement across the continuum need not be linear, and may occur inward from the fourth dimension as well as outward from the first. Upward's writings about the continuum make reference, not only to the work of Giddens, but also to the postmodernist conceptions of Jean-François Lyotard and to ideas about time and/or space put forward in the early 20th century by Samuel Alexander, Henri-Louis Bergson, Albert Einstein and Hermann Minkowski. Although time and space are experienced in human life as separate phenomena, continuum thinking emphasises their inseparability and asks us to perceive them through an Einsteinian lens as undifferentiated spacetime.

Australian advocates of the continuum model often associate it with what they see as a unified discipline of 'recordkeeping'; they prefer to spell this word without a hyphen, and sometimes affirm that the distinctive spelling demarcates a distinctive worldview built on continuum thinking. In this book, I have retained hyphens in 'record-making' and 'record-keeping', partly as a matter of personal preference, but also to suggest that it is possible to take a holistic view of records, and of the contexts in which they are made, kept and used, without necessarily adopting the specific intellectual package promoted by the Australian thinkers.

assemblages of any artefacts or objects deemed significant by those who assemble them, almost any such assemblage can be called an archive, and 'a person['s] or group's archives are whatever they say they are' (Flinn, 2011, 165).[2]

In this book, the focus remains on record-making and record-keeping; later chapters will argue that these activities are still distinctively practised in the 21st century. The book refers to records managers and archivists collectively as 'records professionals', but it also recognises that, in practice, records managers and archivists now often work in largely separate professional groupings. In administrative terms, some records are deemed to be the responsibility of records managers, and some are the responsibility of archivists; there are also many records – and many record-making and record-keeping activities – that fall outside the purview of both professional groups. However, the topics the book seeks to explore, and the questions it tentatively seeks to answer, are very largely applicable to all records, irrespective of who makes them, where they are stored or who is formally in charge of them. Although the chapters that follow are focused on the concerns of our own era, the contexts in which these concerns arise have been shaped by the long history of record-making and record-keeping, and many of the issues raised in these chapters pertain to records made in the past as well as those that are being made today. At a conceptual level, this book is aligned with those who see the field as 'whole and indivisible'.

The records that are being made in the 21st century are, of course, very largely in digital form, and some critics have argued that operational divisions between business and cultural purposes of record-keeping are particularly inappropriate in a digital age. Whether or not this is so, the advent of digital technologies has undoubtedly disrupted many of the traditional ways of working that 20th-century records professionals had learnt to employ. Digital records may sometimes appear to have very different characteristics from their analogue counterparts, and an exploration of the digital realm will be critical to investigate contemporary understandings of records and their place in the wider cultural milieu of the new millennium. The transition from analogue to digital record-making and record-keeping forms a major theme of the next chapter.

Endnotes

1 In Britain, the Public Record Office was re-named The National Archives in 2003.
2 The singular form 'archive' has long been accepted in British usage (cf. Jenkinson, 1922, 36–7, 160), although it has traditionally been deprecated in North America. The words 'archive' and 'archives' (when used to refer to materials rather than institutions) still often convey different nuances from 'record' and 'records'. For example, archives always seem to connote assemblages of some kind; even the concept of a single 'archive' implies an aggregation of items, whereas a 'record' may sometimes stand alone (Yeo, 2011, 17–18). In recent years, understandings of 'archive' and 'archives' have been further complicated by digital librarians, computer scientists, cultural theorists and others who have appropriated these terms for their own purposes. For accounts of the appropriation of 'the archive' by cultural theorists, see Buchanan (2011) and Manoff (2004); for a discussion of earlier metaphorical uses of 'archive', dating back to the 16th and 17th centuries, see Walsham (2016, 14–17).

References

Adler, W. (2012) Christians and the Public Archive. In Mason, E. F. (ed.), *A Teacher for All Generations: essays in honor of James C. VanderKam*, vol. 1, Brill.

Angel, H. E. (1968) Archival Janus: the records center, *American Archivist*, **31** (1), 5–12.

Arlinghaus, F.-J. (2006) Account Books. In Arlinghaus, F.-J., Ostermann, M., Plessow, O. and Tscherpel, G. (eds), *Transforming the Medieval World*, Brepols.

AS 4390.1-1996 *Records Management, Part 1: general*, Standards Australia.

Baker, J. H. (1989) Records, Reports and the Origins of Case-Law in England. In Baker, J. H. (ed.), *Judicial Records, Law Reports and the Growth of Case Law*, Duncker & Humblot.

Bautier, R.-H. (1968) La Phase Cruciale de l'Histoire des Archives: la constitution des dépôts d'archives et la naissance de l'archivistique, *Archivum*, **18**, 139–49.

Bedos-Rezak, B. M. (2003) From Ego to Imago: mediation and agency in medieval France (1000–1250), *Haskins Society Journal: Studies in Medieval History*, **14**, 151–73.

Benati, G. and Lecompte, C. (2016) New Light on the Early Archives from Ur. In Kaelin, O. and Mathys, H.-P. (eds), *Proceedings of the 9th International Congress on the Archaeology of the Ancient Near East*, vol. 3, Harrassowitz.

Berkhofer, R. G. (2004) *Day of Reckoning: power and accountability in medieval France*, University of Pennsylvania Press.

Birket-Smith, K. (1966–7) The Circumpacific Distribution of Knot Records, *Folk*, **8/9**, 15–24.

Boltz, W. G. (2000–1) The Invention of Writing in China, *Oriens Extremus*, **42**, 1–17.

Boone, E. H. and Urton, G. (eds) (2011) *Their Way of Writing: scripts, signs, and pictographies in pre-Columbian America*, Dumbarton Oaks Research Library.

Brendecke, A. (2010) '*Arca, Archivillo, Archivo*': the keeping, use and status of historical documents about the Spanish *Conquista*, *Archival Science*, **10** (3), 267–83.

Brenneke, A. (1953) *Archivkunde: ein Beitrag zur Theorie und Geschichte des europäischen Archivwesens*, Koehler & Amelang.

Buchanan, A. (2011) Strangely Unfamiliar: ideas of the archive from outside the discipline. In Hill, J. (ed.), *The Future of Archives and Recordkeeping*, Facet Publishing.

Carroll, L. (1872) *Through the Looking Glass, and What Alice Found There*, Macmillan.

Cartledge, P. (2009) *Ancient Greek Political Thought in Practice*, Cambridge University Press.

Casanova, E. (1928) *Archivistica*, Lazzeri.

Charpin, D. (2010) *Reading and Writing in Babylon*, Harvard University Press.

Chrisomalis, S. (2009) The Origins and Co-Evolution of Literacy and Numeracy. In Olson, D. R. and Torrance, N. (eds), *The Cambridge Handbook of Literacy*, Cambridge University Press.

Chrisomalis, S. (2010) *Numerical Notation: a comparative history*, Cambridge University Press.

Clanchy, M. T. (1980–1) Tenacious Letters: archives and memory in the Middle Ages, *Archivaria*, **11**, 115–25.

Clanchy, M. T. (2013) *From Memory to Written Record: England 1066–1307*, 3rd edn, Wiley-Blackwell.

Crabbe, V. (1994) *Understanding Statutes*, Cavendish Publishing.

Davies, W. and Fouracre, P. (eds) (1986) *The Settlement of Disputes in Early*

Medieval Europe, Cambridge University Press.

Duchein, M. (1992) The History of European Archives and the Development of the Archival Profession in Europe, *American Archivist*, **55** (1), 14–25.

Duchein, M. (1993) Archives, Archivistes, Archivistique: définitions et problématique. In Favier, J. (ed.), *La Pratique Archivistique Française*, Archives Nationales.

Duranti, L. (1996) Archives as a Place, *Archives and Manuscripts*, **24** (2), 242–55.

Duranti, L. (1997) Archival Science. In Kent, A. (ed.), *Encyclopedia of Library and Information Science*, vol. 59, Marcel Dekker.

Eidem, J. (2011) *The Royal Archives from Tell Leilan*, Nederlands Instituut voor het Nabije Oosten.

Englund, R. K. (1998) Texts from the Late Uruk Period. In Bauer, J., Englund, R. K. and Krebernik, M. (eds), *Mesopotamien*, Vandenhoeck & Ruprecht.

Fentress, J. and Wickham, C. (1992) *Social Memory*, Blackwell.

Fink, R. O. (1971) *Roman Military Records on Papyrus*, Case Western Reserve University.

Flinn, A. (2011) The Impact of Independent and Community Archives on Professional Archival Thinking and Practice. In Hill, J. (ed.), *The Future of Archives and Recordkeeping*, Facet Publishing.

Geary, P. J. (1999) Land, Language and Memory in Europe 700–1100, *Transactions of the Royal Historical Society*, 6th series, **9**, 169–84.

Gelb, I. J., Steinkeller, P. and Whiting, R. M. (1991) *Earliest Land Tenure Systems in the Near East: ancient kudurrus*, Oriental Institute of the University of Chicago.

Hallam, E. M. (1986) *Domesday Book through Nine Centuries*, Thames & Hudson.

Hallam, E. M. and Roper, M. (1978) The Capital and the Records of the Nation: seven centuries of housing the public records in London, *London Journal*, **4** (1), 73–94.

Harris, W. V. (1989) *Ancient Literacy*, Harvard University Press.

Herskovits, M. J. (1932) Population Statistics in the Kingdom of Dahomey, *Human Biology*, **4** (2), 252–61.

Hofman, H. (2005) The Archive. In McKemmish, S., Piggott, M., Reed, B. and Upward, F. (eds), *Archives: recordkeeping in society*, Charles Sturt University.

Horsfall, N. (1991) Statistics or States of Mind? *Journal of Roman Archaeology*, supplementary series, **3**, 59–76.

Hudson, M. and Wunsch, C. (eds) (2004) *Creating Economic Order: record-keeping, standardization, and the development of accounting in the ancient Near East*, CDL Press.

Jacobsen, L. E. (1983) Use of Knotted String Accounting Records in Old Hawaii and Ancient China, *Accounting Historians Journal*, **10** (2), 53–61.

Jenkinson, H. (1922) *A Manual of Archive Administration*, Clarendon Press.

Jenkinson, H. (1948) *The English Archivist: a new profession*, H. K. Lewis.

Jenkinson, H. (1957) Modern Archives: some reflexions, *Journal of the Society of Archivists*, **1** (5), 147–9.

Jones, M. J. (2009) Origins of Medieval Exchequer Accounting, *Accounting, Business & Financial History*, **19** (3), 259–85.

Ketelaar, E. (2007) Muniments and Monuments: the dawn of archives as cultural patrimony, *Archival Science*, **7** (4), 343–57.

Lagercrantz, S. (1968) African Tally-Strings, *Anthropos*, **63**, 115–28.

Lagercrantz, S. (1973) Counting by Means of Tally Sticks or Cuts on the Body in Africa, *Anthropos*, **68**, 569–88.

Larsen, M. T. (1989) What They Wrote on Clay. In Schousboe, K. and Larsen, M. T. (eds), *Literacy and Society*, Akademisk Forlag.

Lodolini, E. (2013) *Storia dell'Archivistica Italiana*, 7th edn, FrancoAngeli.

MacNeil, H. (2006) From the Memory of the Act to the Act Itself: the evolution of written records as proof of jural acts in England, 11th to 17th century, *Archival Science*, **6** (3–4), 313–28.

Manoff, M. (2004) Theories of the Archive from across the Disciplines, *portal: Libraries and the Academy*, **4** (1), 9–25.

Martin, G. H. (1990) The Future of the Public Records. In Martin, G. H. and Spufford, P. (eds), *The Records of the Nation*, Boydell Press.

Martínez García, L. (1999) El Archivo de Simancas en el Antiguo Régimen: secreto, patrimonio, justificación y legitimidad real, *Boletín de la ANABAD*, **49** (2), 77–116.

Mauntel, C. (2015) Charters, Pitchforks, and Green Seals: written documents between text and materiality in late medieval revolts. In Enderwitz, S. and Sauer, R. (eds), *Communication and Materiality: written and unwritten communication in pre-modern societies*, De Gruyter.

McKitterick, R. (1989) *The Carolingians and the Written Word*, Cambridge University Press.

Menninger, K. (1969) *Number Words and Number Symbols: a cultural history of numbers*, MIT Press.

Meyer, E. A. (2015) Writing in Roman Legal Contexts. In Johnston, D. (ed.),

The Cambridge Companion to Roman Law, Cambridge University Press.

Morelle, L. (2000) The Metamorphosis of Three Monastic Charter Collections. In Heidecker, K. (ed.), *Charters and the Use of the Written Word in Medieval Society*, Brepols.

Muller, S., Feith, J. A. and Fruin, R. (1898) *Handleiding voor het Ordenen en Beschrijven van Archieven*, Van der Kamp.

Nissen, H. J., Damerow, P. and Englund, R. K. (1993) *Archaic Bookkeeping*, University of Chicago Press.

Nora, P. (1989) Between Memory and History: les lieux de mémoire, *Representations*, **26**, 7–24.

Norton, M. C. (1975) The Scope and Function of Archives. In Mitchell, T. W. (ed.), *Norton on Archives: the writings of Margaret Cross Norton on archival & records management*, Southern Illinois University Press.

Oppenheim, A. L. (1959) On an Operational Device in Mesopotamian Bureaucracy, *Journal of Near Eastern Studies*, **18** (2), 121–8.

Palaima, T. (2003) Archives and Scribes and Information Hierarchy in Mycenaean Greek Linear B Records. In Brosius, M. (ed.), *Ancient Archives and Archival Traditions*, Oxford University Press.

Panitch, J. M. (1996) Liberty, Equality, Posterity? Some archival lessons from the case of the French revolution, *American Archivist*, **59** (1), 30–47.

Pérotin, Y. (1966) Administration and the 'Three Ages' of Archives, *American Archivist*, **29** (3), 363–9.

Posner, E. (1940) Some Aspects of Archival Development since the French Revolution, *American Archivist*, **3** (3), 159–72.

Postgate, N. (2013) *Bronze Age Bureaucracy: writing and the practice of government in Assyria*, Cambridge University Press.

Radoff, M. (1956) What Should Bind Us Together, *American Archivist*, **19** (1), 3–9.

Reinburg, V. (2016) Archives, Eyewitnesses and Rumours: writing about shrines in early modern France, *Past and Present*, **230**, supplement 11, 171–90.

Rio, A. (2009) *Legal Practice and the Written Word in the Early Middle Ages*, Cambridge University Press.

Salazar Revuelta, M. (1998) La Forma *Litteris* como *Instrumentum* Crediticio en el Derecho Justinianeo, *Revue Internationale des Droits de L'antiquité*, 3rd series, **45**, 501–35.

Sarris, P. (2013) Lay Archives in the Late Antique and Byzantine Near East. In Brown, W. C., Costambeys, M., Innes, M. and Kosto, A. J. (eds),

Documentary Culture and the Laity in the Early Middle Ages, Cambridge University Press.

Schellenberg, T. R. (1956) *Modern Archives: principles and techniques*, F. W. Cheshire.

Schoep, I. (1999) The Origins of Writing and Administration on Crete, *Oxford Journal of Archaeology*, **18** (3), 265–76.

Schwind, F. (1950) *Römisches Recht*, vol. 1, Springer.

Soll, J. (2014) *The Reckoning: financial accountability and the making and breaking of nations*, Allen Lane.

Tanret, M. (2011) Learned, Rich, Famous, and Unhappy: Ur-Utu of Sippar. In Radner, K. and Robson, E. (eds), *The Oxford Handbook of Cuneiform Culture*, Oxford University Press.

Taylor, H. A. (1984) Information Ecology and the Archives of the 1980s, *Archivaria*, **18**, 25–37.

Thorne, S. E. (1968) *Bracton on the Laws and Customs of England*, vol. 2, Harvard University Press.

Tiersma, P. (2008) Writing, Text, and the Law. In Bazerman, C. (ed.), *Handbook of Research on Writing*, Lawrence Erlbaum.

Topic, J. R. (2016) Storerooms, Tokens, and Administrative Devices: an Andean case study. In Manzanilla, L. R. and Rothman, M. S. (eds), *Storage in Ancient Complex Societies: administration, organization, and control*, Routledge.

Upward, F. (1996) Structuring the Records Continuum. Part One: postcustodial principles and properties, *Archives and Manuscripts*, **24** (2), 268–85.

Upward, F. (2005) The Records Continuum. In McKemmish, S., Piggott, M., Reed, B. and Upward, F. (eds), *Archives: recordkeeping in society*, Charles Sturt University.

Urton, G. (2010) Recording Measure(ment)s in the Inka Khipu. In Morley, I. and Renfrew, C. (eds), *The Archaeology of Measurement*, Cambridge University Press.

Urton, G. and Brezine, C. J. (2011) Khipu Typologies. In Boone, E. H. and Urton, G. (eds), *Their Way of Writing: scripts, signs, and pictographies in pre-Columbian America*, Dumbarton Oaks Research Library.

Van Den Hout, T. P. J. (2011) The Written Legacy of the Hittites. In Genz, H. and Mielke, D. P. (eds), *Insights into Hittite History and Archaeology*, Peeters.

Vincent, N. (2004) Why 1199? Bureaucracy and enrolment under John and his contemporaries. In Jobson, A. (ed.), *English Government in the Thirteenth Century*, Boydell Press.

Vincent, N. (ed.) (2009) *Records, Administration and Aristocratic Society in the Anglo-Norman Realm*, Boydell Press.

Walsham, A. (2016) The Social History of the Archive: record-keeping in early modern Europe, *Past and Present*, **230**, supplement 11, 9–48.

Wickham, C. (1986) Land Disputes and their Social Framework in Lombard-Carolingian Italy, 700–900. In Davies, W. and Fouracre, P. (eds), *The Settlement of Disputes in Early Medieval Europe*, Cambridge University Press.

Wolf, J. G. (2004) From the Recent Discovery of Documents in Pompeii: the *tabellae* of Titinia Antracis and the suretyship of Epichares, *Roman Legal Tradition*, **2**, 82–95.

Wolf, J. G. (2015) Documents in Roman Practice. In Johnston, D. (ed.), *The Cambridge Companion to Roman Law*, Cambridge University Press.

Yeo, G. (1986) Record-Keeping at St Paul's Cathedral, *Journal of the Society of Archivists*, **8** (1), 30–44.

Yeo, G. (2011) Rising to the Level of a Record? Some thoughts on records and documents, *Records Management Journal*, **21** (1), 8–27.

Zaid, O. A. (2004) Accounting Systems and Recording Procedures in the Early Islamic State, *Accounting Historians Journal*, **31** (2), 149–70.

CHAPTER 2

Thinking about records and archives; the transition to the digital

Introduction

If archivists or records managers in the early 21st century were asked to conjure up a mental picture of a record, most would probably think of a unit of written text. Textual records have long been at the heart of archival endeavour, and archival institutions now hold vast numbers of them. Conceptually, however, records cannot be confined to textual domains. Particularly in preliterate or semi-literate societies – as the previous chapter suggested – records have often taken the form of three-dimensional artefacts. Drawings, sketches and visual charts can record what happened in the past, and static photographic images have come to fulfil a similar role. Archival scholar Anne Gilliland (2017, 54) has noted how physical artefacts and visual depictions can serve record-keeping needs for those deprived of other means of recording, as in the case of the cloth *arpilleras* woven by women in 20th-century Chile to document their experiences under a repressive government. In contemporary societies, records can also include moving images and sound recordings; video recordings of a meeting or conference, and audio recordings of an interview or telephone conversation, are all recognisable as records of the events concerned. Nevertheless, for most records professionals, these are not the examples that immediately come to mind when the concept of a 'record' is under discussion; in professional discourse, records and written text often seem to belong together. Using terminology developed in the 1970s by psychologist Eleanor Rosch, we may say that – for most archivists and records managers in contemporary western societies – a 'prototypical' record is largely or wholly textual.

American psychologist Eleanor Rosch developed 'prototype theory' as a means of understanding human approaches to categorisation (Rosch, 1978; Smith and Medin, 1981). Rosch and her associates suggested that most conceptual categories have prototypes, which are usually envisaged as mental mappings of typical features: for example, having feathers, an ability to fly and a propensity to build nests might be typical features of a member of the category of 'birds'. A prototype of a bird is likely to be a mental composite of features such as these.

Prototype theory affirms that category membership is graded, and that candidates for membership of a category are assessed in terms of their similarity to a mental prototype. Thus, finches, sparrows and starlings are likely to be judged 'better' members of the category of birds than, for example, owls. Prototype effects usually depend on cultural context; to most people, ostriches and penguins are 'poor' examples of the category of birds, but a penguin might be very close to the prototype for an Antarctic scientist or a South Atlantic islander.

Rosch's ideas can usefully be applied to our conceptual understanding of records (Yeo, 2008). In the 20th century, the usual mental prototype of a record in western cultures was doubtless a paper document kept for business purposes in a structured filing system, but the prototype in medieval Europe was probably a sealed parchment charter; in ancient Mesopotamia, it was presumably a clay tablet of some kind. As digital record-keeping becomes commonplace in the 21st century, the prototype is shifting once again, from paper to digital media. In any age, there are also likely to be many records that do not precisely match the prevailing prototype. Personal papers have often seemed non-prototypical to archivists who have been trained to see issues relating to government records as the core of professional thinking and practice. Similarly, in the modern world, audiovisual resources frequently have a marginal role in professional perceptions of record-keeping. Some 21st-century materials, such as social media postings, are so distant from the record prototype that their status as records is often a matter of dispute.

As we saw in Chapter 1, records have been created using many different media in different places across the centuries. In medieval Europe, the wooden tablets and papyrus used in ancient Rome and Egypt were discontinued in favour of parchment, made from animal skins, which offered a more durable material. In its turn, parchment was largely superseded by paper at the end of the Middle Ages. Long before this, paper had been known and used in China and other parts of eastern Asia. After its arrival in Europe, for more than 400 years paper remained the medium of choice for almost all written record-making and record-keeping.

In recent decades, audiovisual and computing technologies have brought new media and new means of making records, and the use of paper – although by no means obsolete – now appears to be in steep decline. In organizational settings, filing cabinets and shelving units for paper storage are rapidly being made redundant, as digital approaches to record-keeping have become the norm. Many pundits have forecast the near-total displacement of paper and the imminent arrival of the paperless office; although paper-free working environments may still prove chimerical, the 'less-paper' office has already become a reality in most countries around the world.

The shift to digital record-making and record-keeping has introduced powerful new methods of accessing and sharing records, but has also brought new challenges, both for records managers concerned with the capture of records and for archivists concerned with preserving them over time. The intangibility of digital objects, their seeming ephemerality and their separation of messages from fixed media all appeared to threaten the viability of long-term preservation. Particularly in the 1990s, doomsayers often foresaw a 'digital dark age', in which no records would survive for more than a short period of time and no archival legacy would be left for the use of future historians. Today, however, it seems clear that these predictions were unduly pessimistic. Most of the preservation challenges can generally be overcome, and the cost barriers of digital preservation programmes are almost certainly lower than was once thought. Arguably, the biggest challenge that the advent of digital technology has brought for records professionals is the evident weakening, in many organizations, of what might be called a record-keeping mentality; many people, it seems, cease to recognise a need for record capture when they no longer have to deal with paper files or accommodate other tangible media. The transition to the digital world has disrupted traditional working methods, and new approaches will be needed if 21st-century records are to be secured.

It is ever more apparent that record-making practices are now moving away from paper and other analogue media, and that in future the great majority of records will be created, maintained and used in digital form. Some observers have suggested that this transition will require us to reject older understandings of records and replace them with newer concepts. This chapter examines aspects of the digital environment that have led observers to propose a need for a new conceptual understanding; in particular, it discusses questions of mutability and fluidity, which some recent commentators have seen as altering the fundamental characteristics of records and record-keeping. It also reviews changing 'paradigms' in archival thinking, including the emerging paradigm of information.

Fixity and fluidity in the digital domain

At the end of the 20th and the start of the 21st centuries, long-standing notions of records as stable objects appeared to have been challenged, and perhaps overturned, by the fluidity and variability seemingly inherent in digital technologies. In an intellectual climate that attaches little value to fixity, many critics have been led to suggest that today's watchword should be remixability, not stability. In an essay on literature and music, science-fiction novelist William Gibson sweepingly dismissed the term 'record' as:

> antique . . . [and] archaically physical. The record, not the remix, is the anomaly today. The remix is the very nature of the digital. . . . The recombinant (the bootleg, the remix, the mash-up) has become the characteristic pivot at the turn of our two centuries.
>
> (Gibson, 2005)

Gibson was not writing about archives or records management, but his words have been repurposed by other writers and have been used to introduce or illustrate the disruptive forces that the records profession faces in the digital era (McLeod, 2008, 4, citing Keen, 2007; Research Councils UK, 2017).

For some commentators, the starting point for new thinking is the alleged fluidity of *documents* in the digital realm. In the late 20th and early 21st centuries, many critics argued that digital technologies had 'sounded the death knell' for the fixed textual document (Levy, 2001, 35). Documents were said to have become fundamentally unstable, with dynamic capabilities that made them 'transient, fluid, [and] constantly evolving' (Schamber, 1996, 670), not least because computing technologies allowed them to be repeatedly edited and reformatted, both by human editors and by automated processes, with an ease and rapidity that were previously unavailable. The notion that documents were 'stable, static and pre-defined artefacts' was widely perceived as outdated (Prior, 2003, 2) and treated with disdain.

In the 1990s, some analysts of contemporary culture claimed that the evolution of hypertext systems was liberating documents, or readers of documents, from linearity and the 'intimidating figure' of the author (Bolter, 1991, 153; Landow, 1992, 178). In a world where no text need remain the same from one moment to another, and where every document can be individually customised for every user, there need be no predetermined order of reading, and readers of documents – it was said – would no longer be constrained by the power of authors to dictate documentary rigidity. More recently, in a broadly similar fashion, 21st-century social media and Web 2.0 technologies have been heralded as erasing distinctions between authors and readers of digital documents; if readers wish to alter a document that is presented to them, they can add their own contributions or rewrite it as they wish. The components of web pages or other documents can be reassembled in innumerable different ways and users' experiences of them can be personalised.

Ideas about the fluidity and liberation of documents are not only underpinned by current developments in digital technology, but also resonate with prominent strands in the thinking of cultural critics such as Roland Barthes, Michel Foucault and their many followers, who sought to release the document (or 'text') from dependency on 'original' authors and initial moments of creation, and to emphasise instead its fluctuating significance for current users. In the absence of definitive authorial control, texts are dynamic, meanings are never final and users are 'free to enter the text from any direction' (Selden, Widdowson and Brooker, 2005, 150) and to follow, change or reinterpret it at will.

Several writers have adopted or adapted these ideas about the instability of documents or texts and applied them to *records*. Australian advocates of the records continuum model have frequently affirmed that records are 'always in a process of becoming' and 'never in a final state of being' (McKemmish, 1994, 200; Upward, 2004, 40). According to Canadian archivist Jacques Grimard (2005, 159), digital records are 'never static, never materially fixed'. By the early 21st century, British archivists Valerie Johnson and David Thomas (2013, 459) claimed, 'the nature of records had changed, so that in the digital context records could be dynamic . . . and . . . exist in a fluid state'. Johnson and Thomas did not argue that records were obsolescent, as Gibson's work had perhaps suggested, but they proposed that 'classic concepts' of records and archives needed to be drastically revised to make them fit for the digital era. The apparent fluidity of digital archives has sometimes been presented as a return to the 'unstable, plastic, living entities' that characterised oral cultures and were supposedly lost when writing was interposed (Lane and Hill, 2011, 18).

To support their argument, Johnson and Thomas cited the example of company records of shareholders, which are continuously updated because of the 'millions of shares changing hands electronically every day'. Such records, they said, are 'in a state of constant flux', which 'demands a new definition of what a record is' (Johnson and Thomas, 2013, 459). This is a radical claim, and its challenge to traditional understandings of 'what a record is' calls for further investigation. Let us assume that the ABC Company uses a database containing records of its shareholders and their holdings. Many of these shareholders are corporate institutions that own thousands, perhaps millions, of shares and may trade them frequently; much share trading is computer-driven and takes place at high speed; but some shares are owned by individuals who have smaller holdings and rarely buy or sell. When the stock exchanges are open, the database is updated and a new record is added whenever shares in ABC are traded. The frequency of trading by speculators and financial institutions means that the database as a whole is subject to 'continuous' updating; but if I own 100 shares in ABC, the record that relates to my individual holding will persist within the database until I trade them in a new transaction. If the stock exchanges are closed, the whole database is static; no records are added to it, and none deleted. Despite the appearance of constant flux, the database – and each of the records within it – will be as stable as it needs to be, and for as long or as short a period of time as it needs to be. If this were not so, it would not function as a record.

Underlying this discussion are questions about how long records are required to last. Might a particular record need to be preserved without limit of time? Or does a moment arrive when its retention is no longer necessary? As records managers and archivists know, these questions are not as simple as they appear. Records professionals have attempted to provide conceptual criteria for resolving questions of retention and destruction: some have spoken of assessing the continuing *value* of records (Schellenberg, 1956), while others, especially in recent years, have emphasised assessment of the *risks* attaching to their destruction or survival (Lemieux, 2015). In practice, however, these criteria are never easy to apply. Their application can be particularly difficult when the content of a record appears to have been superseded as a result of changing circumstances. In ABC's database, what should be the destiny of records of shareholdings that have been disposed of, or records of former shareholders who have sold all their shares? Might such records need to be kept for some further period of time, or should they simply be discarded as soon as their content is judged to be outdated?

Questions about the retention or destruction of records are not new. Decisions on whether to preserve records or destroy them have had to be made since the earliest days of record-keeping, and destruction after a short retention period has always been an option. Even in the ancient world, as we saw in Chapter 1, many accounting records were routinely discarded within a year of their being made. The change brought by today's digital technology is that we now have automated systems with the capability to retain records for only a very brief period of time – a period that can be measured in hours, minutes, or seconds rather than months or years – in an environment where new records are created in unprecedented numbers at an extremely rapid pace. A record is a record even if it is kept merely 'for a split second' (Upward, 1996, 276) or for a few minutes or hours, but the period of retention is so abbreviated that it gives the impression of a record system in 'constant flux'.

Databases and other computer systems are often developed on the assumption that 'outdated' or non-current records are of no further consequence and can simply be overwritten or deleted. They are often designed so that overwriting or deletion takes place more or less automatically, in ways that were impossible in analogue environments. However, computer technology also allows us to design systems that can offer their users the option of retaining non-current records, by ensuring that new records are created alongside their older counterparts and do not overwrite them. Typically, a system of this kind will store non-current records separately, or will offer an interface that hides them from those users who prefer not to view them. In the case of ABC's shareholder database, most users will probably only want access to records that are current, but there will be many occasions when access to older records will be required: for example, when questions are asked about the date on which institution X sold its shares, what the database claimed that institution Y paid for them, or whether person Z was recorded as a shareholder at the time she received a dividend or voted at a shareholders' meeting. There may also be occasions when questions are asked about the state of all the shareholdings at specific past moments. Helping users to recall or discover what happened in the past has been a function of records for several millennia, and this function has not changed in the digital realm.

Technical possibilities of overwriting or altering records are not unique to the digital environment. In ancient Rome, messages inscribed on wooden tablets with malleable wax surfaces could easily be overwritten or amended; in 16th-century Peru, the knotted cord records known as *khipu* (see Chapter 1) ostensibly offered few safeguards against knots being untied or added to a cord. In both instances, methods were devised to help secure records against tampering. The Romans wrote on wax on the interior faces of two wooden tablets hinged together, and then applied seals to a string wound around or through them (Meyer, 2015, 86–7). *Khipu* are a more complex case; some may have been designed to allow records to be kept for a short term and then 'updated' when circumstances changed (Salomon, 2002, 310), but to prevent unauthorised alterations the Inka sometimes made multiple identical *khipu* and stored each of them separately, thus allowing for evidential comparison (Urton, 2005).

In the digital era, a range of cryptographic tools can be used to inhibit the unauthorised altering of records, but the keeping of multiple copies also remains available as a security mechanism. The possibility of overwriting previously created content and the recognition that measures are sometimes needed to reintroduce a degree of persistence are not new. The innovations brought by digital technology are of speed, frequency and scale. When overwriting can occur almost instantaneously and constantly, records professionals find that retention decisions – especially decisions about long-term preservation – become considerably more challenging.

If digital records were wholly and constantly fluid – if they lacked stability of any kind – they would be unable to communicate their messages either across time or across space. Human society, however, continues to require records that offer these capabilities in the 21st century. In the digital era, we still need records that have the power to underwrite accountability, to testify to past events and statements, and to sustain rights, obligations, agreements and commitments (Bell, 2014; Jimerson, 2009, 319–20; Thibodeau, 2009). In the world of share trading, under the European Union's *MiFID2* regulations,[1] financial institutions are required to keep records of client orders, decisions to deal, transactions and order processing for at least five years; neither the rapid volumes of trading nor the constant changes in share ownership diminish the requirements for records retention. Cultures of accountability require many other industries to operate under similar constraints.

The fluidity that seems inherent in much digital technology does not obviate the need for records, nor does the transition to the digital world offer organizations a licence to ignore record-keeping requirements. Records, it appears, still need to be made and kept, even when digital technology obliges us to seek new practical methods and techniques for underwriting their persistence and integrity over time. This necessity has led records managers to call on commercial vendors who can offer stabilising technologies for record-keeping in the digital world: first through the once-popular EDRM (electronic document and records management) systems, and more recently through add-ons to Microsoft's SharePoint application, both well documented in records management literature in recent years. Moves to embed record-keeping functionality in business systems (Cunningham, 2011), the development of the PDF/A file format for digital preservation (Noonan, McCrory and Black, 2010), the introduction of cryptographic controls and proposals to use blockchain and distributed ledger technologies for record-keeping (Lemieux, 2016) are all further manifestations of the same need.

At the same time, it is appropriate to recognise that mainstream digital systems are not *wholly* fluid; there are elements of stability in the world of computer technology outside the domain of record-keeping add-ons and special preservation formats. In my private life, I feel no need for an EDRM system or even for PDF/A; standard home or office technology largely fulfils my modest needs for record-keeping. I can read e-mails and other digital documents dating back about 20 years without having to use any specialised technological aids, and they generally remain accessible until I choose to delete them. I may regret their lack of sufficient metadata, and I may be unsure how long they will remain accessible in the future, but I do not normally perceive them as unstable or plastic. Unlike paper records, they are easily movable across physical media – indeed, my e-mails have recently been moved from my university's own servers to a storage facility in the 'cloud' – but this does not render them wholly dynamic or irredeemably unstable; they are sufficiently stabilised to meet my day-to-day requirements.

Adventures over time

Nevertheless, it is possible to identify a number of senses in which records – whether digital or analogue – can appropriately be seen as mutable or fluid. In particular, we must acknowledge that people – owners, records managers, archivists, conservators, users and others – treat (and sometimes mistreat) records in ways that affect how the records appear to those who encounter them subsequently. As time passes, records may be filed and refiled, arranged and rearranged, and housed and rehoused in different places; links between one record and another may be made and broken. Variabilities of this kind seem especially characteristic of digital records, but they also occur – albeit usually at a much slower pace – in analogue domains. In archival institutions, users are presented with analogue records and physical media that have been subjected to conservation treatment, rehoused in chemically neutral packaging, labelled and rendered orderly. Measures such as these attempt to arrest or postpone the degradation and decay that affect all media over time, but their deferral of one kind of transformation is achieved by introducing transformations of another kind; records that have been taken from their former environment, transferred to an archival institution and processed by archivists can no longer be encountered in the way they once were. Much the same can be said of the conversion of digital records to preservation-friendly file formats such as PDF/A; paradoxically, archival procedures can help to stabilise the record, but only at the cost of subtly – or not so subtly – changing it.

Records – analogue as well as digital – are also subject to fluidity of interpretation. Over time, as they acquire new users and new uses, they generate a range of interpretations and new symbolic meanings. In Frank Upward's words (2004, 58), records are 'always being stretched spatially and temporally . . . through their use'. They can be understood in ways that their makers did not foresee and brought into relationships that their makers could not have expected. The openness of records to new meanings and interpretations has been asserted by innumerable scholars in recent years, but there are differing views on how these new meanings and interpretations affect the record. One view is that they become indissoluble from, and thus formative of, the record itself. Another view might be that the record becomes encircled by these meanings but remains to some degree independent of them.

Many commentators now acknowledge that records are subject to processes of re-contextualisation arising from the interventions of successive custodians and users. For Dutch archival scholar Eric Ketelaar (2001, 137), every interrogation of records is an 'activation' that helps shape their meaning to their subsequent users, and re-contextualisation occurs 'at every stage of a record's life and in every dimension of the records continuum'. For Brien Brothman (2006, 246), records involve continual activity, a 'process of flux and transformation over time'; for Michelle Caswell (2016), they exist in 'a constantly shifting process of re-contextualization'. These critics lay emphasis on uses and reuses of already existing records (especially, perhaps, records encountered in long-term archival settings), rather than on what happens when a record is made or first inscribed: on the ways that people engage with records in continuing present moments, rather than on the action or actions that people undertook at the specific past moment when a record was born. In the words of social anthropologist Penelope Papailias (2005, 12), the 'unfolding beyond the singularity of the original event constitutes the time of the archive'; an essay by Hans Hofman (2005, 136) implies that it may be the archive, as much as or more than the record, that is ever-forming, always in a process of becoming.

As records are moved, handled, used and interpreted, they acquire new or additional contexts, but allusions to 're-contextualisation' should not be taken to imply that a record's new contexts exclude its older contexts or render them redundant. Records continue to support, and to be supported by, the multiple contexts of their making, keeping and previous use. With each interaction, a record gains further layers of context that add to, but do not supersede, the contexts it has inherited from the past. Records have many adventures, and recent professional literature has often called on archivists to work towards documenting the complex contexts that records accumulate through their ongoing use, their appraisal and their shifting custodial histories, as well as their initial creation (MacNeil, 2009; Nesmith, 2011; Yeo, 2009).

The journals of Richard Stonley, a 16th-century Exchequer official in London, offer an interesting case study of records that garner new contexts of ownership and use. In a series of volumes, Stonley recorded his day-to-day activities and his purchases of foodstuffs, clothing and other items. After his death, they passed through various private hands, and by the end of the 18th century the series had been broken up; only three volumes (covering 1581–2, 1593–4 and 1597–8) seem to have survived. On at least two occasions, the three surviving journals were acquired by booksellers, who sold them to new owners. Some later owners pasted their own bookplates in the volumes, thus affirming a new status for Stonley's journals as part of their owners' collections; others added annotations, paginated the volumes or made transcripts of their contents. The actions of each owner added new layers of context to the variety of contexts that had already accrued (Preston, 2014, 85–7; Scott-Warren, 2016, 155–9).

One entry in the second volume, however, has attracted more attention than any other. In the journal for 1593–4, next to an entry recording the purchase of buttons, is an entry that records Stonley's purchase of a copy of William Shakespeare's *Venus and Adonis*, and it is this entry – the earliest known record of a purchase of a work by Shakespeare – that has largely defined the re-contextualisation of the three volumes. In 1972, they were acquired by the Folger Shakespeare Library in Washington. Since then, they have been increasingly used by researchers, and they have recently been digitised. As literary historian Jason Scott-Warren noted:

> The Shakespeare reference has become, in a sense, the point of the journals, and has even started to shape their material form. While the first and third volumes have been left in a state of advanced decay, the second has been carefully conserved. . . . The volume's perceived value is tied to Shakespeare's exceptional status. (Scott-Warren, 2016, 156)

Since 1972, the journals have also served to enhance the reputation of the Folger Library as an international centre for Shakespearean scholarship. They continue to function as records of Richard Stonley's daily life and financial outlays – indeed, they owe their existence to Stonley's assiduous record-making – but their allusion to a famous poet and playwright has transformed their place in the world.

As Australian archivists Michael Piggott and Sue McKemmish (2002, 12) observed, the contexts of a record become larger and richer over time, but 'a record's content . . . can be seen as fixed'. Their Australian colleague Barbara Reed (2005, 128) suggested that we are faced with an enigma: records, in her opinion, are fluid and ever-forming, but they nonetheless 'aim to fix the elements that structure their formation'. Current intellectual fashion problematises notions of fixity, and we may prefer to take the view, suggested by cultural historian Adrian Johns (1998, 19), that 'fixity exists only inasmuch as it is recognized and acted upon by people'. Nevertheless, it is the apparent fixity of representational content that allows us to use records to look back to the record-making activity that gave rise to them. Records offer this capacity regardless of whether they have survived for many millennia, like the clay tablets that have been excavated from the soil of Mesopotamia, or only for very short periods of time, like some of the share records in ABC's shareholder database. There is considerable scope for fluidity in our interpretation of record-making activity and its circumstances, but the content of the record influences, shapes and ultimately constrains the interpretations to which records are subject and the range of meanings we can find in them.

Record aggregations

Although each record that we encounter is distinct from other records, and each has its own history of creation, keeping and use, records are rarely found in isolation. In practice, we usually encounter them in company with other records. Aggregations of records – rather than single records standing alone – are seemingly the norm.

In the past, such aggregations were often said to grow more or less naturally, because records are generated and accrue in the course of organizational business or daily life. Organizations and individuals, it was claimed, exercise little or no conscious judgement in accumulating records, which come together 'by a natural process' (Jenkinson, 1944, 358). In most countries, the records accrued over time by a particular organization, family or individual are known to archivists as a *fonds*, and the importance that archivists attached to respecting and maintaining intact *fonds* was often said to rest on an understanding of the *fonds* as a natural accumulation.

The principle that came to be known as *respect des fonds* was formally promulgated in France in 1841. Many keepers of records had observed it in practice at earlier dates, but its formal enunciation in 1841 has often been seen as an important landmark in the history of archival ideas. In the years that followed, *respect des fonds* – sometimes interpreted more broadly as the principle that aggregations of records should be maintained in accordance with their origins and managed in ways that protect and preserve knowledge of the contexts of their creation – came to be accepted around the world as a core principle of archival science and a basis for arranging records. More recently, archival thinkers have observed that the contexts of records are more complex than practitioners in the 19th and early 20th centuries generally recognised (Scott, 1966; Cook, 1992). The *fonds* has remained a key concept in archival theory, but is no longer universally thought to provide the only correct basis for arranging records; other ways of safeguarding context have increasingly been sought (Yeo, 2017).

However, there is increasing recognition that records and record aggregations are not as natural as was once commonly believed, but are shaped by the decisions and actions of their originators and custodians. In organizational contexts, records at granular (or 'item') level are purposefully constructed to undertake or provide documentation of business. Aggregations of records are then created by administrators or records managers, who decide which records will be captured for short-term or long-term retention and where and how these records will be grouped and stored. Archivists have also come to acknowledge the formative role of their own interventions in selecting, arranging and delivering records. The forces that determine the shape, content and scope of record aggregations are not natural processes; they are purposive choices based on fallible human judgement.

In the analogue world, record aggregations are enlarged when items are added to them, and may be subject to occasional reordering, but often appear largely stable and unchanging. Rearrangement of the components of an aggregation tends to be discouraged, partly because of lingering beliefs about the 'naturalness' of records' ordering, but also because of the physical effort that any rearrangement requires. In digital environments, however, reordering and rearrangement is much less cumbersome, and aggregations need never be immutable. Aggregations of digital records can be constructed on demand. Users of records can be empowered to construct personalised aggregations as they wish, and their experience of records need not be limited to viewing aggregations that have been predefined by the records' creators or custodians (Yeo, 2012). Fluidity of *use* and fluidity of *interpretation* are phenomena of the analogue as much as the digital realm, but digital technology enables fluidity of *aggregation* on a scale previously unknown. Contextualisation remains an important concern,[2] and records at item level are or should be endowed with an appropriate degree of stability to allow them to fulfil the roles that society requires of them, but record aggregations can now be formed and re-formed at will to meet the changing needs of their users.

Records, then, are not obsolescent in the digital world, as Gibson's (2005) description of them as 'antique' and 'archaically physical' seemed to imply. Nor does the apparent fluidity of the digital environment mean that 'the nature of records [has] changed' from fixity to 'a state of constant flux' (Johnson and Thomas, 2013). Some of the assumptions that characterised archival practices in the past, such as the suppositions that a record must remain affixed to a single medium or that records must be maintained in stable aggregations, were undoubtedly constrained by the physical structure of records in the paper era. The notion that the collective management of records in immutable *fonds* forms an essential principle of archival science can now be seen as flawed; arguably, keepers of paper records adopted a pragmatic response to the need to manage physical objects collectively and elevated it to the status of theory (Bearman, 1996, 197). But at item level – at what might be called the level of the 'elementary record' (Yeo, 2008, 133; 2012) – societal requirements for records with an appropriate degree of stability and contextualisation remain unchanged. The traditional functions of records have not been superseded, and we need not see digital records as somehow different in nature from the records created in earlier eras. Long-standing conceptions of 'what a record is' and of the purposes it serves still hold good in the digital age.

Archival mind-sets

In one of his last published papers, Terry Cook (2013) described four successive phases that he perceived in archival thinking. In attempting what he called a 'historical sociology' of archives and archivists, Cook used the word 'paradigms', borrowed from the work of philosopher Thomas Kuhn, to label the mind-sets, mental models or 'ways of imagining archives and archiving' that he identified among writers in the archival discipline during the past 100 or 150 years. He claimed that, over time, these paradigms had shifted from evidence to memory, and then to identity (or societal engagement) and community archiving:

> The archivist has been transformed, accordingly, from passive curator to active appraiser to societal mediator to community facilitator. The focus of archival thinking has moved from evidence to memory to identity and community, as the broader intellectual currents have changed from premodern to modern to postmodern to contemporary.
>
> (Cook, 2013, 95)

The archival discipline, Cook said, traditionally emphasised the acquisition, description and preservation of records as evidence; the rigorous application of principles such as *respect des fonds* was believed to allow records to serve as trustworthy evidence of actions, facts and ideas. According to Cook, this first mind-set dominated archival discourse until the 1930s, although it has also had many adherents in more recent times (Cook, 2013, 97, 100, 107).

Thomas Kuhn was a 20th-century American physicist, historian and philosopher of science. In his book *The Structure of Scientific Revolutions*, he argued that scientific investigation does not proceed in a continuous linear fashion, but is subject to 'paradigm shifts', which intermittently transform scientists' modes of understanding (Kuhn, 1962). Kuhn's approach has sometimes been criticised as overly simplistic, especially when applied to disciplines outside the hard sciences, but it has remained influential and is often cited. Writers on archives who have adopted Kuhn's language, or used some of his ideas, include Hugh Taylor (1987–8), Heather MacNeil (1994), Frank Upward (2000) and Fiorella Foscarini (2017). In addition to Terry Cook's 2013 article 'Evidence, Memory, Identity, and Community: Four Shifting Archival Paradigms', which is discussed here, Cook wrote about archival paradigm shifts in at least two of his earlier essays (1984–5 and 1997).

In Cook's second paradigm, which (he said) flourished from the 1930s to the 1970s, appraisal of records became an accepted and increasingly widespread practice, and the archivist 'became an active selector of the archive . . . and thereby consciously created public memory' (Cook, 2013, 108–9). The key concept of this second paradigm was memory, but 'with memory comes the inevitable privileging of certain records and records creators' (Cook, 2013, 101).

In his third paradigm, archival materials, activities and professionals began to offer more direct responses to the diverse and contingent nature of human society:

> Archives became increasingly linked to justice and human rights. . . .
> Recordkeeping systems are now consciously designed to prevent
> future abuses and to promote better accountability for public affairs
> and governance through creating and maintaining better records,
> especially in a digital world.   (Cook, 2013, 111)

Cook saw identity as the key concept of this paradigm, reflecting archivists' search for their own identity as well as the multiple identities that can be underpinned by records in the wider society. He also associated the third paradigm with the idea that digital records were less stable than records of earlier times, affirming that 'the record itself, now overwhelmingly electronic and computer-generated . . . was also much more fluid and transient' (Cook, 2013, 110). The two earlier paradigms survived into the digital era, but lost their dominant status and coexisted somewhat uneasily with these newer perspectives.

Cook's essay addressed only the period between the late 19th and early 21st centuries: the period that witnessed the increasing maturity, if not the birth, of the archival profession. As we have seen, understandings of records in terms of memory and evidence are not a product of recent times, but go back to the early days of record-keeping. Although Cook recognised evidence as the initial paradigm within the period that he studied, it seems almost certain that memory – the potential for records to help counteract human forgetfulness – was the driver for the very first attempts at record-making and record-keeping. The role of records in constructing or reinforcing identity is also far from new; when medieval charters were furnished with impressive seals and read aloud or presented at church altars in public ceremonies, they not only served to fix the solemnity of the occasion in the minds of those who were present, but can also be seen (by modern scholars, at least) as a means by which the persons who issued them proclaimed their identity and social status.

Cook's perspective, however, was very largely of the 21st century, particularly when he insisted that memory is a tool for making sense of the present as much as, or more than, an aid to recalling the past. This view, which links memory to the shaping of present-day identities, is indicative of the presentism that pervades much contemporary thinking, but does not seem to reflect the perspectives or mind-sets of the scribes and jurists of earlier generations, whose thoughts about memory we met in Chapter 1; as far as we can tell, when writers such as Henry de Bracton advocated making records 'for perpetual remembrance', they looked to the future, in the belief that record creators could anticipate possible needs for recollection and corroboration of past events. Also new, of course, are the explicit acknowledgement of these various mind-sets by 21st-century scholarship, their recognition as subjects of analytical study and the development of a distinctive vocabulary to describe them.

The fourth paradigm that Cook discussed was the making and keeping of records in ways that are believed to empower communities and bind them together. He argued that record-making and record-keeping by informal organizations, citizen groups and community activists was giving rise to a new mind-set or model, although not yet a fully formed paradigm. In an age of new communication patterns and a new social ethos, Cook affirmed (2013, 114–16), archives were being democratised and archivists needed to develop a sensitivity to communitarian perspectives and an awareness of the multiple ways in which communities value their records.

Perhaps more sharply than the others, this fourth paradigm offers every appearance of a decisive break with past ideas and past practice, especially when it is seen in terms of democratisation. Although scholars have argued that concepts of 'community' are problematic (Evans, 2015, 2–3; Muehlmann, 2014, 582–3), and it remains debatable whether records and archives are truly able to empower or unite communities at grass-roots level, the shift from formerly exclusive modes of record-keeping to new democratic understandings seems real enough. In the past, most records were made by or for rulers, aristocrats or elite institutions and were kept to serve the interests of the elite. Most of the activities that typically led to the creation of records – the buying and selling of land, the administration of justice, the collection of rents and taxes – were activities undertaken by people with wealth and power or by agents acting at their behest. Individuals at lower levels of society may have had their names entered in official records when they were born, married or died, or when they appeared before a court of law, but they met with relatively few occasions to make or keep records of their own.

We must not exaggerate the extent to which ordinary lives were isolated from record-keeping cultures. In ancient Mesopotamia, non-elite workers were able to keep written records of the property they owned (Larsen, 1989, 139); in medieval Europe, freed serfs could rely on records to prove their free status (Rio, 2009, 13–14). The use of written records and oral traditions were often intertwined. Nevertheless, records were more commonly kept and used by the powerful, and the evidence that records provided – following Cook's 'first paradigm' – was usually employed to buttress the interests and privileges of the elite. Before the 20th century, the memorial role of records was acknowledged primarily in legal and administrative contexts, rather than in terms of individual, communal or wider societal memory. Insofar as early records played a part in constructing or promoting identities, we may infer that the identities at issue were almost always those of rulers and persons in authority.

Probably the best-known exemplar of the historic exclusivity of records and archives is pre-Revolutionary France, where they were an 'instrument placed at the disposition of those in power' (Bautier, 1968, 141; Panitch, 1996, 33). The so-called *feudistes* who specialised in organising and arranging archives under the *ancien régime* had done so with the specific aim of enabling landowners to assert their feudal rights against their tenants and rivals (Friedrich, 2016, 55, 64). Echoing the destruction of records at the time of the English 'Peasants' Revolt' (see Chapter 1), the leaders of the French Revolution at first set out to burn many records that they saw as symbols of subjugation and servitude, only later coming to recognise the records' continuing cultural interest (Kingston, 2011; Panitch, 1996). The symbolism attached to these records was directly associated with the oppressive circumstances of their creation and former use. Modern or postmodern critics who seek to deprecate the role of record creators in order to focus on records' later re-contextualisations are liable to overlook the asymmetries of power that shaped the initial production of most records in the past.

When national archival institutions were first established and their holdings made available to the public, they may notionally have been open to all comers, but in practice almost all of their users were legal investigators or scholars using older records to undertake historical research. The customer base of a typical archival institution in the 19th or early 20th century was very small and usually very homogeneous. During the 20th century, however, the range of scholarly users – and the interests of archivists themselves – expanded, as historical scholarship outgrew its traditional confinement to early political, constitutional and military affairs, and academic researchers in other disciplines found that records might be useful in their work. In the second half of the century, archival institutions began to attract a wider variety of visitors; professional scholars were joined by large numbers of non-academic users undertaking self-directed research, especially in the fields of genealogy and local history, which became popular leisure pursuits at this time. By the end of the century, 'leisure' users, particularly genealogists, formed the majority of users in many archival institutions, and much of the work of archivists was re-focused to accommodate these new user groups. In addition, wider socio-cultural changes in developed countries in the 20th century – especially the advent of mass literacy – opened up the benefits and obligations of written record-keeping to all individuals in those countries in their private lives. In contrast to the restricted availability of record-keeping and the closed archives characteristic of most earlier ages, the making and keeping of written records became available to all, and publicly funded archival institutions in democratic societies felt able to proclaim that they served the needs of all, or at least a wider cross-section, of the human population.

In the 21st century, many socially engaged commentators have felt a need to re-orient the archival discipline, moving beyond the 'serving' of users – providing them with access to records curated by an archival institution on its own terms – and seeking to establish participatory cultures in which users become active contributors in the co-production of archival enterprise. Building on broader trends toward increased public involvement in areas of social life previously considered exclusive, those formerly identified as 'users' are reconceptualised as partners and are encouraged to participate in appraisal, description, preservation and other aspects of archival endeavour. As British archivist Alexandra Eveleigh (2017, 300) has noted, developments in participatory archives are often heralded as a means of revealing multiple meanings and perspectives, including those of traditionally excluded minority groups. While acknowledging that participatory approaches have sometimes been seen as endangering the function of archivists as trusted custodians, Eveleigh (2017, 306–7) identified the move toward participatory archives as an evolving paradigm that aims not only to embrace wider audiences, but also to transpose curatorial processes into a more democratic context. Although records managers continue to serve more restricted groups of users in the worlds of government and corporate business, and it remains unclear how far users of archives will be readily inclined to adopt the new roles envisaged for them, many archivists in the early 21st century appear to welcome a new democratic or communitarian paradigm. Some may perceive it, as Fiorella Foscarini (2017, 126) has suggested, as 'the archival paradigm characterizing our time'.

Information: a fifth paradigm?

In an essay published in the 1980s, Terry Cook had written about *knowledge* as 'an intellectual paradigm for archives' and had suggested that archivists should engage in a 'quest for knowledge rather than mere information' (Cook, 1984–5, 28, 49). But in his later article on the 'four paradigms' he said nothing about either knowledge or information as a paradigm for thinking about archives or records. This was perhaps not part of the story that Cook wanted to tell in 2013. Others, however, might argue that information seems to have become a prevailing paradigm for records professionals in the 21st century (Pierce Owen, 2016). Largely absent from older discussions, allusions to information and its presumed relationship to records are ubiquitous in the professional literature of the past 30 years, especially the literature of records management. At an earlier date, Theodore Schellenberg (1956, 139) had promoted the idea that records have informational as well as evidential values, but the emphasis on information that characterises much writing of the past three decades does not seem to be rooted in Schellenberg's work. The new discourse rarely presents information in terms of 'value'; much of it is associated with the transition to the digital realm, with assumptions that the primary function of computers is to manage or manipulate information, and with beliefs that information has roles to play in the evolving digital world that transcend its role in the analogue past.

Among the first to position records and archives in this kind of information context was Hugh Taylor, who affirmed that 'there can be no society without information' (Taylor, 1987–8, 15) and that what he called the 'ecology of information' provided archivists with an opportunity to move out of their 'historical shunt' and re-establish the importance of archival record-keeping in the eyes of government and private-sector policy makers (Taylor, 1984, 34; for the so-called 'historical shunt', see Chapter 1 above). Others who advocated an information-centric view of records in the 1980s included Richard Kesner (1984–5) and Michael Cook (1986) in the field of archives, and Betty Ricks and Kay Gow (1984) and Patricia Wallace and her colleagues (Wallace et al., 1987) in records management.

In the early 1990s, much thinking about record-keeping was influenced by the work of a technical panel of the Advisory Committee for the Co-ordination of Information Systems (ACCIS), which was set up to advise the United Nations on the management of digital records. The panel had an interdisciplinary membership including several computing experts. Its reports described records managers and archivists as 'information service providers' (ACCIS, 1990, 25) and asserted the utility of treating a record as an 'information object' (ACCIS, 1992, 7). Guided by archival consultant David Bearman, the panel was careful to nuance these opinions and to suggest that records are created by transactions in which information is received or sent (ACCIS, 1990, 20).[3] However, despite the influence of the panel's report, other writers in the later 1990s who made associations between records and information often paid little heed to the transactional aspects of records and saw them simply as a 'category of information' (Penn, Pennix and Coulson, 1994, 4).

At the start of the 21st century, the emerging information paradigm was reflected in the definition of records that appeared in the international standard for records management, ISO 15489. According to the first edition of this standard, published in 2001, records are 'information created, received and maintained as evidence and information by an organization or person, in pursuance of legal obligations or in the transaction of business' (ISO 15489-1: 2001, clause 3.15). In this form, the definition may seem questionable, not least because of the circularity of its allusion to 'information . . . maintained as . . . information'. Nevertheless, it was widely quoted in records management literature, presumably because it carried the cachet of approval in an international standard. In a companion standard, ISO 30300, published in 2011, the wording of this definition was altered and records were re-defined as 'information created, received and maintained as evidence and as an asset by an organization or person . . .' (ISO 30300: 2011, clause 3.1.7). The revised wording adopted the currently fashionable notion of information as an 'asset', which we will meet again in Chapter 4. The definition in its revised form also seems likely to enjoy a wide circulation, especially since it has been used in a new edition of ISO 15489 published in 2016 (ISO 15489-1: 2016, clause 3.14).

According to North American archivist Brien Brothman (2008, 150), the view 'that records are information entities or information objects residing in information systems' is now common, perhaps even reflexive, among archival professionals. His comment seems close to the mark; understandings of records in terms of information have been widely enunciated in writings by archivists and records managers in the early 21st century. For Michael Moss (2006, 228), 'the management of records is concerned with the control of flows of information'. According to Steve Bailey (2008, 59), 'any student of archives or records management will tell you' that 'all records are information'. Nicole Convery (2011, 207–8) expressed the opinion that records managers, archivists, knowledge managers and librarians 'all essentially manage information in its various guises' and are members of 'fractured information professions' whose activities, she believed, should be united 'under the umbrella of information management'.

The period in which these views have come to the fore has coincided with the period when many traditional approaches to record-making and record-keeping were disrupted by the arrival of digital technology. As we will see in later chapters, this was also a period in which ideas about the pervasiveness and societal importance of information were discussed and promoted in numerous public fora. Today, writings about information offer a number of different perspectives on its characteristics and availability that may engage the attention of records professionals. Because information is often said to be fluid, unstable and constantly changing in digital environments (Dearstyne, 1999, 5–6; Gauld, 2017, 238), a paradigm that views records in informational terms may have a particular appeal to those professionals who perceive records as increasingly volatile.[4] It can also be linked to notions of democratisation and egalitarianism in the digital realm; writers who adopt a libertarian focus often affirm that information, previously controlled and guarded by specialists, is now a commodity available to everyone and a resource to which everyone can contribute. In other writings about information, especially those aimed at business audiences, models of control continue to be advocated; in this literature, it is often said that information is at risk of becoming overabundant, unruly or insecure and is therefore in need of systematic management or governance. From this perspective, too, an informational paradigm can easily seem applicable to the record-keeping discipline, since organizational records management practices are largely predicated on a belief that records must be methodically controlled if they are to remain accessible, usable and trustworthy.

Information, then, can be seen as a fifth paradigm or mental model that has come to operate alongside Cook's four paradigms of evidence, memory, identity and community, in shaping understanding of and discourse about records and archives. It is a model that many records professionals have found attractive in the early years of the 21st century. In writings such as Convery's, however, information is presented as something more than a mental model; information and its management are perceived as larger entities into which records and record-keeping could (and perhaps should) be subsumed. Convery (2011, 208) stressed that she saw a place for distinct professional specialisms within an 'information management framework', but other writers have contended that such distinctions are no longer needed and that former divisions between information and records are becoming, or have become, blurred in a digital environment (Bailey, 2008, 146; Clarke, 2009, 121; Trombley, 2016, 50). For Lorrie Luellig (2012, 32), writing from an American perspective, the rapid growth of information systems and technologies means that 'defining a record is . . . becoming unnecessary'. In Britain, Valerie Johnson and David Thomas (2013, 461) saw this as a question or questions awaiting an answer ('In the digital world, can there be such a thing as an archive repository? Are there not simply caches of information?'), but Victoria Lane and Jennie Hill (2011, 18) seem to have believed that the answer was already clear, quoting with apparent approval the claim by two Dutch critics that 'what used to be . . . archive-systems' have become 'immaterial information-banks'.

It seems that proponents of these ideas are not simply seeking a change of terminology, substituting the word 'information' for the words 'archives' and 'records', much as 'archives' and 'records' had displaced seemingly quainter words such as 'muniments'. What some commentators now advocate goes far beyond this; we are asked to acknowledge that a fundamental shift in understanding has taken place and that records are no longer a distinct conceptual category. Information, and particularly digital information, we are told, has absorbed them.

In reality, most archivists – and probably most records managers – are unlikely to accept that, after 10,000 years of record-making and record-keeping, the body of understanding that has grown up around these practices has become redundant. Nevertheless, notions about the overarching role of information have pervaded large parts of the professional discourse in the late 20th and early 21st centuries. As we will see in later chapters, in much of the recent literature that might be expected to address organizational record-keeping concerns, records are rarely mentioned and the language and concepts of information management predominate. Record-keeping principles and practices, though not extinct, certainly appear to be under threat. Chapter 3 seeks to explore in more detail how ideas about information have penetrated the record-keeping discipline, to identify different strands of thinking about information and to examine how records managers and archivists have responded to them.

Endnotes

1 See www.esma.europa.eu/policy-rules/mifid-ii-and-mifir.
2 For a discussion of how context can be documented and protected in a world of fluid aggregations, see Yeo (2014, 176–80).
3 The idea that records are – or are created by – transactions in which information is communicated is also found in some of Bearman's later

work (cf. Bearman, 1994, 133, 189–90). The United Nations panel presented this view alongside 'another common definition' that a record is any information generated in the course of official business (ACCIS, 1990, 28), but it did not consider the possibility that records might represent transactions unconcerned with communicating information.

4 Others, however, have argued that the contrast between mutable information and stabilised records may provide a 'fundamental point of separation' between them (Bell, 2014, 239). Craig Gauld (2017, 238) seemingly attributes the view that 'information is unstable in an online environment' to me, but the perspective that he articulates is his own.

References

ACCIS (Advisory Committee for the Co-ordination of Information Systems) (1990) *Management of Electronic Records: issues and guidelines*, United Nations.

ACCIS (Advisory Committee for the Co-ordination of Information Systems) (1992) *Strategic Issues for Electronic Records Management: towards open systems interconnection*, United Nations.

Bailey, S. (2008) *Managing the Crowd: rethinking records management for the Web 2.0 world*, Facet Publishing.

Bautier, R.-H. (1968) La Phase Cruciale de l'Histoire des Archives: la constitution des dépôts d'archives et la naissance de l'archivistique, *Archivum*, **18**, 139–49.

Bearman, D. (1994) *Electronic Evidence: strategies for managing records in contemporary organizations*, Archives and Museum Informatics.

Bearman, D. (1996) Item Level Control and Electronic Recordkeeping, *Archives and Museum Informatics*, **10** (3), 195–245.

Bell, A. (2014) 'Participation vs Principle: does technological change marginalize recordkeeping theory? In Brown, C. (ed.), *Archives and Recordkeeping: theory into practice*, Facet Publishing.

Bolter, J. D. (1991) *Writing Space: the computer, hypertext and the history of writing*, Lawrence Erlbaum.

Brothman, B. (2006) Archives, Life Cycles, and Death Wishes: a helical model of record formation, *Archivaria*, **61**, 235–69.

Brothman, B. (2008) Review of Pekka Henttonen, *Records, Rules and Speech Acts*, *Archival Science*, **8** (2), 149–56.

Caswell, M. (2016) 'The Archive' Is Not an Archives: acknowledging the intellectual contributions of archival studies, *Reconstruction*, **16** (1), https://escholarship.org/uc/item/7bn4v1fk.

Clarke, S. (2009) Crowded Out: records management and the Web 2.0 phenomenon, *Archives and Manuscripts*, **37** (1), 118–33.

Convery, N. (2011) Information Management, Records Management, Knowledge Management: the place of archives in a digital age. In Hill, J. (ed.), *The Future of Archives and Recordkeeping*, Facet Publishing.

Cook, M. (1986) *The Management of Information from Archives*, Gower.

Cook, T. (1984–5) From Information to Knowledge: an intellectual paradigm for archives, *Archivaria*, **19**, 28–49.

Cook, T. (1992) The Concept of the Archival *Fonds*: theory, description, and provenance in the post-custodial era. In Eastwood, T. (ed.), *The Archival Fonds: from theory to practice*, Bureau of Canadian Archivists.

Cook, T. (1997) What is Past is Prologue: a history of archival ideas since 1898, and the future paradigm shift, *Archivaria*, **43**, 17–63.

Cook, T. (2013) Evidence, Memory, Identity, and Community: four shifting archival paradigms, *Archival Science*, **13** (2–3), 95–120.

Cunningham, A. (2011) Good Digital Records Don't Just 'Happen': embedding digital recordkeeping as an organic component of business processes and systems, *Archivaria*, **71**, 21–34.

Dearstyne, B. W. (1999) Records Management of the Future: anticipate, adapt, and succeed, *Information Management Journal*, **33** (4), 4–16.

Evans, K. (2015) *Community and the Problem of Crime*, Routledge.

Eveleigh, A. (2017) Participatory Archives. In MacNeil, H. and Eastwood, T. (eds), *Currents of Archival Thinking*, 2nd edn, Libraries Unlimited.

Foscarini, F. (2017) Archival Appraisal in Four Paradigms. In MacNeil, H. and Eastwood, T. (eds), *Currents of Archival Thinking*, 2nd edn, Libraries Unlimited.

Friedrich, M. (2016) The Rise of Archival Consciousness in Provincial France: French feudal records and eighteenth-century seigneurial society, *Past and Present*, **230**, supplement 11, 49–70.

Gauld, C. (2017) Democratising or Privileging: the democratisation of knowledge and the role of the archivist, *Archival Science*, **17** (3), 227–45.

Gibson, W. (2005) God's Little Toys. *Wired*, July, www.wired.com/2005/07/gibson-3.

Gilliland, A. J. (2017) Archival and Recordkeeping Traditions in the Multiverse and Their Importance for Researching Situations and Situating Research. In Gilliland, A. J., McKemmish, S. and Lau, A. J.

(eds), *Research in the Archival Multiverse*, Monash University.

Grimard, J. (2005) Managing the Long-Term Preservation of Electronic Archives or Preserving the Medium and the Message, *Archivaria*, **59**, 153–67.

Hofman, H. (2005) The Archive. In McKemmish, S., Piggott, M., Reed, B. and Upward, F. (eds), *Archives: recordkeeping in society*, Charles Sturt University.

ISO 15489-1: 2001, *Information and Documentation – Records Management. Part 1: general*, International Organization for Standardization.

ISO 15489-1: 2016, *Information and Documentation – Records Management. Part 1: concepts and principles*, International Organization for Standardization.

ISO 30300: 2011, *Information and Documentation – Management Systems for Records – Fundamentals and Vocabulary*, International Organization for Standardization.

Jenkinson, H. (1944) Reflections of an Archivist, *Contemporary Review*, **165**, 355–61.

Jimerson, R. C. (2009) *Archives Power: memory, accountability, and social justice*, Society of American Archivists.

Johns, A. (1998) *The Nature of the Book: print and knowledge in the making*, University of Chicago Press.

Johnson, V. and Thomas, D. (2013) Digital Information: 'let a hundred flowers bloom . . .'. Is digital a cultural revolution? In Partner, N. and Foot, S. (eds), *The Sage Handbook of Historical Theory*, Sage.

Keen, A. (2007) *The Cult of the Amateur: how today's internet is killing our culture*, Doubleday.

Kesner, R. M. (1984–5) Automated Information Management: is there a role for the archivist in the office of the future? *Archivaria*, **19**, 162–72.

Ketelaar, E. (2001) Tacit Narratives: the meanings of archives, *Archival Science*, **1** (2), 131–41.

Kingston, R. (2011) The French Revolution and the Materiality of the Modern Archive, *Libraries and the Cultural Record*, **46** (1), 1–25.

Kuhn, T. (1962) *The Structure of Scientific Revolutions*, University of Chicago Press.

Landow, G. P. (1992) *Hypertext: the convergence of contemporary critical theory and technology*, Johns Hopkins University Press.

Lane, V. and Hill, J. (2011) Where Do We Come From? What Are We? Where Are We Going? Situating the archive and archivists. In Hill, J. (ed.), *The Future of Archives and Recordkeeping*, Facet Publishing.

Larsen, M. T. (1989) What They Wrote on Clay. In Schousboe, K. and Larsen, M. T. (eds), *Literacy and Society*, Akademisk Forlag.

Lemieux, V. L. (2015) Risk Management (Records). In Duranti, L. and Franks, P. C. (eds), *Encyclopedia of Archival Science*, Rowman & Littlefield.

Lemieux, V. L. (2016) Trusting Records: is blockchain technology the answer? *Records Management Journal*, **26** (2), 110–39.

Levy, D. M. (2001) *Scrolling Forward: making sense of documents in the digital age*, Arcade.

Luellig, L. (2012) A New Game Plan for Building a Retention Strategy that Works, *Information Management*, **46** (1), 31–4.

MacNeil, H. (1994) Archival Theory and Practice: between two paradigms, *Archivaria*, **37**, 6–20.

MacNeil, H. (2009) Trusting Description: authenticity, accountability, and archival description standards, *Journal of Archival Organization*, **7** (3), 89–107.

McKemmish, S. (1994) Are Records Ever Actual? In McKemmish, S. and Piggott, M. (eds), *The Records Continuum: Ian Maclean and Australian Archives first fifty years*, Ancora.

McLeod, J. (2008) *Why Am I a Records Manager?*, http://nrl.northumbria.ac.uk/8298/1/McLeodInauguralLecture.pdf.

Meyer, E. A. (2015) Writing in Roman Legal Contexts. In Johnston, D. (ed.), *The Cambridge Companion to Roman Law*, Cambridge University Press.

Moss, M. (2006) The Function of the Archive. In Tough, A. and Moss, M. (eds), *Record Keeping in a Hybrid Environment*, Chandos.

Muehlmann, S. (2014) The Speech Community and Beyond. In Enfield, N. J., Kockelman, P. and Sidnell, J. (eds), *The Cambridge Handbook of Linguistic Anthropology*, Cambridge University Press.

Nesmith, T. (2011) Documenting Appraisal as a Societal-Archival Process: theory, practice, and ethics in the wake of Helen Willa Samuels. In Cook, T. (ed.), *Controlling the Past: documenting society and institutions*, Society of American Archivists.

Noonan, D. W., McCrory, A. and Black, E. L. (2010) PDF/A: a viable addition to the preservation toolkit, *D-Lib Magazine*, **16** (11–12), www.dlib.org/dlib/november10/noonan/11noonan.html.

Panitch, J. M. (1996) Liberty, Equality, Posterity? Some archival lessons from the case of the French Revolution, *American Archivist*, **59** (1), 30–47.

Papailias, P. (2005) *Genres of Recollection: archival poetics and modern Greece*, Palgrave Macmillan.

Penn, I. A., Pennix, G. and Coulson, J. (1994) *Records Management Handbook*, 2nd edn, Gower.

Pierce Owen, M. (2016) From the Chair: ring in the new! *IRMS Bulletin*, **189**, 3.

Piggott, M. and McKemmish, S. (2002) *Recordkeeping, Reconciliation and Political Reality*, http://staging-infotech.monash.edu.au/research/groups/rcrg/publications/piggottmckemmish2002.pdf.

Preston, A. (2014) *Moving Lines: the anthropology of a manuscript in Tudor London*, MA thesis, University of Akron.

Prior, L. (2003) *Using Documents in Social Research*, Sage.

Reed, B. (2005) Records. In McKemmish, S., Piggott, M., Reed, B. and Upward, F. (eds), *Archives: recordkeeping in society*, Charles Sturt University.

Research Councils UK (2017) *Record DNA: reconceptualising the life of digital records as the future evidence base*, http://gtr.rcuk.ac.uk/projects?ref=AH%2FP006868%2F1.

Ricks, B. R. and Gow, K. F. (1984) *Information Resource Management*, South-Western Publishing.

Rio, A. (2009) *Legal Practice and the Written Word in the Early Middle Ages*, Cambridge University Press.

Rosch, E. (1978) Principles of Categorization. In Rosch, E. and Lloyd, B. B. (eds), *Cognition and Categorization*, Lawrence Erlbaum.

Salomon, F. (2002) Patrimonial Khipu in a Modern Peruvian Village. In Quilter, J. and Urton, G. (eds), *Narrative Threads: accounting and recounting in Andean khipu*, University of Texas Press.

Schamber, L. (1996) What is a Document? Rethinking the concept in uneasy times, *Journal of the American Society for Information Science*, **47** (9), 669–71.

Schellenberg, T. R. (1956) *Modern Archives: principles and techniques*, F. W. Cheshire.

Scott, P. J. (1966) The Record Group Concept: a case for abandonment, *American Archivist*, **29** (4), 493–504.

Scott-Warren, J. (2016) Early Modern Bookkeeping and Life-Writing Revisited: accounting for Richard Stonley, *Past and Present*, **230**, supplement 11, 151–70.

Selden, R., Widdowson, P. and Brooker, P. (2005) *A Reader's Guide to Contemporary Literary Theory*, 5th edn, Pearson.

Smith, E. E. and Medin, D. L. (1981) *Categories and Concepts*, Harvard University Press.

Taylor, H. A. (1984) Information Ecology and the Archives of the 1980s, *Archivaria*, **18**, 25–37.

Taylor, H. A. (1987–8) Transformation in the Archives: technological adjustment or paradigm shift? *Archivaria*, **25**, 12–28.

Thibodeau, K. (2009) The Survival of Records (and Records Management) in the Twenty-First Century. In Tibbo, H. R., Hank, C., Lee, C. A. and Clemens, R. (eds), *Digital Curation: practice, promise and prospects. Proceedings of DigCCurr 2009*, University of North Carolina.

Trombley, S. (2016) Self-Reinvention: the next step for future-forward information professionals, *IRMS Bulletin*, **194**, 50–1.

Upward, F. (1996) Structuring the Records Continuum. Part One: postcustodial principles and properties, *Archives and Manuscripts*, **24** (2), 268–85.

Upward, F. (2000) Modelling the Continuum as Paradigm Shift in Recordkeeping and Archiving Processes, and Beyond: a personal reflection, *Records Management Journal*, **10** (3), 115–39.

Upward, F. (2004) The Records Continuum and the Concept of an End Product, *Archives and Manuscripts*, **32** (1), 40–62.

Urton, G. (2005) Khipu Archives: duplicate accounts and identity labels in the Inka knotted string records, *Latin American Antiquity*, **16** (2), 147–67.

Wallace, P. E., Schubert, D. R., Lee, J. A. and Thomas, V. S. (1987) *Records Management: integrated information systems*, 2nd edn, John Wiley & Sons.

Yeo, G. (2008) Concepts of Record (2): prototypes and boundary objects, *American Archivist*, **71** (1), 118–43.

Yeo, G. (2009) Custodial History, Provenance, and the Description of Personal Records, *Libraries and the Cultural Record*, **44** (1), 50–64.

Yeo, G. (2012) Bringing Things Together: aggregate records in a digital age, *Archivaria*, **74**, 43–91.

Yeo, G. (2014) Contexts, Original Orders, and Item-Level Orientation: responding creatively to users' needs and technological change, *Journal of Archival Organization*, **12** (3–4), 170–85.

Yeo, G. (2017) Continuing Debates about Description. In MacNeil, H. and Eastwood, T. (eds), *Currents of Archival Thinking*, 2nd edn, Libraries Unlimited.

CHAPTER 3

Archivists, records managers and the rise of information

Introduction

In October 1947, Sir Hilary Jenkinson, the doyen of 20th-century English archivists, gave a lecture to inaugurate the newly established archival education programme at University College London. Jenkinson used this auspicious occasion to describe the curriculum that he thought appropriate for students of archives. In the part of his lecture devoted to 'the attainments necessary for the Complete Archivist' (Jenkinson, 1948, 14), he expounded the need for prospective archivists to study administrative history, diplomatic, palaeography and repository methods and techniques. He emphasised the importance of conservation and custody, and spoke of the use of records in academic research and the relations between the archivist and the historian. He also addressed the subject of evidence, and – in a resounding conclusion to the lecture – proclaimed the 'sanctity of evidence' as the archivist's creed.

But Jenkinson said nothing about *information* as a subject of study for archivists; it played no part in his proposed curriculum. Although he knew the word 'information' and used it occasionally in other contexts, he probably never expected that, over time, information would become a significant motif in archival discourse. Today, however, the study of information seems predominant. In the early 21st century, archival education appears to have found a home in the iSchools movement, which seeks to provide scholarly environments where 'issues of information' are addressed and expertise in the use of information is developed (Cox and Larsen, 2011, 13, 26). At University College London, the School of Librarianship and Archives (as it was called in Jenkinson's day) has been renamed the Department of Information Studies. It now claims to educate students for 'the information professions' and its website describes archives and records management as an 'information discipline'.[1]

These changes reflect wider trends that can be observed in contemporary society and in the world of record-keeping. In recent years, records management organizations in several countries have changed their names or adjusted their preferred terminology. The Records Management Society of Great Britain has become the Information and Records Management Society. The former Records Management Association of Australasia is now Records and Information Management Professionals Australasia. In the USA, members of the professional association ARMA International have also largely rejected the term 'records management' in favour of 'records and information management' as a label for their disciplinary practice.

Similar trends can be observed in the changing terminology used in published literature. Figure 3.1 on the opposite page is derived from Google Books Ngram Viewer, which purports to measure the frequency of particular terms used in publications scanned by Google; it demonstrates an apparent rise in the use of the term 'records management' in literature of the 1970s and 1980s, followed by a decline in its use since the 1990s. Figure 3.2 shows how Ngram Viewer depicts the rapidly growing popularity of the term 'records and information management' over the same period.[2] The trend indicated in Figure 3.2 will doubtless be familiar to most people who have worked in the records profession in English-speaking countries in recent decades.

After replacing 'records' by 'records and information', the next step for some professional associations has been to move toward seemingly abandoning the word 'records'. ARMA International has been in the forefront of this movement. In 1999, it relabelled its periodical, the *Records Management Quarterly*, as the *Information Management Journal*. Three years later, it published a booklet for American corporate executives, addressing what it would once have called records management concerns, under the title *Information Management: a Business Imperative* (ARMA International, 2002). More recently, the

Figure 3.1 *Ngram Viewer: usage of the term 'records management'*

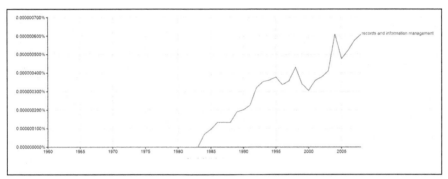

Figure 3.2 *Ngram Viewer: usage of the term 'records and information management'*

same trend has been observable in Britain, where the Information and Records Management Society issued a new mission statement that made no mention of records; in 2014, the society announced its aim 'to be the home of all those engaged in the management, governance or utilisation of information' (Information and Records Management Society, 2014, 4). The society's *Bulletin* now carries a strapline promoting itself as 'the interactive hub of the information world'.

Although changes of this kind seem to have met with broad approval among members of the associations concerned, they have not been entirely uncontroversial. This chapter sets out to examine the thinking that underlies these changes, to look more widely at the contexts in which ideas about 'the management, governance or utilisation of information' came to the attention of records professionals and to analyse some of the responses that these ideas have evoked.

Accentuating information in contemporary culture

Today, records managers often contend that the term 'information' has a broader appeal than 'records'. In informal conversations, many records managers have told me that they now think it essential to use the language of information in order to communicate effectively with colleagues, 'keep up with the times' or avoid marginalisation in the workplace. ARMA International's decision to substitute 'information' for 'records' in the title of its journal was said to emanate from a desire 'to position our field in a strategically advantageous manner' (Dearstyne, 1999, 4). Other commentators, too, have observed that an emphasis on information can be seen as a way of bolstering the professional profile of records managers, enhancing their influence and overcoming the poor visibility of records management (Cox, 2005, 206; Kahn and Blair, 2009, 6).

These aspirations are supported by a cultural and economic environment in which governments and commercial interests constantly promote the importance of information and affirm its social and economic benefits. Advertisements and consultants' sales pitches regularly tell us that it is the most valuable commodity in business. British government publications claim that, in the 21st century, information is 'the force powering our democracy', the foundation of effective policy making and 'the lifeblood of virtually every service we use as citizens' (UK Government, 2008, 1–2; UK Government, Cabinet Office, 2017, 3). As social historian Theodore Roszak (1994, 3, xiv) noted, before the Second World War 'information was nothing to get excited about', but since then it 'has had a remarkable rags-to-riches career' and 'has come to be connected with a historic transition in our economic life'.

Above all, for many people, 'information' now evokes the world of computing. Computer scientists have come to see themselves as purveyors of information systems, and use the term 'information technology' to reiterate the informational aspects of their role. Unlike the dusty image that has often been associated with records and archives, the predominant image of computing is of a field that is vibrant, exciting and up-to-the-minute. It is scarcely surprising if records professionals are frequently tempted to use the vocabulary of information technology in the hope that some of the resources and influence it attracts will come their way.

Figure 3.3 is a further Ngram, which portrays the changing usage of 'information' and 'record' in published literature over the past 140 years, and the rising popularity of 'information' since the 1950s. If this Ngram is to be believed, the fortunes of the two terms have been very different.

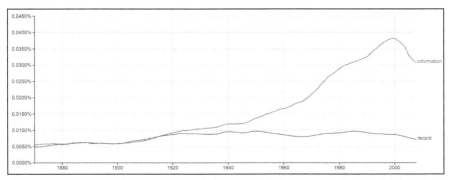

Figure 3.3 *Ngram Viewer: usage of the terms 'information' (upper line) and 'record' (lower line)*

The desirability and high status attributed to information have also been reflected in numerous pronouncements about the emergence of an Information Society. Much heralded in recent decades, the Information Society is supposedly a new type of society in which technological tools produce and manage unprecedented quantities of information, and economies are characterised by post-industrial workforces that use and share information in creative ways (Duff, 2000; Karvalics, 2008; Wilson, Kellerman and Corey, 2013). Scholars sometimes treat this thesis with suspicion, but to many in the popular media, in the world of business and in political circles, this is a powerful message.

The notion of progress towards an Information Society is often equated with the growing deployment of digital technology. Many commentators assert that the Information Society has arrived, and that it is the form of society in which we now live. As early as 1982, the American Office of Technology Assessment proclaimed that 'the United States has become an information society' (Roszak, 1994, 23). For others, however, it remains an aspiration, or work in progress. When the United Nations World Summit on the Information Society first met in 2003, it declared its 'common desire and commitment to build a[n] . . . Information Society, where everyone can create, access, utilize and share information and knowledge'.[3] A study published in 2013 affirmed that the Information Society is 'still unfolding' (Wilson, Kellerman and Corey, 2013, 11). Although much of the current discourse about the Information Society seems to be driven by the concerns of computer scientists, records and archives have made intermittent appearances; for example, the World Summit's 2003 'Plan of Action' included proposals to develop a framework for secure storage of digital records, together with 'policies and laws to ensure that libraries, archives . . . and other cultural institutions can play their full role . . . in the Information Society'.[4]

Records management and information governance

In many respects, records managers' enthusiastic adoption of the term 'information' can be seen as a response, not just to the explosion of technology or to notions of an incipient Information Society, but also to the growth of what might be called the compliance agenda. In many countries, an important factor has been the arrival of measures to enhance accountability and transparency in public administration, and especially of laws that purport to give citizens rights of access to information held by governments and public-sector organizations. Laws of this kind have been adopted in more than 100 countries during the past half-century (Lemieux and Trapnell, 2016; Shepherd, 2017). Although these are usually called 'freedom of information', 'right to information' or 'access to information' laws, some commentators observe that citizens normally gain access to *records* rather than information (Sprehe, 2000, 24); legislators, however, have generally assumed that 'information' is the right word to use.

In the USA, a similar transition has occurred in connection with the growth of e-discovery (the practice of identifying and safeguarding digital materials that are needed to respond to lawsuits). Since the beginning of the 21st century, a significant community of e-discovery specialists has emerged; it includes technical experts and lawyers as well as people whose professional background is in records management or related fields. Members of this community usually speak of the discovery of 'electronically stored information' rather than digital records. In the discourse of its adherents, the phrase 'electronically stored information' is usually abbreviated to 'ESI', and it has been claimed that ESI was the factor that 'changed the science of records management to the point that a new term . . . *records and information management*' had to be coined (Kahn and Blair, 2009, 65).

Organizational compliance with laws and regulations, and the need to preserve and locate records required for litigation, have long been recognised as crucial areas to which records management contributes, but have recently been bundled up with a broader range of concerns that are often labelled 'information governance'. While the Ngram in Figure 3.2 suggests that the rise of 'records and information management' was a gradual phenomenon that occurred over two decades, Figure 3.4 implies that the term 'information governance' acquired sudden popularity at the start of the 21st century. Its growing popularity can also be seen in the chart in Figure 3.5 on the next page, derived from another of Google's analytical tools (Google Trends). This chart represents the relative numbers of online searches for 'information governance' that were made using the Google search engine in 2006, 2011 and 2016. Charts such as these need to be treated with caution, but they illustrate a development that many records professionals will have observed.

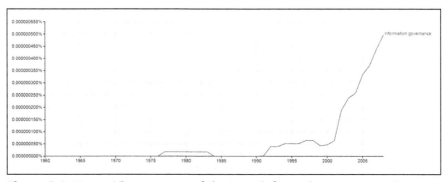

Figure 3.4 *Ngram Viewer: usage of the term 'information governance'*

The rise to prominence of 'information governance' had its origins in a report published in England in 2001 by the Information Policy Unit of the Department of Health, which proposed it as a label for a new strategic framework embracing system and process management, records management, data quality, data protection and controlled

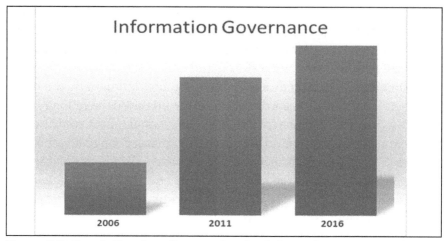

Figure 3.5 *Google Trends: online searches for 'information governance'*

information sharing within the National Health Service in the UK (Department of Health, 2001, 32). The term 'information governance' was well established in the British health sector by 2004 (Donaldson and Walker, 2004; Keyser and Dainty, 2005), and had attracted the attention of some senior staff at The National Archives of the UK by 2005 (Blake, 2005), but it did not come to the notice of mainstream records managers in North America until about 2009, the year in which the Gartner consultancy published an information governance toolkit (Logan and Geragas, 2009). The term seems to have made its first appearance in ARMA International's professional journal in that year (Lanter, 2009). Since then, it has been adopted by the e-discovery community in the USA and by many records management practitioners and professional bodies.

Some critics insist that information governance, as promoted in the second decade of the 21st century, is simply a rebranding of records management (Lueders, 2014). Others, however, see it as encompassing a wider range of concerns, or as offering a strategic framework within which records management activities are performed (Saffady, 2015). For Jason Baron (2015), information governance 'is best viewed as a coordinating function for a variety of important interests within the corporate enterprise'. A cross-disciplinary consortium, the Information Governance Initiative, has suggested that the components of information governance include not only the compliance and privacy issues that are familiar to records managers and archivists, but also matters such as information security, which are more usually associated with managing computer systems. In practice, interpretations of information governance can vary from one organization – or one type of organization – to another, but it is often viewed in terms of risk management; information governance programmes generally seek to identify and mitigate the risks that would arise if issues relating to information security, privacy, confidentiality or legal compliance are inadequately addressed. Information governance has been heralded as 'a new discipline that . . . represents a major evolutionary shift in how organizations understand, use, and . . . govern their information' (Information Governance Initiative, 2014).

However, there is also a sense in which the practice of information governance seems more restrictive than records management, which has often sought to address ways in which records can add value to an organization's activities, as well as the risks that an organization may incur and the controls deemed necessary to counteract them. Information governance does not focus on knowledge sharing, supporting corporate memory, improving decision-making or contributing to business performance or service delivery. It usually emphasises threats rather than opportunities, and is most likely to be effective in highly regulated organizations where compliance, account-ability and risk mitigation are seen as essential. As British records manager Stephen Harries (2012, 6, 13) has noted, a concentration on regulatory compliance can 'easily become a battle against innovation, in which records managers are . . . always in the position of saying No'. The management of records, or information, then becomes a burden rather than a value-adding activity for organizational employees. James Lappin (2014) has made a similar point, arguing that the information governance model neglects aspirations to design records systems that benefit internal users, in favour of an emphasis on risk management and compliance with the requirements of external stakeholders.

Nevertheless, the concept of information governance has become influential both in the public sector and among private-sector organizations, and the term is now widely used in the UK and North America. While some commentators have seen its adoption by records managers primarily as a profile-raising exercise – an attempt 'to get a seat at the table of senior executives' (Hagmann, 2013, 229) – others affirm with apparent conviction that notions of record-keeping as a distinct practice are obsolescent and that records management should be, or has been, absorbed into information governance. Particularly in the USA, it has become commonplace to assert that this change has now occurred. Organizations, we are told, have abandoned '20th century records management protocols . . . to embrace a broader, interconnected scope of information governance as a unifying business priority' (Ritter, 2015).

Information and archives

Much of the recent discourse gives the impression that records management is being overtaken by more exciting developments in the contemporary world of information. However, it is not only the records management field whose future has been challenged or called into question; broadly similar trends can also be observed in official pronouncements about archival institutions that keep records primarily for cultural reasons. In 1998, the director of informatics of Unesco (the United Nations Educational, Scientific and Cultural Organization) told an international meeting of archivists that 'archives should not remain on the margins of the Information Society as mere repositories of historical records', but 'should become central information and content providers . . . for the sake of the common good' (Quéau, 1998, 26). In 2000, the British government announced that it expected 'the archives sector' to 'adapt itself to the information revolution' (UK Government, 2000, 17); in 2008, the chief executive of The National Archives of the UK affirmed that the model of a contemporary archival institution 'needs to shift from records to information', and that 'archives are about managing, collecting, preserving and enabling access to information' (Ceeney, 2008, 68–9). As we have seen in Chapter 2, many archivists might argue that archives are at least as much about evidence, memory, identity or community as 'about . . . information', but the rhetoric of information has often prevailed in government circles in recent years.

The language of information has also been used to support arguments that archival institutions should seek to converge with museums and libraries. The similarities and common interests, real or supposed, among archives, museums and libraries have been much discussed. Some commentators have argued a case for convergence based on a shared interest in cultural heritage (Martin, 2007), memory (Robinson, 2012) or digital curation (Higgins, 2013; Tammaro, Madrid and Casarosa, 2013), but for many advocates of convergence the unifying elements are the beliefs that 'archives, libraries and museums all deal with information' (Usherwood, Wilson and Bryson, 2005, 90) and that their personnel all belong to 'information-focused professions' (Given and McTavish, 2010, 26; Marty, 2014, 617).

This line of thinking was strongly developed in the work of W. Boyd Rayward (1996), who affirmed that archives, libraries and museums are all components of what he called 'information infrastructure', differentiated only by the format of the materials they collect and manage. Many supporters of multidisciplinary convergence have followed Rayward's arguments about the need for integrated approaches to information, contending (for example) that in professional education 'there appears to be space for archival and museum studies under the information-related "umbrella"' (Given and McTavish, 2010, 25). Perhaps unsurprisingly, most promoters of these views are librarians or information scientists rather than archivists or museum curators; in claiming that the days of separate library, archive and museum professions are numbered, some have argued that the leading role in the proposed unified future falls naturally to libraries (Prasad, 2011, 209).

Although proponents of convergence often make no mention of records management, some commentators have also included records management in their list of disciplines that should or will come together with librarianship in the unified future that they foresee. As Adrian Cunningham (1998, 420) has noted, many librarians – and many records managers with library backgrounds – tend to believe 'that records management and librarianship share common if not identical goals and . . . principles' that centre on the management of information. Convergence arguments, however, are rarely left to rest on goals and principles alone. The decisive factor is often said to be the digital information revolution. Many convergence advocates argue that technology now leads users to expect seamless access to records, museum objects and library materials, and to become impatient of their traditionally separate access routes; some go further and claim that digital resources no longer fall into these distinct conceptual categories. When 'all media have converged into bitstreams' (Naughton, 2012, 152), it seemingly becomes possible to affirm that records and library materials have been homogenised and that separate curatorial institutions are no longer needed.

Like records managers, archivists have sometimes appeared keen to reposition their discipline within the emerging world of information. In the USA, for example, David Bearman and Richard Lytle (1985–6, 14) encouraged the archival profession to 'make a transition to the modern information culture', and Randall Jimerson (1989, 340) argued that archivists must strive to become part of the Information Society. Former National Archivist James Rhoads (1989) claimed that both current records and historical archives are significant components of a nation's information resources and 'should be integral parts of the national information system'. In a paper published in a Swiss journal, Frank Boles and Mark Greene (2001, 435) argued forcefully that 'the broader objective of archives, as the mainstream of US archivists sees it, is . . . to preserve and make available information'. In Britain, Michael Cook (1999, 11) affirmed that archives belong to the universe of information media, and Nicole Convery (2011, 207) advocated 'an inclusive view of the realm of archivists as . . . part of the . . . information management arena'. In the view of all these commentators, archival work is – or should now be – aligned with what they see as a larger domain of information resources.

Some records professionals have warned of the risks of embracing the information agenda. When Canadian archivist Terry Cook (1990–1b, 127) warned that archives must not become 'the McDonald's of information', he was perhaps expressing anxiety about archival institutions attempting to mimic a fast-food outlet's approach to mass-marketing, rather than about contemporary perceptions of an information culture. But other records professionals have perceived the march of information as dangerous. Over 30 years ago, Gordon Dodds (1984, 272) asked whether archives were 'in danger of . . . dissolving into an enormous cauldron of informational resources'. More recently, Stephen Harries (2012, 15), without quoting Dodds, answered his question in the affirmative: 'there is a danger that the concept of records becomes diluted in a sea of information'. Margaret Pember and Roberta Cowan (2009, 2) used a different metaphor when they warned of records becoming 'lost in the information fog'. In his book *Archives & Archivists in the Information Age*, Richard Cox (2005, 206) enquired how often records professionals have 'been duped into thinking that their primary responsibility is information rather than records'. Nevertheless, these are perhaps minority opinions; the prevailing view in much of Europe and North America seems to be that, as Bruno Delmas (2001, 29) expressed it, 'the society of information in which we are today compels us to reconsider archival science'.

Making connections between records and information: diverse views

In this climate, many scholars and practitioners have been led to examine, or at least to make affirmations about, the conceptual relationships between records and information. A widely held view is that records are a *type* of information. Dutch archival educator Theo Thomassen (2001, 374) characterised them as 'information that is generated by and linked to work processes'. For Gillian Oliver and Fiorella Foscarini (2014, 20, 95), records are 'information as evidence', as opposed to the 'information for knowledge and awareness' that concerns librarians. For the authors of *The Sedona Guidelines* on records management, a record is 'information deemed to have some enduring value . . . and warranting special attention concerning retention, accessibility, and retrieval' (The Sedona Conference, 2007, 3). Other authors have equated records management to 'dealing with internally generated proprietary information' (McLeod and Hare, 2006, 11), or record-keeping to 'managing unpublished information objects in context' (Tough and Moss, 2006). All these authors indicate or imply that (in their opinion) records are a type of information, but they have differing views on what might distinguish records from other information types; there is no agreement on whether records are information that has not been published, or information that is evidential, or proprietary, or process-bound, or of continuing value.

As we saw in Chapter 2, the compilers of the international standard for records management (ISO 15489-1: 2016) define records as 'information created, received and maintained . . . by an organization or person, in pursuance of legal obligations or in the transaction of business'; this definition, too, suggests that a record is a particular type of information. Broadly similar definitions can be found in the *Glossary* produced by ARMA International (2016) and in the archival description standard *ISAD(G)* (International Council on Archives, 2000). Some records management textbooks likewise affirm that records are a type or category of information (Kahn and Blair, 2009, 23; Penn, Pennix and Coulson, 1994, 4). Other authors, however, describe records as a *subset* of information (Borglund and Öberg, 2006, 2; Franks, 2013, 57). Depending on the perspective adopted by the author, information is seen either as a genus of which records are a species, or as a whole of which records are a part.

Such views are not universally shared. Some professionals define a record as a type of *document*; in the work of the InterPARES project based at the University of British Columbia, records are described as documents made or received in the course of activity and set aside (Duranti, 2005, 363; Duranti and Preston, 2008, 832). Others have preferred to define records in terms of *evidence* (Bearman, 1994, 15; Australian Public Service Commission, 2007, 4), typically characterising them as evidence of business transactions and emphasising the roles they can play in supporting accountability. Definitions like these reflect distinctive understandings of records and implicitly differentiate them from information. Indeed, in the 1990s, writers who emphasised the evidential function of records often stated that records are 'more than information' or that they are 'not information' at all.[5] Terry Cook (1990–1a, 176) and Glenda Acland (1992, 58) both forcefully promoted the view that 'archivists . . . are in the *understanding* business, not the *information* business'.

However, in the new millennium, these voices are muted; linking records with information is commonplace, both in Europe and in North America. Many records managers now use the words 'information' and 'records' interchangeably. In his book *Managing the Crowd*, British records manager Steve Bailey (2008, xiv, 146) noted that he had deliberately referred to 'information' where readers might have expected the word 'records', because the 'rationale for making a distinction between records and information is steadily disappearing' and only 'purists . . . still want to distinguish the record from other information'. In North America, both in professional literature and in guidance issued to users, statements such as 'records management programs . . . manage organizational information' (Federal Aviation

Administration, 2012) and 'the discipline of records management . . . govern[s] information from creation to final disposition' (Hoke, 2011, 29) have become almost routine.

Even in Australia, where the view that records are evidence rather than information was most loudly promoted, the website of the National Archives of Australia now affirms that records management practices are essential to ensure that 'business information is well managed' and explains that the National Archives will assist government agencies in improving information management.[6] The 'recordkeeping informatics' approach now advocated by a number of academics in Australia (Upward et al., 2013) seems to conceptualise the keeping of records as a specialised form of information management and has adopted the word 'informatics' in order to situate it in an information environment (Cumming, 2015, 322; Upward, 2015, 337).

Managing information 'as a record'

Another notion often proposed by records managers is that information, or particular kinds of information, can or should be 'managed as a record'. In the USA, the Institute of Certified Records Managers (2017) asserts a need for qualified professionals to 'know what metadata is required to define, classify, and manage information as a record'. The Australian National Audit Office (2015) contends that 'information created and captured as evidence of . . . business should be managed as a record'. The international standard on *Management Systems for Records* (ISO 30300: 2011) also advocates the 'systematic management of information as records'. Although seemingly absent from the first edition of the longer-established records management standard ISO 15489 (2001), this mode of thinking has found its way into the second edition, which affirms that 'any set of information, regardless of its structure or form, can be managed as a record' (ISO 15489-1: 2016, clause 5.1). The origins of the phrase 'managed as a record' do not appear to be known, but the idea has become resilient; it is usually linked to the view that records must be managed in special ways to ensure their continuing trustworthiness and integrity.

Traditionally, records managers assumed that these qualities are best protected by moving or capturing records into formal record-keeping systems, although more recently it has been argued that capture is often inessential and records can be maintained within business systems where they originate. Proponents of capture generally affirm that a formal record-keeping system can ensure that records are stabilised and safeguarded against premature destruction, inadvertent alteration or malicious tampering, and they often seek to restrict the term 'records' to materials that have been captured into a system that offers these capabilities. In digital environments, until lately, records managers usually labelled uncaptured items as 'documents'; those documents deemed to merit special protection were declared to be records when they were captured in a record-keeping system and formally passed into corporate control (ANSI/AIIM/ARMA TR48-2004, 18). Today, however, the word 'document' seems to have fallen out of favour in the records management community. Instead, we are sometimes told that *information* can be declared as a record and managed according to special rules (Goodyear, 2013, 11; Kahn and Blair, 2009, 11, 15).

In the past few years, many of those who see records as 'information . . . managed according to special rules' have begun to argue that decisions to designate certain information for special treatment are arbitrary and that commercial and governmental organizations need to control the whole of the information relating to their business operations (Convery, 2011, 209; Franks, 2013, 62; Hagmann, 2013, 229). Proponents of the notion that organizations should change, or are changing, 'from management of declared records to management of all . . . information' (AIIM Industry Watch, 2014, 7) often see a reflection of this change in the terminological shift from 'records management' to 'information governance'. They argue that – in jurisdictions where privacy or freedom of information laws are in force – all of an organization's information may be subject to those laws, that it is all potentially discoverable in the event of litigation, and that litigants and other users are unlikely to care whether information has been declared as a record or not (AIIM Industry Watch, 2014, 4; Bailey, 2008, 56; Franks, 2013, 241).

Outside the records management community, notions that information can be declared or managed 'as a record' are largely unknown; even among records managers, this mode of thinking is not universally accepted. Indeed, a newcomer observing our field might be surprised when practitioners connect records and information in this manner. In everyday language, speakers and writers refer to a record *of* something, but information *about* something; we can speak of having 20 or 200 records, but English idiom does not allow us to speak of 20 or 200 informations. Records and information may both be matters of importance, but they do not seem to behave in the same way.

An observer might also remark that, despite the widespread and growing practice of associating records with information, practitioners' views on the nature of this supposed association are very disparate and sometimes appear incompatible. For example, the view that information can be managed as a record does not seem easily reconcilable with the opinion that governance of information is superseding the management of records; the view that records are a distinct type or subset of information seems incompatible with the perception that differences between records and information are vanishing. Professional literature has rarely attempted to resolve these conflicts.

In much recent literature, the presumed relationships between records and information tend to be asserted rather than argued or analysed. There are many conceptual questions that require deeper investigation if we are to reach useful conclusions about connections or divergences between records and information. To what do we refer when we speak of 'information'? What might be meant by a 'record'? Are information and records commensurate? The following chapters seek to unpick some aspects of the concepts of 'information' and 'records', and to ask how far, and in what ways, distinctions between them might remain valid in the digital world.

Endnotes

1 See www.ucl.ac.uk/dis/; www.ucl.ac.uk/dis/study.
2 These figures are reproduced by courtesy of Google Books Ngram Viewer, http://books.google.com/ngrams/info.
3 See www.itu.int/wsis/docs/geneva/official/dop.html.
4 See www.itu.int/wsis/docs/geneva/official/poa.html. It is unclear how far attempts have been made to implement this plan.
5 The view that records are 'more than information' was prominently

affirmed in early versions of the New South Wales *Government Recordkeeping Manual*, which has now been removed from the website of State Records New South Wales.

6 See www.naa.gov.au/information-management/information-governance/evidence/;
www.naa.gov.au/information-management/selecting-national-archives/;
www.naa.gov.au/information-management/information-management-standard/im-standard-document.aspx.

References

Acland, G. (1992) Managing the Record Rather than the Relic, *Archives and Manuscripts*, **20** (1), 57–63.

AIIM Industry Watch (2014) *Automating Information Governance: assuring compliance*, Association for Information and Image Management.

ANSI/AIIM/ARMA TR48-2004 *Framework for Integration of Electronic Document Management Systems and Electronic Records Management Systems*, American National Standards Institute, Association for Information and Image Management and ARMA International.

ARMA International (2002) *Information Management: a business imperative*, https://netdiligence.com/wp-content/uploads/2017/03/rim_imperative.pdf.

ARMA International (2016) *Glossary of Records Management and Information Governance Terms*, 5th edn, ARMA International.

Australian National Audit Office (2015) *Records Management in Health*, www.anao.gov.au/work/performance-audit/records-management-health.

Australian Public Service Commission (2007) *Note for File: a report on recordkeeping in the Australian public service*, www.apsc.gov.au/__data/assets/pdf_file/0014/51224/noteforfile.pdf.

Bailey, S. (2008) *Managing the Crowd: rethinking records management for the Web 2.0 world*, Facet Publishing.

Baron, J. R. (2015) *Information Governance to Take Centre Stage*, https://ethicalboardroom.com/information-governance-to-take-centre-stage.

Bearman, D. (1994) *Electronic Evidence: strategies for managing records in contemporary organizations*, Archives and Museum Informatics.

Bearman, D. A. and Lytle, R. H. (1985–6) The Power of the Principle of

Provenance, *Archivaria*, **21**, 14–27.

Blake, R. (2005) *ERM Compliance Review Methodology*, http://dlmforum.typepad.com/Paper_RichardBlake_ ERMcompliancereviewmethodology.pdf.

Boles, F. and Greene, M. (2001) Confusing the Bun for the Burger: rehabilitating the role of content in the archival context, *Schweizerische Zeitschrift für Geschichte*, **51**, 424–47.

Borglund, E., and Öberg, L.-M. (2006) *Operational Use of Records*, www.itu.dk/iris29/IRIS29/6-3.pdf.

Ceeney, N. (2008) The Role of a 21st-Century National Archive: the relevance of the Jenkinsonian tradition, and a redefinition for the Information Society, *Journal of the Society of Archivists*, **29** (1), 57–71.

Convery, N. (2011) Information Management, Records Management, Knowledge Management: the place of archives in a digital age. In Hill, J. (ed.), *The Future of Archives and Recordkeeping*, Facet Publishing.

Cook, M. (1999) *The Management of Information from Archives*, 2nd edn, Gower.

Cook, T. (1990–1a) Rites of Passage: the archivist and the information age, *Archivaria*, **31**, 171–6.

Cook, T. (1990–1b) Viewing the World Upside Down: reflections on the theoretical underpinnings of archival public programming, *Archivaria*, **31**, 123–34.

Cox, R. J. (2005) *Archives & Archivists in the Information Age*, Neal-Schuman.

Cox, R. J. and Larsen, R. L. (2011) *iSchools and Archival Studies*, revised version, http://d-scholarship.pitt.edu/5851/4/iSchools_%26_Archival_Studies.pdf.

Cumming, K. (2015) Recordkeeping. In Duranti, L. and Franks, P. C. (eds), *Encyclopedia of Archival Science*, Rowman & Littlefield.

Cunningham, A. (1998) Review of Brittain, J. M. (ed.), *Introduction to Information Management*, *Archives and Manuscripts*, **26** (2), 418–21.

Dearstyne, B. W. (1999) Records Management of the Future: anticipate, adapt, and succeed, *Information Management Journal*, **33** (4), 4–16.

Delmas, B. (2001) Archival Science Facing the Information Society, *Archival Science*, **1** (1), 25–37.

Department of Health (2001) *Building the Information Core: protecting and using confidential patient information*, www.igt.hscic.gov.uk/KnowledgeBaseNew/NHSNumber-Building%20the %20information%20core%20protecting%20and%20using%20confidential% 20patient%20information%20a%20strategy%20for%20the%20NHS.pdf.

Dodds, G. (1984) Review of Orwell, G., *Nineteen Eighty-Four*, *Archivaria*, **18**, 268–72.

Donaldson, A. and Walker, P. (2004) Information Governance: a view from the NHS, *International Journal of Medical Informatics*, **73** (3), 281–4.

Duff, A. S. (2000) *Information Society Studies*, Routledge.

Duranti, L. (ed.) (2005) *The Long-Term Preservation of Authentic Electronic Records: findings of the InterPARES project*, Archilab.

Duranti, L. and Preston, R. (eds) (2008) *International Research on Permanent Authentic Records in Electronic Systems (InterPARES 2)*, Coop Libraria Editrice Università di Padova.

Federal Aviation Administration (2012) *Why Records Management? Ten business reasons*, www.faa.gov/about/initiatives/records/what/why_records_management.

Franks, P. C. (2013) *Records and Information Management*, American Library Association and Neal-Schuman.

Given, L. M. and McTavish, L. (2010) What's Old Is New Again: the reconvergence of libraries, archives, and museums in the digital age, *Library Quarterly*, **80** (1), 7–32.

Goodyear, S. (2013) *Practical SharePoint 2013 Enterprise Content Management*, Apress.

Hagmann, J. (2013) Information Governance – Beyond the Buzz, *Records Management Journal*, **23** (3), 228–40.

Harries, S. (2012) *Records Management and Knowledge Management: a handbook for regulation, innovation and transformation*, Chandos.

Higgins, S. (2013) Digital Curation: the challenge driving convergence across memory institutions. In Duranti, L. and Shaffer, E. (eds), *The Memory of the World in the Digital Age: digitization and preservation*, Unesco.

Hoke, G. E. J. (2011) Records Life Cycle: a cradle-to-grave metaphor, *Information Management*, **45** (5), 28–32.

Information and Records Management Society (2014) The Executive Sets a Course, *IRMS Bulletin*, **181**, 4–5.

Information Governance Initiative (2014) *2014 Annual Report Sneak Peak: the facets of information governance*, http://iginitiative.com/2014-annual-report-sneak-peek-the-facets-of-information-governance.

Institute of Certified Records Managers (2017) *Records and Information: creation and use*, www.icrm.org/annotated-outline-part-2.

International Council on Archives (2000) *ISAD(G): general international standard archival description*, 2nd edn, International Council on Archives.

ISO 15489: 2001, *Information and Documentation – Records Management*, International Organization for Standardization.

ISO 15489-1: 2016, *Information and Documentation – Records Management. Part 1: concepts and principles*, International Organization for Standardization.

ISO 30300: 2011, *Information and Documentation – Management Systems for Records – Fundamentals and Vocabulary*, International Organization for Standardization.

Jenkinson, H. (1948) *The English Archivist: a new profession*, H. K. Lewis & Co.

Jimerson, R. C. (1989) Redefining Archival Identity: meeting user needs in the Information Society, *American Archivist*, **52** (3), 332–40.

Kahn, R. A. and Blair, B. T. (2009) *Information Nation: seven keys to information management compliance*, 2nd edn, Wiley Publishing.

Karvalics, L. Z. (2008) Information Society – What Is It Exactly? The meaning, history and conceptual framework of an expression. In Pintér, R. (ed.), *Information Society: from theory to political practice*, Gondolat.

Keyser, T. and Dainty, C. (2005) *The Information Governance Toolkit*, Radcliffe Publishing.

Lanter, A. (2009) Committing to Good Information Governance, *Information Management*, **43** (3), 4.

Lappin, J. (2014) *The Strengths and Weaknesses of the Information Governance Approach to Records Management*, http://thinkingrecords.co.uk/2014/03/21/the-strengths-and-weaknesses-of-the-information-governance-approach-to-records-management.

Lemieux, V. L. and Trapnell, S. E. (2016) *Public Access to Information for Development*, World Bank.

Logan, D. and Geragas, D. (2009) *Toolkit: information governance project*, www.gartner.com/doc/933912.

Lueders, D. (2014) Records Management, Information Governance and the Future of Information Lifecycle Management, *IRMS Bulletin*, **180**, 27–9.

Martin, R. S. (2007) Intersecting Missions, Converging Practice, *RBM: A Journal of Rare Books, Manuscripts, and Cultural Heritage*, **8** (1), 80–8.

Marty, P. F. (2014) Digital Convergence and the Information Profession in Cultural Heritage Organizations: reconciling internal and external demands, *Library Trends*, **62** (3), 613–27.

McLeod, J. and Hare, C. (2006) *How to Manage Records in the e-Environment*, Routledge.

Naughton, J. (2012) *From Gutenberg to Zuckerberg: what you really need to know about the internet*, Quercus.

Oliver, G. and Foscarini, F. (2014) *Records Management and Information Culture*, Facet Publishing.

Pember, M. and Cowan, R. A. (2009) Where Is the Record We Have Lost in Information? In Pember, M. and Cowan, R. A. (eds), *iRMA Information and Records Management Annual 2009*, Records Management Association of Australasia.

Penn, I. A., Pennix, G. and Coulson, J. (1994) *Records Management Handbook*, 2nd edn, Gower.

Prasad, N. (2011) Synergizing the Collections of Libraries, Archives and Museums for Better User Services, *IFLA Journal*, **37** (3), 204–10.

Quéau, P. (1998) In Search of the Common Good: the Information Society and archives. In *CITRA 1998: proceedings of the 33rd International Conference of the Round Table on Archives*, International Council on Archives.

Rayward, W. B. (1996) Libraries, Museums and Archives in the Digital Future: the blurring of institutional boundaries. In *Multimedia Preservation: capturing the rainbow. Proceedings of the Second National Conference of the National Preservation Office, Brisbane, 28–30 November, 1995*, National Library of Australia.

Rhoads, J. B. (1989) *The Role of Archives and Records Management in National Information Systems: a RAMP study*, revised edn, Unesco.

Ritter, J. (2015) *Information Governance 2015: the year of digital evidence as truth*, http://searchcompliance.techtarget.com/tip/Information-governance-2015-The-year-of-digital-evidence-as-truth.

Robinson, H. (2012) Remembering Things Differently: museums, libraries and archives as memory institutions and the implications for convergence, *Museum Management and Curatorship*, **27** (4), 413–29.

Roszak, T. (1994) *The Cult of Information*, 2nd edn, University of California Press.

Saffady, W. (2015) Records Management or Information Governance? *Information Management*, **49** (4), 38–41.

Shepherd, E. (2017) Right to Information. In MacNeil, H. and Eastwood, T. (eds), *Currents of Archival Thinking*, 2nd edn, Libraries Unlimited.

Sprehe, J. T. (2000) Integrating Records Management into Information Resources Management in US Government Agencies, *Government Information Quarterly*, **17** (1), 13–26.

Tammaro, A. M., Madrid, M. and Casarosa, V. (2013) Digital Curators'

Education: professional identity vs. convergence of LAM (libraries, archives, museums). In Agosti, M., Esposito, F., Ferilli, S. and Ferro, N. (eds), *Digital Libraries and Archives: 8th Italian Research Conference, IRCDL 2012, Bari, Italy, February 9–10, 2012, revised selected papers*, Springer.

The Sedona Conference (2007) *The Sedona Guidelines: best practice guidelines & commentary for managing information & records in the electronic age*, 2nd edn, https://thesedonaconference.org/publication/Managing%20Information%20%2526%20Records.

Thomassen, T. (2001) A First Introduction to Archival Science, *Archival Science*, **1** (4), 373–85.

Tough, A. and Moss, M. (eds) (2006) *Record Keeping in a Hybrid Environment: managing the creation, use, preservation and disposal of unpublished information objects in context*, Chandos.

UK Government (2000) Government Policy on Archives, *Journal of the Society of Archivists*, **21** (1), 11–26.

UK Government (2008) *Information Matters: building government's capability in managing knowledge and information*, https://web.archive.org/web/20130728081227/www.nationalarchives.gov.uk/services/publications/information-matters-strategy.pdf.

UK Government, Cabinet Office (2017) *Better Information for Better Government*, www.gov.uk/government/uploads/system/uploads/attachment_data/file/589946/2017-01-18_-_Better_Information_for_Better_Government.pdf.

Upward, F. (2015) Records Continuum. In Duranti, L. and Franks, P. C. (eds) *Encyclopedia of Archival Science*, Rowman & Littlefield.

Upward, F., Reed, B., Oliver, G. and Evans, J. (2013) Recordkeeping Informatics: re-figuring a discipline in crisis with a single minded approach, *Records Management Journal*, **23** (1), 37–50.

Usherwood, B., Wilson, K. and Bryson, J. (2005) Relevant Repositories Of Public Knowledge? Libraries, museums and archives in the information age, *Journal of Librarianship and Information Science*, **37** (2), 89–98.

Wilson, M. I., Kellerman, A. and Corey, K. E. (2013) *Global Information Society: technology, knowledge, and mobility*, Rowman & Littlefield.

CHAPTER 4

Finding a way through the hall of mirrors: concepts of information

Introduction

Although in recent decades many archivists and records managers have wanted to characterise records in terms of information, few of them have felt it necessary to examine the possible meaning or meanings of the word 'information' or to discuss its significance in any detail. Information is often heralded as a concept that can help to explicate records and archives, but is seldom presented as a concept that may itself be in need of explication. Similarly, advocates of the new discipline of information governance sometimes offer definitions of 'governance' but rarely trouble to define the concept of information. Even the *Encyclopedia of Archival Science* (Duranti and Franks, 2015), which includes entries for 'information assurance', 'information governance', 'information management' and 'information policy', has no entry for 'information'.

Why are records professionals so reluctant to scrutinise a concept that their profession has embraced with such apparent enthusiasm? One possible explanation is that information has proved difficult to delineate. As American philosopher Fred Dretske (1981, ix) remarked, 'it is much easier to talk about information than it is to say what it is you are talking about'. But the most probable explanation of professional reticence is simply that the word 'information' has come to be so widely used in the discourse of contemporary society that most records professionals now perceive it as self-explanatory. We live in an information culture, in which we hear information mentioned so frequently that most of us feel no need to ask what kind of phenomenon it is.

Outside the field of archives and records, however, many scholars and practitioners have recognised that information is not a concept that we can simply take for granted. In the twin disciplines of librarianship and information science, in recent decades, numerous writers have taken up the challenge of elucidating what we might mean when we talk about information. Even a brief inspection of the writings on this subject reveals the scale of the difficulties that Dretske observed; the literature on the meaning of information is extensive but remains largely inconclusive. According to a philosopher of information science, 'it has become a cliché to note that as many definitions of information have been suggested as there are writers on the topic' (Furner, 2015, 364).

A leading information scientist has admitted that, although information seems 'as ubiquitous as air, or heat, or water, . . . no one seems to know exactly what information is' (Fox, 1983, 3). Another has written that 'when we try to define information, we become lost in a hall of mirrors occupied by human reflections' (Morville, 2005, 47). Every way that we look at information seems to open up several other possible ways of defining it. In contemplating ideas about information, this chapter sets out to find a path through this hall of mirrors and to seek a basis for developing some tentative understandings of the connections and disjunctions between information and records.

Information and its reification

As far as we can tell, the word 'information' first appeared in the English language in the late Middle Ages. Many of its early uses referred to incriminatory intelligence brought against an accused person (a meaning still apparent today in words such as 'informer' and 'informant').[1] But the earliest use of 'information' cited in the *Oxford English Dictionary* is from a reference to the biblical 'five books of Moses' in a 14th-century translation of Ranulph Higden's *Polychronicon*, where it was said that 'five books came down from heaven for information of mankind'. The phrase 'information of mankind' may perhaps have carried connotations of 'formation', in the sense of 'giving form to', as well as suggesting that these books played a part in the 'informing' or 'instruction' of humanity.

Other meanings of 'information' developed over time, and the *Oxford English Dictionary* offers several different definitions of the word. Most are variations on the themes of communicative acts and imparted knowledge; information is said to be 'that of which one is apprised or told; intelligence, news'. Similar definitions can be found in many other dictionaries, including the famous dictionary of 1755 compiled by Samuel Johnson, who defined information as 'the act of informing' and as 'intelligence given' (Weller and Bawden, 2006, 139). A common feature of all these definitions is that information is perceived as abstract and intangible.

A more recent interpretation sees it rather differently: as a 'thing', a material form into which intelligence is encoded. In the early 1990s, this reified view of information was explored by Anglo-American information scientist Michael Buckland, who noted that the word 'information' has increasingly been used attributively for objects that are regarded as informative. Buckland (1991, 351–2) observed that this usage is characteristic of the world of information systems, which are posited on assumptions that information exists in physical shape and can be 'handled and operated upon'. The view that information is a material 'thing' marks a distinct break with traditional usages, and still receives scant recognition in most English dictionaries. To its supporters, however, information is a constituent of physical reality (Bawden and Robinson, 2013); it appears that 'we have only to look around us to establish . . . that information exists in the form of physical objects' (Case and Given, 2016, 73).

Although it does not seem to have been explicitly discussed by information scientists until the 1990s, the perception of information as a material 'thing' or object can be traced in studies of a technical nature undertaken in the USA several decades earlier. In their work on mathematical information theory, uncertainty reduction and signal transmission, electrical engineer Claude Shannon and mathematician Warren Weaver (1949) alluded to information in a distinctly mechanistic fashion; their ideas have been widely cited in the fields of communications and cybernetics, and have sometimes been interpreted as implying that the word 'information' can refer to anything that a sender can encode to transmit to a receiver. Shortly

Typologies of conceptual understandings of 'information' have been proposed by a number of information scientists. Michael Buckland, professor of library and information studies at the University of California, Berkeley, identified three 'principal uses' of the word 'information' (Buckland, 1991, 351):

- information as process
- information as knowledge
- information as thing.

The first two of these 'principal uses' assume that information is abstract and intangible; only the third sees it as a reified entity.

While Buckland's typology has remained influential, alternatives have been suggested by other information scientists who have analysed differing interpretations of 'information' within and beyond their discipline. Marcia Bates (2010) proposed seven types of 'conceptions of information':

- information in a communicatory or semiotic frame
- information as event
- information as a proposition or claim about the world
- information as a kind of structure
- information as socially embedded
- information as a term with multiple meanings
- deconstructive approaches to information.

From another perspective, Jonathan Furner (2015, 364) offered five definitions:

- information as data
- information as content
- information as propositional content
- information as knowledge
- information as news.

Although these typologies share some common features, they reflect different intellectual approaches to understanding information and for the most part they resist attempts at consensus. Buckland's conception of 'information as thing' underpins much of the discussion in this chapter. Some of the other conceptions will be considered in later chapters of this book.

after Shannon and Weaver's work was published, the term 'information retrieval' was invented by American computer scientist Calvin Mooers. However, the information retrieval systems that Mooers promoted in the early 1950s were designed to retrieve books and documents in libraries, and critics complained that he had confused information with literature (Mooers, 1954, 112; Swanson, 1988, 92). Users had needs for information, which might be met by matching their requests to books or other items in a library, but it was far from clear that the books themselves could be said to constitute the information that users sought. However, in the late 20th and early 21st centuries, many librarians found it politically convenient to position libraries as repositories of information rather than repositories of books, and Buckland's formulation of 'information as thing' appeared to legitimise this usage.

At the start of the new millennium, the growth of digital technology offered further encouragement, since it seemed to promise a world where books and other traditional physical media would increasingly disappear. Some information scientists contended that computers are able to offer transparent environments enabling humans to interact directly with information, and that information retrieval was being – or had been – superseded by a new discipline of 'human–information interaction', modelled on the study of human–computer interaction (Marchionini, 2004; 2008). One of its proponents argued that, if human–information interaction means interaction with 'a string of symbols that has meaning', the term 'information' must refer, not to the meanings that are ascribed, but to the symbols that supposedly bear them (Fidel, 2012, 6); information, then, is perceived as 'things', albeit as things that are encountered in digital rather than traditional physical form.

Another approach to information addresses the concept of 'information flow': the idea that information has movements that can be identified and tracked. This mode of thinking dates back to the 1960s and the work of German computer scientist Carl Adam Petri (1963). In the 1970s and 1980s, computer scientists adapted Petri's ideas about information flow to office settings and developed information flow models to support the automation of office work. Of the numerous models developed at that time, the best known is probably Clarence Ellis's 'information control nets' model, described as 'a mathematical flow model which provides a formal description of the information flow within an office' (Auramäki, Hirschheim and Lyytinen, 1992; Ellis, 1979). Since the 1990s, developments in the field of computer science have tended to address 'workflow' (the flow of units of work from one user or workstation to another in structured work processes) rather than information flow; however, notions of information flow persist in library studies and information science, where they are often associated with the practice of 'information audit', the formal examination of the use and movement of information within an organization (Buchanan and Gibb, 2007; Hibberd and Evatt, 2004; Orna, 1990).

Understandings of information 'as thing' also underlie the notion of 'information resource management', which originated in the mid-1970s as a term to describe the management of data, documents and computer technology in government agencies in the USA. The idea that organizations should aim to manage information as a 'resource' was largely driven by a rationalisation agenda and a growing belief among organizational advisers that new systematic approaches would improve an organization's efficiency and effectiveness. In the 1980s and 1990s, information resource management was often promoted by individuals who had built their careers in data processing and computing, and its practical implementation frequently emphasised procedures for the systematic management of hardware and software; but wider ideas about information resource management were also adopted by many whose backgrounds were in librarianship or information science (Bergeron, 1996; Marchand and Horton, 1986; Thibodeau, 1990; Wilson, 2002). Emphasis was often laid on the economic value of information, and efforts were made to explore how information could be made quantifiable in monetary terms and how the practice of information audit could be aligned to financial audits or other audits of measurable commodities.

This line of thought was taken further in 1995, when a group of business leaders in the UK proposed that organizations should identify their 'significant information' for 'consideration as an asset' and that directors and senior managers should be encouraged to address their responsibilities for information assets in the same way as other organizational assets (Hawley Committee, 1995). These proposals – and particularly the recommendation of the terminology of asset management – attracted much attention. In the 21st century, the phrase 'information asset management' has replaced 'information resource management' in most of the discourse, and there has been much talk both about how an organization's 'significant information' should be formally categorised as an asset and about how valuations of information assets should appear on company balance sheets (El-Tawy and Abdel-Kader, 2013; Mancini, 2016; Ward and Peppard, 2002, 486– 502; Wilson and Stenson, 2008).

Records management and new concepts of information

Although the leading advocates of these ideas are chiefly from the information science and information systems fields, their vocabulary has become increasingly influential in records management. For example, records managers who might once have alluded to conducting 'records inventories' (Robek, Brown and Stephens, 1995, 27) or 'records surveys' (Shepherd and Yeo, 2003, 66) now often prefer to speak of 'information audits', a term that is probably thought to give their language a more corporate tone and to endow the activity with a wider scope and a higher status.

Since the 1980s, the rhetoric of resources and assets has often featured in records management literature, and many writers have promoted connections between records management and information resource or asset management. An American records management textbook published in 1984 was entitled *Information Resource Management* (Ricks and Gow, 1984); by 1990, a knowledgeable commentator could describe information resource management as 'the predominant records management approach' in the USA (Thibodeau, 1990, 199; cf. Schwartz and Hernon, 1993, 213–14). Following the terminological shift from 'resources' to 'assets', British records management educators Catherine Hare and Julie McLeod (1997, 7) argued that records are 'the key manifestation of an organisation's information asset', American digital records specialist Kenneth Thibodeau (2009, 26) affirmed that records are 'a distinct class of information assets', and the authors of the international standard *Management Systems for Records* (ISO 30300: 2011, clause 2.3.1) described them as a 'type of information resource, . . . part of the . . . assets of an organization'.

In the UK, the language of information asset management has permeated central government in the early 21st century, and The National Archives has chosen to make reference to 'information assets' rather than 'records' in some of its guidance issued to government departments. In recent guidance, for example, departments have been instructed to make a comprehensive listing of their information assets, identify risks and opportunities associated with each asset, determine how long assets need to be kept and assess whether their sensitivity requires protection (The National Archives, 2017, 17–24). The vocabulary of asset management has also been adopted by many in the information governance movement: we are told, for example, that information governance is 'the discipline of treating information as a strategic corporate asset' (Hulme, 2012, 99), and that the notion of information as an asset 'is fundamental to . . . information governance and its likely success' (Siatiras, 2013, 18).

To promoters of these views, an organization's 'documents, . . . spreadsheets, digital images, multimedia, [and] databases' can or should be managed using 'information asset management . . . principles' (Corrigan and Sprehe, 2010, 27). What these principles are said to be and what management practices they are said to entail usually depend on the environments in which they are advocated or the disciplinary backgrounds of those who advocate them. For information scientists, information asset management generally includes the auditing of information flows, the compilation of an 'information asset register' and perhaps the quantification of the assets' supposed economic value, but writers with a records management background often conclude that information assets should be managed by setting retention periods and undertaking disposal actions using a traditional records life-cycle framework.

All these approaches are predicated on understanding information as a 'thing'. They allow proponents of information asset management or information governance to speak of identifying and categorising information, organising and storing it, auditing it, transferring it to archival repositories, and discarding or destroying it when it is no longer required (Dederer and Dmytrenko, 2015, 32–3; Kahn and Blair, 2009, 11, 17; Leming, 2015, 216; Smallwood, 2013, 15). However, assumptions that information can be measured, organised, audited or discarded remain open to question. What if information resides in people's minds as well as, or instead of, on tangible or digital media? If it is associated with a medium, should it be equated with the medium itself, the content inscribed on the medium or the ideas, meanings or memories that the content conveys? When information is equated with ideas and meanings, measuring it and subjecting it to control are less obviously feasible, and destroying it cannot be simple; as cultural historian Antonio Sennis (2013, 152) noted, 'when we destroy our scripts we do not always destroy the memories that go with them'. Equally, if we surrender our scripts to a third party, our minds can still retain the information we acquired from them before we handed them over. Information cannot simply be correlated with the objects that practitioners seek to manage and govern. We may find that we must consider these objects, not as information *per se*, but as entities from which information can be elicited or derived.

A **shift in understandings of 'information'** can also be seen in official pronouncements about 'reuse of public sector information' and copyright law. In legal tradition, copyright protects 'literary works' and 'expressions', but does not protect ideas or information (Litman, 1992, 185–6). Yet recent guidance on 'public sector information' sometimes promotes a different view. Following European Union directives of 2003 and 2013, the UK government introduced new regulations for the reuse of public sector information in 2015, with the aim of 'unlocking' its economic potential and enhancing transparency and accountability. The National Archives of the UK issued guidelines affirming that the regulations apply to 'information' whose copyright is held by a public sector body, and that 'information whose copyright does not belong to the public sector body' is exempt (The National Archives, 2015, 6–7). The guidelines tacitly equated 'information' with the literary works and expressions that copyright law recognises.

The National Archives seems firmly committed to a reified view of information. In other guidance published on its website, it has affirmed that information is tangible and can be systematically stored, protected and manipulated.[2] However, critics of this approach – and copyright lawyers – might wish to argue that it is mistaken, because it confuses information with its carrier (Buckland, 1991, 351–2; Butterfield, Ngondi and Kerr, 2016, 268; Dinneen and Brauner, 2015, 388–9; Dretske, 2008, 274–5; Lester and Koehler, 2003, 15–17).

Information as content or information as affordance?

As early as 1980, some computer science researchers began to ask in what sense information can be said to 'flow' around an organization. In an era before digital technology was extensively used in the workplace, they interpreted information flow as the flow of *forms*; they argued that information was collected on forms, and the forms then moved from one location or processing unit to another (Auramäki,

Hirschheim and Lyytinen, 1992, 343; Ladd and Tsichritzis, 1980, 533). From this perspective, information *carriers* are the entities that 'flow' or travel within or across organizations. The information – it might be said – is not the forms themselves, but their *content*.

Similarly, there is a resilient strand in archival thinking that sees information as the *content* of a record. Timothy Sprehe (2000, 24), for example, stated that records contain information set down in the context of business operations, and that the purpose of records management is 'to render the information contained in the records more accessible'. To Robert Sanders and Ira Penn (1998, 10), it appeared self-evident that 'the content of all records is information'. Frank Boles and Mark Greene (2001, 426–7) likened records to a 'box' in which information is held. Using language that I might now prefer to avoid, Elizabeth Shepherd and I (2003, 12) wrote that records 'typically contain information relating to . . . an activity'. According to Barbara Reed (2005, 102), records 'definitely consist of information in some form'.

In 2017, a British government publication adopted a broadly similar viewpoint when it described information as 'the raw material from which records are made' (UK Government, Cabinet Office, 2017, 4). Proponents of this view sometimes argue that information originates outside physical media; it is produced or acquired mentally, but is then inscribed on a carrier so that it can be preserved and shared across time or space. Seen in this way, information is not a physical object, but is nevertheless a seemingly objective commodity that can be stored within such an object, thus ensuring that it will be retrievable when it is needed at a future moment (Karvalics, 2008, 33; Salminen, Lyytikäinen and Tiitinen, 2000, 624–5). The simple view is that the object – the record – acts as a secure container for the information and transmits it directly and unambiguously to the reader. A user, it is supposed, may refer to records to obtain the information that the record creator set down in them. Some commentators, however, take a more nuanced view. For Stephen Harries (2012, 56), records are artefacts containing information, but users have to make sense of the information they contain; information is open to interpretation and the user has to contribute something to its understanding.

It is also possible to argue that information does not reside in records, but arises and exists largely or only in the intellects of

The view that a record transmits information unambiguously to any user who is able to read it is sometimes referred to as the 'conduit metaphor' or 'bucket theory'. According to psycholinguist Charles Osgood (1979, 213), adherents to this theory assume that 'words, like little buckets, . . . pick up their loads of meaning in one person's mind, carry them across the intervening space, and dump them into the mind of another'. As computer scientist Jan Dietz (2004, 61) noted, similar assumptions are commonplace in the field of information systems, where the view that 'information is something that is put into and got from an information system' has long been prevalent. In the words of Dutch archivist Pieter van Koetsveld (2009, 47), the presupposition is 'that there is one truth to be recorded, that it can be recorded without distortion . . . by inscribing information onto a carrier, and that this information when retrieved will represent the same truth as the inscriber intended'.

individuals. As science journalist James Gleick (2010) observed, this argument takes us back to the long-established notion that 'information . . . takes place *in the mind*. Our minds are informed; then we have something we lacked before – some idea, some knowledge, some information'. From this perspective, the sense-making task that Harries described *creates* information. It does not merely try to make sense of information that already exists; information is a matter of what users can infer from reading a record, or perhaps from interacting with it as an integral whole, including its form and structure as well as its content. Information, then, is not what records *are*, or what they *contain*, but what we gain from using them; it is 'the product of interpretative activity' (Dousa and Ibekwe-SanJuan, 2014, 11).

In earlier work (Yeo, 2007, 329–30), I proposed that information can be seen as an affordance of records: a capacity that records can supply to a user, or a benefit that can be derived from their use. Something of this view can also be observed in Hilary Jenkinson's (1922, 11) definition of archives (and, by extension, records) as documents drawn up or used in a transaction and preserved 'for their own information by the person or persons responsible for that transaction and their legitimate successors'. The informational aspects of records are not a prominent theme in Jenkinson's writings, but it appears that he saw information in terms of use, or as a purpose for which archives and records are preserved.

Although Jenkinson's definition emphasised provision of infor-mation to the creators of records and their formal successors, other writers have adopted wider perspectives suggesting that the informational capacities of records extend to many other users and uses. For example, a report of the Royal Commission on Historical Manuscripts in the late 19th century advised its readers that the medieval archives of the archbishopric of Dublin 'afford the most authentic information on the arrangements and relations . . . between the archbishops of Dublin and the kings of England' and that the municipal records of Galway 'supply . . . information on the civic, commercial, and social arrangements . . . in the western province of Ireland' (Historical Manuscripts Commission, 1885, 43–5). The use of the records to garner the kinds of information envisaged by the Royal Commission would undoubtedly require some 'interpretative activity' on the part of the users. The expected seekers of such information, we may assume, would seldom be the creators of the records or their successors in office; from the perspective adopted in the Royal Commission's report, the records in question would serve to inform scholarly investigators wishing to research various aspects of Irish history and society.

Almost a century later, a handbook for historical researchers compiled by W. B. Stephens adopted a similar view of records as materials from which information can be gained when they are used appropriately; Stephens (1981, 80, 86) noted that, in England, records such as charters can 'provide . . . information for tracing the evolution of a borough as a unit of local government' and minutes of urban

---

The concept of 'affordance' has its origins in the work of visual psychologist James Gibson (1979) and cognitive scientist and designer Donald Norman (1988). These scholars introduced the term 'affordances' to refer to the functional goods, benefits or capacities that a resource can provide. Following Gibson and Norman, affordance theorists suggest that a single resource can have multiple affordances; although the physical aspect of a resource is common to each individual who encounters it, the resource may offer different affordances to different users (Leonardi, 2011, 153). In some instances, these affordances may be foreseen by the creator of the resource, but affordances may also be perceived anew at the moment of use (Sadler and Given, 2007, 116).

The informational affordances of a record need not be limited to those intended by the record's creator. Each user 'may see . . . information that no one else has seen before' (Latham, 2011, 13), and new informational affordances may come into being when records are used in innovative ways.

council meetings are 'an important source of information . . . on every aspect of town life, political, social, religious, and economic'. Information, in the sense of an affordance that records offer, may be associated with a wide range of use. As historian and archivist James O'Toole (2002) remarked, a record can 'provide information to an open-ended number of inquiries and inquirers'. Records are kept and used for many reasons, but one important reason for keeping and using them is their ability to inform those who encounter and engage with them.

Dissent and debate

Just as there are many ways of conceptualising 'information', there are many differing opinions on the relationship of information to records. Those who wish to see information as a reified entity – a material 'thing' – may have little difficulty in accepting claims that records and information are becoming indistinguishable or that records are a special type or subset of information. However, those who argue that information belongs to the sphere of the mind are unlikely to assent to these suppositions or to accept the claim that information can be unproblematically embedded in a record. They will also be sceptical of the popular notion that information is a commodity that can be governed in a systematic fashion. Records, a critic might argue, can be managed – they can be quantified, classified, stored, retrieved and perhaps ultimately destroyed – but if information is an affordance, a conceptual space for individualised meaning-making (Cope and Kalantzis, 2011, 83), it cannot be the kind of entity that we can hope to manage or control.

There is abundant scope for debate about all these matters, and many of the questions raised in this chapter will be revisited and explored further in the final chapters of this book. Before we can return to the topic of information, however, we must give some thought to the parallel debates that enfold its close relative, *data*. Chapter 5 will ask whether, instead of characterising records in terms of information, we should seek to understand them through a lens of data science. It examines points of connection between records and data, reviews ideas about the 'datafication' of records and investigates the associations of both data and information with objectivity and notions of fact.

Endnotes

1 See the discussion by lexicographer Michael Proffitt at http://public.oed.com/aspects-of-english/word-stories/information.
2 See www.nationalarchives.gov.uk/information-management/manage-information/planning/knowledge-principles; see also Keegan (2016).

References

Auramäki, E., Hirschheim, R. and Lyytinen, K. (1992) Modelling Offices through Discourse Analysis, *Computer Journal*, **35** (4), 342–52.

Bates, M. J. (2010) Information. In Bates, M. J. and Maack, M. N. (eds), *Encyclopedia of Library and Information Sciences*, 3rd edn, vol. 3, CRC Press.

Bawden, D. and Robinson, L. (2013) 'Deep Down Things': in what ways is information physical, and why does it matter for information science?, *Information Research*, **18** (3), http://InformationR.net/ir/18-3/colis/paperC03.html.

Bergeron, P. (1996) Information Resources Management, *Annual Review of Information Science and Technology*, **31**, 263–360.

Boles, F. and Greene, M. (2001) Confusing the Bun for the Burger: rehabilitating the role of content in the archival context, *Schweizerische Zeitschrift für Geschichte*, **51**, 424–47.

Buchanan, S. and Gibb, F. (2007) The Information Audit: role and scope, *International Journal of Information Management*, **27** (3), 159–72.

Buckland, M. K. (1991) Information as Thing, *Journal of the American Society for Information Science*, **42** (5), 351–60.

Butterfield, A., Ngondi, G. E. and Kerr, A. (eds) (2016) *A Dictionary of Computer Science*, 7th edn, Oxford University Press.

Case, D. O. and Given, L. M. (2016) *Looking for Information: a survey of research on information seeking, needs, and behavior*, 4th edn, Emerald.

Cope, B. and Kalantzis, M. (2011) What Does the Digital Do to Knowledge Making? In Cope, B., Kalantzis, M. and Magee, L. (eds), *Towards a Semantic Web: connecting knowledge in academic research*, Chandos.

Corrigan, M. and Sprehe, J. T. (2010) Cleaning Up Your Information Wasteland, *Information Management*, **44** (3), 26–30.

Dederer, M. G. and Dmytrenko, A. (2015) Eight Steps to Effective Information Lifecycle Management, *Information Management*, **49** (1), 32–5.

Dietz, J. L. G. (2004) Towards a LAP-Based Information Paradigm. In

Aakhus, M. and Lind, M. (eds), *Proceedings of the 9th International Working Conference on the Language Action Perspective on Communication Modelling*, Rutgers University.

Dinneen, J. D. and Brauner, C. (2015) Practical and Philosophical Considerations for Defining *Information* as Well-Formed, Meaningful Data in the Information Sciences, *Library Trends*, **63** (3), 378–400.

Dousa, T. M. and Ibekwe-SanJuan, F. (2014) Introduction. In Ibekwe-SanJuan, F. and Dousa, T. M. (eds), *Theories of Information, Communication and Knowledge*, Springer.

Dretske, F. (1981) *Knowledge and the Flow of Information*, Basil Blackwell.

Dretske, F. (2008) The Metaphysics of Information. In Pichler, A. and Hrachovec, H. (eds), *Wittgenstein and the Philosophy of Information*, Ontos.

Duranti, L., and Franks, P. C. (eds) (2015) *Encyclopedia of Archival Science*, Rowman & Littlefield.

El-Tawy, N. and Abdel-Kader, M. (2013) Accounting Recognition of Information as an Asset, *Journal of Information Science*, **39** (3), 333–45.

Ellis, C. A. (1979) Information Control Nets: a mathematical model of office information flow. In *Proceedings of the Conference on Simulation, Measurement, and Modeling of Computer Systems*, ACM Press.

Fidel, R. (2012) *Human Information Interaction: an ecological approach to information behavior*, MIT Press.

Fox, C. J. (1983) *Information and Misinformation: an investigation of the notions of information, misinformation, informing, and misinforming*, Greenwood Press.

Furner, J. (2015) Information Science Is Neither, *Library Trends*, **63** (3), 362–77.

Gibson, J. J. (1979) *The Ecological Approach to Visual Perception*, Houghton Mifflin.

Gleick, J. (2010) *The Information Palace*, www.nybooks.com/daily/2010/12/08/information-palace.

Hare, C. E. and McLeod, J. (1997) *Developing a Records Management Programme*, Aslib.

Harries, S. (2012) *Records Management and Knowledge Management: a handbook for regulation, innovation and transformation*, Chandos.

Hawley Committee (1995) *Information as an Asset*, KPMG.

Hibberd, B. J. and Evatt, A. (2004) Mapping Information Flows: a practical guide, *Information Management Journal*, **38** (1), 58–64.

Historical Manuscripts Commission (1885) *Tenth Report of the Royal Commission on Historical Manuscripts*, Eyre & Spottiswoode.

Hulme, T. (2012) Information Governance: sharing the IBM approach, *Business Information Review*, **29** (2), 99–104.

ISO 30300: 2011, *Information and Documentation – Management Systems for Records – Fundamentals and Vocabulary*, International Organization for Standardization.

Jenkinson, H. (1922) *A Manual of Archive Administration*, Clarendon Press.

Kahn, R. A. and Blair, B. T. (2009) *Information Nation: seven keys to information management compliance*, 2nd edn, Wiley Publishing.

Karvalics, L. Z. (2008) Information Society – What Is It Exactly? The meaning, history and conceptual framework of an expression. In Pintér, R. (ed.), *Information Society: from theory to political practice*, Gondolat.

Keegan, N. (2016) *Knowledge Principles for Government* (2016), http://blog.nationalarchives.gov.uk/blog/knowledge-principles-government.

Ladd, I. and Tsichritzis, D. (1980) An Office Form Flow Model. In *AFIPS '80: Proceedings of the May 19–22, 1980, National Computer Conference*, ACM Press.

Latham, K. F. (2011) Medium Rare: exploring archives and their conversion from original to digital. Part two: the holistic knowledge arsenal of paper-based archives, *LIBRES*, **21** (1), http://libres-ejournal.info/wp-content/uploads/2014/06/Vol21_I1_Latham__EssOp_LIBRES21n1.pdf.

Leming, R. (2015) Why Is Information the Elephant Asset? An answer to this question and a strategy for information asset management, *Business Information Review*, **32** (4), 212–19.

Leonardi, P. M. (2011) When Flexible Routines Meet Flexible Technologies: affordance, constraint, and the imbrication of human and material agencies, *MIS Quarterly*, **35** (1), 147–67.

Lester, J. and Koehler, W. C. (2003) *Fundamentals of Information Studies: understanding information and its environment*, Neal-Schuman.

Litman, J. (1992) Copyright and Information Policy, *Law and Contemporary Problems*, **55** (2), 185–209.

Mancini, J. (2016) *Infonomics: how do you measure the value of information?*, AIIM.

Marchand, D. A. and Horton, F. W. (1986) *Infotrends: profiting from your own information resources*, John Wiley & Sons.

Marchionini, G. (2004) From Information Retrieval to Information Interaction, *Lecture Notes in Computer Science*, **2997**, 1–11.

Marchionini, G. (2008) Human-Information Interaction Research and
    Development, *Library and Information Science Research*, **30** (3), 165–74.
Mooers, C. N. (1954) Choice and Coding in Information Retrieval Systems,
    Transactions of the IRE Professional Group on Information Theory, **4** (4),
    112–18.
Morville, P. (2005) *Ambient Findability: what we find changes who we become*,
    O'Reilly Media.
Norman, D. A. (1988) *The Psychology of Everyday Things*, Basic Books.
Orna, E. (1990) *Practical Information Policies: how to manage information flow in
    organizations*, Gower.
Osgood, C. E. (1979) What Is a Language? In Aaronson, D. and Rieber,
    R. W. (eds), *Psycholinguistic Research: implications and applications*,
    Lawrence Erlbaum.
O'Toole, J. M. (2002) *Comment on 'The Many Meanings of Objects' (Response to
    Elaine Heumann Gurian)*,
    https://web.archive.org/web/20041217001959/www.hfmgv.org/research/
    publications/symposium2002/papers/otoole.asp.
Petri, C. A. (1963) Fundamentals of a Theory of Asynchronous Information
    Flow. In Popplewell, C. M. (ed.), *Proceedings of the IFIP Congress 1962*,
    North Holland Publishing.
Reed, B. (2005) Records. In McKemmish, S., Piggott, M., Reed, B. and
    Upward, F. (eds), *Archives: recordkeeping in society*, Charles Sturt
    University.
Ricks, B. R. and Gow, K. F. (1984) *Information Resource Management*, South-
    Western Publishing.
Robek, M. F., Brown, G. F. and Stephens, D. O. (1995) *Information and
    Records Management*, 4th edn, Glencoe.
Sadler, E. and Given, L. M. (2007) Affordance Theory: a framework for
    graduate students' information behavior, *Journal of Documentation*, **63** (1),
    115–41.
Salminen, A., Lyytikäinen, V. and Tiitinen, P. (2000) Putting Documents
    into Their Work Context in Document Analysis, *Information Processing
    and Management*, **36** (4), 623–41.
Sanders, R. L. and Penn, I. A. (1998) What's in a Name? *Records Management
    Quarterly*, **32** (3), 9–13.
Schwartz, C. and Hernon, P. (1993) *Records Management and the Library*,
    Ablex.
Sennis, A. (2013) Destroying Documents in the Early Middle Ages. In

Jarrett, J. and McKinley, A. S. (eds), *Problems and Possibilities of Early Medieval Charters*, Brepols.

Shannon, C. E. and Weaver, W. (1949) *The Mathematical Theory of Communication*, University of Illinois Press.

Shepherd, E. and Yeo, G. (2003) *Managing Records: a handbook of principles and practice*, Facet Publishing.

Siatiras, K. (2013) Information Governance: new approach or old news?, *IRMS Bulletin*, **176**, 15–19.

Smallwood, R. F. (2013) *Managing Electronic Records: methods, best practices, and technologies*, John Wiley & Sons.

Sprehe, J. T. (2000) Integrating Records Management into Information Resources Management in US Government Agencies, *Government Information Quarterly*, **17** (1), 13–26.

Stephens, W. B. (1981) *Sources for English Local History*, 2nd edn, Cambridge University Press.

Swanson, D. R. (1988) Historical Note: information retrieval and the future of an illusion, *Journal of the American Society for Information Science*, **39** (2), 92–8.

The National Archives [of the UK] (2015) *Guidance on the Implementation of the Re-Use of Public Sector Information Regulations 2015 for Public Sector Bodies*, www.nationalarchives.gov.uk/documents/information-management/psi-implementation-guidance-public-sector-bodies.pdf.

The National Archives [of the UK] (2017) *Identifying Information Assets and Business Requirements*, www.nationalarchives.gov.uk/documents/information-management/identify-information-assets.pdf.

Thibodeau, K. (1990) Information Resources Management in Context and Contest. In Durance, C. J. (ed.), *Management of Recorded Information: converging disciplines*, K. G. Saur.

Thibodeau, K. (2009) The Survival of Records (and Records Management) in the Twenty-First Century. In Tibbo, H. R., Hank, C., Lee, C. A. and Clemens, R. (eds), *Digital Curation: practice, promise and prospects. Proceedings of DigCCurr 2009*, University of North Carolina.

UK Government, Cabinet Office (2017) *Better Information for Better Government*, www.gov.uk/government/uploads/system/uploads/attachment_data/file/584532/2017-01-18_-_Better_Information_for_Better_Government.pdf.

Van Koetsveld, P. (2009) *Valuing Archives*, Master's thesis, Erasmus

University Rotterdam,
https://thesis.eur.nl/pub/6881/thesis_Valuing_Archives_Pieter_van_
Koetsveld.doc.

Ward, J. and Peppard, J. (2002) *Strategic Planning for Information Systems*, 3rd edn, John Wiley & Sons.

Weller, T. and Bawden, D. (2006) Individual Perceptions: a new chapter on Victorian information history, *Library History*, **22** (2), 137–56.

Wilson, R. M. S. and Stenson, J. A. (2008) Valuation of Information Assets on the Balance Sheet: the recognition and approaches to the valuation of invisible assets, *Business Information Review*, **25** (3), 167–82.

Wilson, T. D. (2002) Information Management. In Feather, J. and Sturges, P. (eds), *International Encyclopedia of Information and Library Science*, 2nd edn, Routledge.

Yeo, G. (2007) Concepts of Record (1): evidence, information, and persistent representations, *American Archivist*, **70** (2), 315–43.

CHAPTER 5

Records and data

Introduction

If the writings of contemporary pundits are correct, we live not only in an age of information, but also in an age of data. In literature aimed at the corporate business market, much of the rhetoric that has come to surround concepts of information is often transferred to a parallel discourse about data. We can read, for example, of the importance of efficient enterprise data management, of data governance frameworks and of a need to recognise data as a 'valuable and manageable organizational asset' (Bhansali, 2014, 9–10). In the 2010s, organizations have increasingly sought to take advantage of new data analytic techniques to improve decision-making or business activities; many now aim to 'monetise' data, exploiting their corporate data in creative ways to become more competitive and profitable (Cohen and Kotorov, 2016; Marr, 2017).

Interest in data analysis and exploitation is not confined to commercial enterprises. Governments, political parties, police forces, scientists and health care providers are all now seeking to analyse digital data to enhance their operations. Data science and data administration, although newly emerging as professions, are rapidly expanding areas of employment in many countries, and the worlds of data analysis and curation have become major fields of research. As Jonathan Furner observed:

> There seems to be no doubt that both data science and data studies are here to stay as discrete areas of inquiry. Levels of interest in the development and application of tools and techniques for the analysis of . . . data are high and constantly rising, as are levels of interest in the study of the sociocultural, political, and economic contexts in which data is created and used.   (Furner, 2015, 369)

When European records professionals consider data, they often think of data protection law, whose connections to record-keeping are well established. Records retention, security and privacy must increasingly be addressed in the context of European regulations concerned with trans-border data flows (Montaña, 2016; Sautter, 2011, 25–6). More recently, discussions about data have extended to big data (exponentially growing volumes of analysable data arising from the proliferation of computers across business, government and the wider community), open data (proactive release of public sector data for sharing, redistribution and creative reuse) and other flavours of data that may also appear to be connected with records. Some commentators have begun to argue that records professionals can facilitate open data initiatives by working to ensure that data are accessible, reliable and appropriately contextualised (Shepherd, 2017, 265; Thurston, 2012); others have suggested that records management practices may be able to assist with retention and disposition issues associated with big data and open data (Dale, 2015, 30; McDonald and Léveillé, 2014). References to data have become increasingly common in literature about digital records, and in 2015 the archives and records management subcommittee of the International Organization for Standardization reported that it had set up working groups to investigate 'how to manage data as a record' and to study relationships between open data and records management methods and principles.[1]

Although the authors of professional standards and glossaries have usually defined records in terms of information rather than data, points of connection between records and data may not seem difficult to identify. Some archivists have remarked that the qualities often said to be found in, or required of, records – qualities such as reliability, authenticity, contextual integrity and usability – appear equally relevant to data (Ellis, 1996, 326; Evans et al., 2014, 219). Others have noted that, like organizational records, organizational data are generated and used in business processes (McDonald and Léveillé, 2014, 111). Like records, but unlike information, data are – theoretically, at least – countable. English-language usage does not allow us to have 200 'informations', but we can have 200 or 200,000 data. Data can be encountered in units of any size, and we can constitute specific sets of data. To many observers, claims that data can be systematically managed and controlled may seem more convincing than similar affirmations about the management and control of information.

The common ground that appears to connect data and records warrants further investigation. Rather than identifying records as a type or subset of information, might we now find it more fruitful to seek to explain or characterise records in terms of data? This chapter looks at the world of data science and data management, and asks whether and how far recent work in this area may be relevant to our understanding of records and archives. The word 'data' is often used to denote the 'structured' contents of datasets or databases, but data are not always perceived in this way; this chapter also examines different conceptions of data and different views of the relationships between data, information and factuality.

The 'datafication' of records

Stories about the convergence of records and data began to circulate as early as the 1980s, when Canadian records manager Terry Campbell (1989, 147) wrote that 'the functions of records management . . . and data administration . . . begin to blend and merge' and his Canadian colleague John McDonald (1989, 5) boldly asserted that 'records management and data management . . . mean the same thing'. However, a more frequently held view is that 'all records are data, but not all data are records' (Anderson, 2013, 363). This perspective was reflected in Chris Hurley's (1994, 338) definition of electronic records as 'so much of the data on a system . . . [as] is used for record-keeping purposes'. Others have seen data as building blocks or components from which digital records are constructed (O'Shea, 1996; Thibodeau, 2009), or data processing as a means by which records are made (Smit, 2017, 252–4). Since about 2006, many e-discovery specialists in the USA have adopted the terms 'data mapping' and 'data profiling', and it can be assumed that North American records managers who have recently begun to use these terms in place of 'records survey' or 'information audit' (cf. Franks, 2013, 91–3; McGann, 2013) are willing to perceive records as data or aggregates of data.

Understandings of records as data also underlie research initiatives such as the British 'Traces through Time' project, which aimed to employ 'tools for navigating Big Data [to] equip . . . historians to . . . trace the paths of individuals across the landscape of the official record' (Ranade, 2016; Research Councils UK, 2015). Another research initiative in the UK, the Administrative Data Research Network (2017), has affirmed that administrative data can include 'social security payment records, educational attainment records, health records, court records, [and] tax records'. While a generalised perception of records as data for research is of long standing in some scholarly disciplines, initiatives of this kind view records from the specific perspective of 21st-century data science and see them as candidates for participation in projects that employ new computational and analytical techniques from the worlds of big data and artificial intelligence. It is widely asserted that, by using these techniques to detect and analyse themes, patterns and relationships in and among digital materials, innovative modes of discovery and investigation can be opened up.

Commentators on technological development have often referred to this trend as 'datafication', a term popularised during the 2010s by the writings of Kenneth Cukier and Viktor Mayer-Schönberger. To 'datafy a phenomenon', in the words of these writers, is to put it in a format that allows it to be tabulated and analysed; the 'datafication of everything' permits an 'endless stream of textual analysis' (Mayer-Schönberger and Cukier, 2013, 78, 84, 94). Datafication, it seems, can be understood in at least two senses: in practical terms, it can be interpreted as an imperative to create resources in, or convert them into, datafied forms; at a more conceptual level, it implies an intellectual reframing of all digital objects as data that are amenable to computation (Padilla, 2016, 1). Some commentators have associated datafication with a supposed democratisation of data, as well as with the increasing use of data analysis to guide organizational decision-making or offer competitive advantage to commercial enterprises (Lycett, 2013, 382). It has often been remarked that these changes are also having an impact on scholars and the ways in which they study the world. Before the word 'datafication' became popular, digital librarian Sayeed Choudhury (2010, 194) wrote of a shift towards a 'datacentric view of scholarship'; more recently, other commentators have written of the 'datafication of the humanities' and the advent of 'computational social sciences' (Blanke and Prescott, 2016, 190; Kitchin, 2014a, 1).

Many records professionals, especially those with technical interests or expertise, have been alert to these developments and have seen their relevance to records and archives. In 2016, in North America, Richard Marciano and his colleagues at the University of Maryland announced the arrival of 'computational archival science', an interdisciplinary field that aims to apply computational methods to the processing, preservation and use of archival records (Marciano, 2016). In Britain, archivists advocating datafication have argued that reconceptual-isations of archives as data – or possibly transformations of archival materials into data – are moving us to 'a world in which . . . the whole record can be mined and analysed' (Ranade, 2016, 1; Thomas, Fowler and Johnson, 2017, 93–4, 166–7). It is also argued that, for this transition to be successful, digitisation procedures for analogue textual records will have to be restructured to generate computer-processable data rather than mere digital images of the originals. Born-digital records can be expected to present fewer difficulties, since many should be fully processable as they are; others, it is said, may perhaps need to be converted to new digital formats that are more hospitable to data analytics. At the same time, proponents of datafication and compu-tational archival science affirm, efforts can be made to persuade creators of records to use analytics-friendly formats, and archivists and records managers should be encouraged to acquire new skills and mind-sets that will allow them to integrate computational ideas with archival thinking.

Further perspectives on data and record-keeping

Until recently, in contrast to the current vocal support for 'datafication', there was often a feeling among records professionals that data were, at best, marginal to record-keeping. A report published in 2008 by the InterPARES project at the University of British Columbia described 'data, databases and related information' as 'entities that . . . are not generally considered records, except in very special and limited circumstances' (Roeder et al., 2008, 165). This view reflected a perception of data that largely associated them with database technologies; more particularly, it reflected an awareness that the contents of databases may change over time and a belief that such changeability does not march well with understandings that records are or should be unalterable. Looked at in this way, data were perceived as unstable or ephemeral entities of little interest to records managers or archivists.

Another perception of data associates them with the inputs and outputs of automated processing systems that are focused on statistical calculation or other forms of quantified measurement. Data can be created by people or by mechanical devices such as computers; they can also be *processed* by people or computers, although automated processing is now the norm. When existing data are processed or analysed, quantities of new data – sometimes called 'computational data' – are likely to be created. In complex scientific fields, multiple stages of processing are often involved, with each stage representing a higher degree of refinement or aggregation. Thus, data can be said to exist at different levels in a chain of processing; for example, the National Aeronautics and Space Administration in the USA has identified six levels to which data can be processed (Borgman, 2015, 21–2). Processed or computational data are highly valued in many scientific and research domains, but organizational records managers have often viewed them as largely unconnected to record-keeping missions.

Although there are signs that these perceptions are now beginning to change, concerns about the relevance of data – and data management practices – to the keeping of records have not wholly disappeared. According to Barbara Reed (2016), even when data are recognised as objects that can be captured for preservation, terms such as 'data curation' still do not resonate well in the field of record-keeping. However, archivists and records managers in the 21st century have increasingly recognised that many commercial and governmental transactions are now recorded in databases or database-like systems (Bantin, 2008; Yeo, 2011). The database used to maintain records of the ABC Company's share transactions, which we encountered in Chapter

2, is an example of this phenomenon, albeit a fictitious example. Data held in a system of this kind can be expected to remain stable for as long as their retention is deemed necessary. So-called 'research data' (data assembled for use in, or as a product of, scientific or other research projects) are also likely to appear stabilised – they will almost certainly be stable if they are retained after the completion of a research project – and there has been increasing recent interest in efforts to secure their long-term preservation (Evans et al., 2014; Grant, 2017). Even processed data, when maintained in stable or persistent forms, may be perceived as relevant to record-keeping enterprise insofar as they can be seen as records of computational processes and their outcomes.

Computing specialists often use the term 'data' to refer to the contents of datasets or relational databases and the inputs and outputs of formalised analysis and processing methods. But it also has wider connotations; it is sometimes used to refer to any content, other than program code, that is held in a computer. Data in this sense can be perceived as the content that computers present to users, as opposed to the executable code that remains largely invisible and is supposedly of interest only to technologists and programming experts. While some computer scientists exclude narrative text from their interpretation of 'data', others consider that the term embraces narrative documents such as letters, memoranda and reports, at least when they exist in digital forms. In the computing industry, documents of this kind are often described as 'unstructured' data, in contrast to the 'structured' data that are characteristic of database-like systems. Some commentators further extend the scope of 'data' to include audiovisual materials as well as alphanumeric data (Stair and Reynolds, 2016, 5).

A similar variety of opinions exists in the record-keeping domain. Some records professionals insist on a firm differentiation between documents and data, but others have accepted that a broader definition of data includes documents, and that the universe of data can thus encompass records in documentary or narrative form (Coleman et al., 2011, xix-xx).

Another view, often put forward by professionals concerned with records management in developing countries, is that records are a *source* of data. From this perspective, records and data are distinct phenomena, but data are frequently extracted or derived from the

'Structured' data in computer systems are granularised, with each item of data usually comprising a label and a value: for example, *'Number of students:* 100'; *'Name of student:* John Smith'. Tools such as Extensible Markup Language (XML) can also be seen as providing a format for 'structured' (or, some might say, 'semi-structured') data: <student>John Smith</student>.

A record of Smith's examination result could be formulated as a document ('I am able to report that John Smith has achieved a mark of 95% . . .'), but could equally be formulated as 'structured' data:

Name of student: Smith, John
Course: Archival Studies
Mark: 95%
Grade: Distinction.

The notion that content not formulated in this way is 'unstructured' seems misleading, since letters, reports and other documents have internal structures of their own, albeit structures that differ from those used in databases. Nevertheless, so-called 'structured' data are popular among data analysts and advocates of reusability, because they are easier to process and are often thought to allow deeper or more multidimensional analysis than 'unstructured' text. Techniques for mining and analysing 'unstructured' resources, however, are rapidly becoming more powerful and reliable. Datafication is sometimes understood as a movement to convert existing materials from 'unstructured' to 'structured' form, but the need for such conversion may diminish as new analytic techniques are developed for 'unstructured' digital formats. Data scientists' interests and analytic projects now increasingly extend to 'unstructured' as well as 'structured' data.

content of organizational records; employees or contractors identify appropriate details within the content of a series of records, format or code them as data and input them into a 'structured' database system, where they may be used for a range of purposes including statistical analysis, administrative and financial control, strategic planning and open government. For example, employment data can be derived from records of staff appointments, and disease data from records of medical diagnoses; such data are then used, or are intended to be used, for purposes beyond those that led to the initial making of the records. Those who adopt this view see the making of records as prior to the creation of data; a poorly kept record, they affirm, will result in misleading data (Cain, 1999; McDonald and Léveillé, 2014, 103; Thurston, 2012).

To its critics, however, this view may appear to be a legacy of an earlier era when data were associated only with structured automated systems, records were largely identified with paper documents and databases were often populated from pre-existing paper sources. Alternative points of view are undoubtedly possible. Instead of contending that data first come into existence when entries are made in a structured database, it could be argued that data already exist – albeit perhaps in unprocessed or non-aggregated forms – within the 'unstructured' records from which these entries are derived. It might also be suggested that the need to translate data to structured databases is now obsolescent, because analytical tools can increasingly be used with 'unstructured' as well as structured resources. In new environments, where records are largely digital and where powerful analytical tools can be applied directly to them, records themselves may be viewed as data that can be mined, analysed, reused and repurposed.

If concepts of datafication now imply a refashioning of all digital objects as data, questions must inevitably arise about older ideas that see records and data as more or less distinct entities. Have we arrived at a moment when archivists and records managers should abandon these ideas and frame their understandings in a different way? Should records now be viewed partly or wholly through the lenses provided by data science? Might records – or, more specifically, digital records – perhaps be *defined* as data, or as a subset of data? Should we conclude that records and data are indistinguishable? These questions will remain contentious, and unanimity among records professionals seems highly unlikely, but we can certainly expect growing numbers of professionals to accept a closer association between data and records than has been usual in the past.

Some records professionals, however, may wish to question whether *non-digital* records can usefully be described as data. Although it originated long before the invention of computer technology, the term 'data' has been appropriated by the computing industry, and some records professionals may believe that data can only be created or maintained digitally. Others are likely to acknowledge that, in pre-computer eras, data were kept in the form of card indexes, paper registers or ledgers, but may still be reluctant to recognise a wider range of analogue records as data. If all records – not merely digital records – were to be defined in terms of data, it would be necessary to look beyond ledgers, registers and card indexes, and to accept that data also include narrative reports on paper, handwritten letters, sealed parchment charters, clay tablets and wooden tally sticks. It seems likely that some professionals would be more willing than others to conceptualise data in this way.

Data and information: some conflicting views

At this point, we may feel a need for further elucidation of the possible meaning or meanings of 'data', and we may again be tempted to turn to a dictionary. The *Oxford English Dictionary* indicates that the word 'data' has been in use since the 17th century and the birth of what might be called scientific modernity, but its earliest usages predominantly reflected the word's Latin origins – data were matters that might be considered as 'given' – and were chiefly confined to numerical and scientific contexts (Rosenberg, 2013). In recent times, of course, the word has been used more widely, especially in computing and information studies, and there have been numerous attempts to characterise data in relation to information. Data have been defined as 'forms of information' (Borgman, 2015, 18), 'the raw material of information' (Brotby, 2009, 7), 'pieces of information stored in a structured way' (Administrative Data Research Network, 2015, 7) and 'the smallest meaningful units of information' (Duranti and Preston, 2008, 807; Léveillé and Timms, 2015, 158). The *Oxford English Dictionary* likewise offers 'items of information' as one of its definitions.

Data and information have sometimes been treated as more or less identical; the terms 'data privacy' and 'information privacy', for example, have both become popular in recent years and are often used interchangeably. The view of 'information as data' that was briefly introduced in Chapter 4 – one of five definitions, according to Furner (2015, 364), that are broadly accepted among information scientists – also seems to imply that there is little distinction to be made between data and information. An alternative view, equally well known in the fields of information studies and management science, is that data can be *converted into* information, and perhaps then further transformed into a higher state of knowledge, by means of some process of concentration, organization or improvement.

Data, information and knowledge are often depicted in textbooks as three discrete elements in a hierarchical model. Different versions of this model vary in points of detail, but data are usually presented as the lowest level; they are said to be distillable or improvable into information, which in turn can be processed further to create knowledge (Hey, 2004; Rowley, 2007). Following the widely cited lines from T. S. Eliot's play *The Rock*,

'Where is the wisdom we have lost in knowledge? Where is the knowledge we have lost in information?'   (Eliot, 1934, 7)

wisdom is frequently added as an additional term at the peak of the hierarchy, and the resulting four-part model is known as the DIKW (data, information, knowledge, wisdom) model. Its popularity in textbooks on information management and related fields is probably due to its apparent simplicity and its potential for visual presentation; it is usually depicted in the form of a pyramid. At its apex, wisdom is sometimes replaced or supplemented by other terms such as intelligence or enlightenment. The higher levels of the model are variously said to entail deeper reflection, greater connectedness or a larger role for the human mind.

Despite its renown, the DIKW model seems open to many of the same criticisms that have been applied to the records life-cycle model (Chapter 1). Like the life-cycle model, the standard DIKW model implies a linear progression and identifiable points of change, but critics have noted that the terms it uses – and the concepts underlying them – are not fully discrete, and that it seems impossible to determine exact points at which data might be turned into information or information into knowledge. Suggested alternatives, however, have not generally drawn on continuum thinking. Instead, some commentators have proposed replacements that invert or subvert the standard model. Rather than seeking to convert data into information, proponents of 'datafication' have sometimes advocated converting information into data to facilitate analysis and reuse (Mai, 2016, 193; Mayer-Schönberger and Cukier, 2013, 15, 96). According to archival consultant Laura Millar (2017, 5), data are transformable into knowledge, which can then be shared and turned into information. Data have also been said to emerge from knowledge (Tuomi, 1999–2000, 107), and information can be seen as knowledge that has been stored or communicated (Orna, 2004, 7). As this diversity of opinion indicates, data, information and knowledge are contested constructs, and their supposed relationships and transformations can be interpreted in many different ways.

In contrast to writers who emphasise the informational aspects of data, others have claimed that data have little meaning or significance (Ratzan, 2004, 2; Wilson, Kellerman and Corey, 2013, 12) or are 'simple sequences of signs and symbols that have no further meaning' (Hoppe et al., 2011, 585). Technologists often use the word 'data' to refer to strings or clusters of binary signals stored or communicated on particular digital media. When they speak of 'data streams' or 'data packets', they envisage data as assemblages of bits and bytes that – potentially, at least – can be identified, measured, preserved or deleted; in this sense, data may be perceived as a substance, 'a solid, physical thing with an objective existence' (Hey, 2004, 6), which is manageable and capable of being subjected to retention controls in much the same way as records. Notions of the materiality of data also underpin the discipline of digital forensics, which utilises material traces to reveal forensic evidence in computer systems (Blanchette, 2011, 1045). But when computing specialists describe a single bit or byte as 'the smallest unit of data a computer can handle' (Laudon and Laudon, 2012, 239; Wempen, 2014, 22), the word 'data' is seemingly used to allude to low-level digital signals without any consideration of their possible semantics. A collection of bits and bytes might be found meaningful by humans, but could equally be gibberish.

Nevertheless, to most people, allusions to 'data' undoubtedly connote a level of semantic meaning. Data protection laws, the open data movement and the burgeoning world of data analytics all rest on assumptions that data are meaningful. The idea that data can or should be reliable and authentic (Ellis, 1996, 326; Evans et al., 2014, 219) is also posited on a belief that data convey meaning and are not merely material aggregations of bits and bytes. The issues to which these beliefs and assumptions give rise are similar to some of the quandaries we encountered in Chapter 4 with regard to information. If data are thought to be meaningful, how far – if at all – are they independent of any platform in which meaning may appear to be captured? Can data be understood as meaning apart from media, or as media apart from meaning? How should we interpret the concept of 'data' when ostensibly similar content has been captured in two or more separate media?

Definitive answers to these questions appear to be beyond our reach. However, so strong is the popular association between data and perceived meaning that when, for example, Paul has typed 'The sky is blue' into his data storage system and Sylvie has typed 'The sky is blue' into hers, many observers would affirm that – although the material signals are distinct and housed in different locations – each of them has entered *the same data*. Many would say that the data remain identical even if saved in different file formats. Some might even claim that the data are the same if Paul has typed 'The sky is blue' and Sylvie has typed 'Le ciel est bleu'. Others, however, would almost certainly insist that Sylvie and Paul have created and stored separate data. These examples may seem trivial, but they are indicative of the difficulty of deciding what we might mean by the word 'data' when we use it in larger contexts, or how we might interpret it when we hear 'data' spoken of as an organizational resource. When the author of a computing textbook noted that 'often . . . the same data are stored in several different memories' (Watson, 2002, 22), his mode of thinking was scarcely compatible with the view that data are specific sets of binary code identifiable on particular computers. We seem to have arrived in another hall of mirrors; whichever way we choose to look, there is always another way of looking. In many respects, the concept of 'data' appears as insecure and problematic as 'information' as a foundation for our understanding of records.

Factuality

One of the biggest difficulties with seeing records either as information or as data is the frequent association of information and data with uncritical notions of fact. When data are perceived as offering some degree of meaning, they are often defined as 'raw facts' (Bantin, 2008, 67) that 'provide no judgment or interpretation' (Davenport and Prusak, 2000, 3). According to management scientists Peter Checkland and Sue Holwell (2006, 51), 'there are myriad facts about the world . . . and . . . the obvious word for the mass of facts is "data"'. In textbooks, examples of unprocessed 'raw' data are typically said to be customers' names and addresses, numbers of hours worked by an employee or numbers of units on a production line (Coronel and Morris, 2015, 15; Stair and Reynolds, 2016, 5). Information, too, is sometimes described as 'a collection of facts' (Shim, 2000, 1). According to an information management textbook, 'information is as close to the truth as one can get. It is not subjective or biased but . . . factual and impartial' (McGonigle and Mastrian, 2012, 20).

   Claims of this kind presuppose a world in which data and

information are independent of context, facts are transparent and elements of language correspond more or less precisely to external realities. Knowledge, it is assumed, can be set down in a way that is unmarked by any trace of the knower and requires no interpretation on the part of the reader or user. Data that take the form of numbers often seem especially free of creative or interpretative dimensions; because little or none of their content is framed as text or language, they appear to resist the biases that are frequently associated with theory and conjecture (Poovey, 1998, xii, 4). The presumptions that data 'speak for themselves' (Kitchin, 2014b, 136) and that their meaning will be self-evident to anyone who encounters them underpin much mainstream thinking in computer science and information management. In proclaiming the objectivity of data and seeking to isolate them from social and contextual influences, this mode of thinking is emblematic of rationalism and modernity.

In the discourse of corporate information systems, data are often associated with notions of authoritativeness and truth, and the belief that it may be possible for data management experts to identify particular data as 'sources of truth' has been widely promoted in recent years. For example, on the UK Government's Digital Service Blog (Downey, 2015), a register of government data was described as an 'authoritative list of information you can trust' and a 'canonical source of truth'. Language of this kind is frequently associated with attempts to define files of 'master data' that supposedly provide users with a single point of reference. According to the information technology division of an Australian university, the 'classification and description of master data identifies the authoritative source of truth' (Charles Sturt University, 2014). Similar ideas have often prevailed in the world of commercial business, where information specialists may set out to identify data 'that everyone . . . agrees is the real, trusted number' and a 'single source of truth' to guide organizational decision-making (Kosur, 2015; Murphy, 2011). When promoted by software vendors or consultancy firms, the notion that data control systems may make it possible to create or find a 'single source of truth' can seem highly attractive to managers seeking definitive solutions to business problems.

However, data are rarely as uncomplicated or univocal as literature aimed at business managers tends to suggest. Even ostensibly simple data such as customers' addresses often prove to be less straightforward than they at first appear. When an organization's customer database presents us with the datum that 'Paul's address is Windy Ridge', we must acknowledge that it could be wrong (if he has never set foot there) or out-of-date (if he has moved away). Moreover, even if we suppose that Paul has a current association with Windy Ridge, we may find it appropriate to ask what this datum might mean or to question our interpretation of it. Does Paul live there all the time, or might the Windy Ridge property be his second home? Does he reside in the property himself, or is he an absentee owner who has let his house to a tenant? What is Paul's address during the weeks when he stays in a hotel, lodges with a friend or camps in the backwoods? What are we to make of the datum that Sylvie's address is a Post Office Box number? We may surmise that the organization has agreed to send mail or goods to Paul and Sylvie at named locations, but this does not mean that data such as 'Paul's address is Windy Ridge' or 'Sylvie's address is P. O. Box 1234' are unambiguous, independently valid or reusable in any circumstance we wish. The data remain open to dispute; even when they are repurposed or remixed, their content is still moulded by the context or contexts in which it was made.

Large-scale processed data and other more complex forms of data are subject to similar concerns and constraints. Historian William Sewell and sociologists Norma Williams and Andrée Sjoberg have cited the example of a 19th-century statistical report on work and industry in Paris. Many historians have accepted the report at its face value, but a more thoughtful investigation has demonstrated that it must be approached more cautiously. The numbers and statistics that it presents cannot be treated as an objective source of knowledge of Parisian social life; this report and others like it are shaped by the categories and interpretations that were chosen by their compilers (Scott, 1999; Sewell, 2005, 50; Williams and Sjoberg, 1993, 189–90). All too often, statistical categorisations – although seemingly a technical matter – are found to be highly political; they valorise particular assumptions and particular ways of looking at the world.

In 19th-century Paris, statistical data had to be processed manually, but computer-processed data of the 20th and 21st centuries are equally open to critical judgement. At first sight, computer processing and data analytics may give every appearance of objective calculation untainted by bias or failings of perception, but the outputs of automated processing systems are not neutral; they are always dependent both on the choices that were made regarding input and on the choices made in designing the processing algorithms. Even in the realm of artificial intelligence, where computers and other 'intelligent' devices are increasingly being designed to make decisions without any direct human intervention, the chains of reasoning always begin with the design choices made by computer scientists and developers. Human responsibility lies behind 'smart' or 'intelligent' machines, and the data that such machines produce and use are not immune from ambiguity, partiality or political influence.

Growing numbers of scholars now argue that data are constructed within and conditioned by the practices used to generate them. According to José van Dijck (2015, 202), data are cultural objects generated for specific purposes and embedded within a social system. For Rob Kitchin (2014b, 2), they are 'framed technically, economically, ethically, temporally, spatially, and philosophically'. Lisa Gitelman (2013, 2) affirmed that, even in an era when the phrase 'raw data' seems ubiquitous, data 'are always already "cooked" and never entirely raw'. Following Geoffrey Bowker (2005, 184), Gitelman described raw data as an oxymoron; their rawness is a fiction that is often convenient but does not stand up to examination.

The data from Google's analytic tools depicted in Chapter 3 (Figures 3.1–3.5) were certainly cooked. Critics of Google have noted that its Ngrams do not reflect an unbiased sampling of published works or the cultural popularity of each publication (Pechenick, Danforth and Dodds, 2015, 23); the numbers that underlie Ngrams are not derived directly from the books Google scanned, but are dependent on potentially unreliable optical character recognition techniques and on normalisation procedures imposed by the software designers.[2] Similarly, Google itself issued a warning that the results produced by its Google Trends tool 'may contain inaccuracies for a number of reasons, including data-sampling issues and a variety of approximations that are used to compute results' (Hubbard, 2011, 84). The overall trends shown in Figures 3.1–3.5 may be convincing, but the details cannot be depended on. Data are never autonomous; they are often equivocal, and are always shaped by the circumstances that led to their creation.

In technological circles, however, concerns such as these rarely carry much weight. Despite the wealth of sceptical argument, foundationalist and seemingly unreflective ideas about truth, accuracy and objectivity have continued to find new expression in discourses about computing. For example, many advocates of emerging blockchain technologies have adopted the rhetoric of 'sources of truth', and speak of the primary purpose of blockchains as the creation of a 'permanent source of truth' or an agreed 'state of truth for data' (Dwyer, 2017; Roon, 2016). Datafication, too, is often presented as a neutral paradigm that leads to unbiased insights and objective understandings of the world. Proponents of new data-centric technologies typically affirm that the use of data analytics will enable 'reliable and provable knowledge' (Keim et al., 2008, 155; Naranjo, Sánchez and Villalobos, 2013, 29), or that data linkage techniques can be used to create an 'accurate picture of society' (Administrative Data Research Network, 2017). In the world of scholarship, some datafication enthusiasts have gone so far as to argue that a focus on data allows established critical and theoretical frameworks – in the humanities and social sciences as well as the physical sciences – to be abandoned in favour of mathematically based models and research questions derived from numerical patterns (Anderson, 2008; cf. Blanke and Prescott, 2016, 187–8). Similar unbridled optimism about the objective benefits of new techniques for analysing, quantifying and linking data is widespread in writings targeted at business organizations and government agencies. The notion that digital data and the algorithms that can be applied to them are free from human prejudice is too useful to organizations and their advisers to allow them to relinquish it.

Contested concepts

It seems we must conclude that, like the concepts of information discussed in earlier chapters of this book, concepts of data are – and are likely to remain – a matter of contestation. As information scientist Christine Borgman (2015, 28) noted, 'the term *data* has yet to acquire a consensus definition'. Although writers about data are sometimes reluctant to acknowledge the diversity of opinion, the term is capable of bearing a wide variety of meanings and interpretations, both within and across disciplines. This polysemy tends to cloud any exploration of the domain of data and its possible relationships to the field of records.

As we have seen, forays into the literature of the expanding world of data scholarship reveal unresolved tensions between those scholars who perceive data as social phenomena and those who are primarily interested in the technical challenges and opportunities of data management and analysis. The goal of most research in the data domain, as Jonathan Furner (2015, 370) observed, is not to enhance understanding of the concept of data but to specify methods that data curators can use to administer data more efficiently or deploy them to better effect. Data and data-centric technologies have acquired increasingly high profiles in the early 21st century, but ideas and concepts derived from data science and data studies can seemingly offer us only a shifting foundation on which to build our comprehension of record-making and record-keeping. Chapter 6 will propose that, if we wish to gain fuller understandings of records and the roles they fulfil in human society, we need to adopt a different approach.

Endnotes

1 See https://committee.iso.org/sites/tc46sc11/home/news/content-left-area/news-about-standarization-in-t-1/how-to-manage-data-as-a-record.html and https://committee.iso.org/sites/tc46sc11/home/news/content-left-area/news-about-standarization-in-t-1/open-data-and-records-management.html.

2 Furthermore, Google's Ngram tools do not fully disambiguate variant meanings that may be assigned to a single word or phrase. In Figure 3.3, for example, the data underlying the line that purports to depict usage of the word 'record' almost certainly include allusions to gramophone records and to world records achieved in sport. Cf. Lin et al. (2012, 169); Pal and Saha (2015).

References

Administrative Data Research Network (2015) *ADRN Glossary*, https://adrn.ac.uk/media/1166/adrn018-glossary_0008_pub.pdf.

Administrative Data Research Network (2017) *Administrative Data*, http://adrn.ac.uk/get-data/administrative-data.

Anderson, C. (2008) The End of Theory: the data deluge makes the scientific method obsolete. *Wired*, 23 June, www.wired.com/2008/06/pb-theory.

Anderson, K. (2013) The Footprint and the Stepping Foot: archival records, evidence, and time, *Archival Science*, **13** (4), 349–71.

Bantin, P. C. (2008) *Understanding Data and Information Systems for Recordkeeping*, Neal-Schuman.

Bhansali, N. (ed.) (2014) *Data Governance: creating value from information assets*, CRC Press.

Blanchette, J-F. (2011) A Material History of Bits, *Journal of the American Society for Information Science and Technology*, **62** (6), 1042–57.

Blanke, T. and Prescott, A. (2016) Dealing with Big Data. In Griffin, G. and Hayler, M. (eds), *Research Methods for Reading Digital Data in the Digital Humanities*, Edinburgh University Press.

Borgman, C. L. (2015) *Big Data, Little Data, No Data: scholarship in the networked world*, MIT Press.

Bowker, G. C. (2005) *Memory Practices in the Sciences*, MIT Press.

Brotby, K. (2009) *Information Security Governance*, John Wiley & Sons.

Cain, P. (1999) Automating Personnel Records for Improved Management of Human Resources: the experience of three African governments. In Heeks, R. (ed.), *Reinventing Government in the Information Age*, Routledge.

Campbell, T. M. (1989) Archives and Information Management, *Archivaria*, **28**, 146–50.

Charles Sturt University (2014) *Information and Data Standards*, www.csu.edu.au/__data/assets/pdf_file/0003/1314696/Data-Standards.pdf.

Checkland, P. and Holwell, S. (2006) Data, Capta, Information and Knowledge. In Hinton, M. (ed.), *Introducing Information Management*, Elsevier.

Choudhury, S. (2010) Data Curation: an ecological perspective, *College and Research Libraries News*, April, 194–6.

Cohen, G. and Kotorov, R. (2016) *Organizational Intelligence: how smart companies use information to become more competitive and profitable*, Information Builders.

Coleman, L., Lemieux, V. L., Stone, R. and Yeo, G. (eds) (2011) *Managing Records in Global Financial Markets*, Facet Publishing.

Coronel, C. and Morris, S. (2015) *Database Systems*, 11th edn, Cengage.

Dale, K. L. (2015) RIM's Role in Harnessing the Power of Big Data, *Information Management*, **49** (4), 29–32.

Davenport, T. H. and Prusak, L. (2000) *Working Knowledge: how organizations manage what they know*, Harvard Business School Press.

Downey, P. (2015) *Registers: authoritative lists you can trust*, UK Government Digital Service Blog, https://gds.blog.gov.uk/2015/09/01/registers-authoritative-lists-you-can-trust.

Duranti, L. and Preston, R. (eds) (2008) *International Research on Permanent Authentic Records in Electronic Systems (InterPARES 2)*, Università di Padova.

Dwyer, C. (2017) *Is Blockchain a 'Future of Work' Gamechanger?*, http://cporising.com/2017/02/03/is-blockchain-a-future-of-work-gamechanger-2.

Eliot, T. S. (1934) *The Rock*, Harcourt, Brace and Company.

Ellis, S. (1996) Four Travellers, Two Ways, One Direction: where to now for archival practice? *Archives and Manuscripts*, **24** (2), 322–9.

Evans, J., Reed, B., Linger, H., Goss, S., Holmes, D., Drobik, J., Woodyat, B. and Henbest, S. (2014) Winds of Change: a recordkeeping informatics approach to information management needs in data-driven research environments, *Records Management Journal*, **24** (3), 205–23.

Franks, P. C. (2013) *Records and Information Management*, American Library Association and Neal-Schuman.

Furner, J. (2015) Information Science Is Neither, *Library Trends*, **63** (3), 362–77.

Gitelman, L. (ed.) (2013) *'Raw Data' Is an Oxymoron*, MIT Press.

Grant, R. (2017) Recordkeeping and Research Data Management: a review of perspectives, *Records Management Journal*, **27** (2), 159–74.

Hey, J. (2004) *The Data, Information, Knowledge, Wisdom Chain: the metaphorical link*, www.dataschemata.com/uploads/7/4/8/7/7487334/dikwchain.pdf.

Hoppe, A., Seising, R., Nurnberger, A. and Wenzel, C. (2011) Wisdom: the blurry top of human cognition in the DIKW-model? In Galichet, S., Montero, J. and Mauris, G. (eds), *EUSFLAT 2011: proceedings of the 7th Conference of the European Society for Fuzzy Logic and Technology*, Atlantis Press.

Hubbard, D. W. (2011) *Pulse: the new science of harnessing Internet buzz to track threats and opportunities*, John Wiley & Sons.

Hurley, C. (1994) Data, Systems, Management and Standardisation, *Archives and Manuscripts*, **22** (2), 338–59.

Keim, D., Andrienko, G., Fekete, J., Görg, C., Kohlhammer, J. and Melançon, G. (2008) Visual Analytics: definition, process, and challenges,

Lecture Notes in Computer Science, **4950**, 154–75.

Kitchin, R. (2014a) Big Data, New Epistemologies and Paradigm Shifts, *Big Data & Society*, **1** (1), 1–12.

Kitchin, R. (2014b) *The Data Revolution*, Sage.

Kosur, J. (2015) *CFOs Need to Define a 'Single Source of Truth' for All of their Business Needs*, http://uk.businessinsider.com/cfos-need-to-define-the-single-source-of-truth-2015-10.

Laudon, K. C. and Laudon, J. P. (2012) *Management Information Systems*, 12th edn, Pearson.

Léveillé, V. and Timms, K. (2015) Through a Records Management Lens: creating a framework for trust in open government and open government information, *Canadian Journal of Information and Library Science*, **39** (2), 154–90.

Lin, Y., Michel, J.-B., Aiden, E. L., Orwant, J., Brockman, W. and Petrov, S. (2012) *Syntactic Annotations for the Google Books Ngram Corpus*, www.anthology.aclweb.org/P/P12/P12-3029.pdf.

Lycett, M. (2013) Datafication: making sense of (big) data in a complex world, *European Journal of Information Systems*, **22** (4), 381–6.

Mai, J.-E. (2016) Big Data Privacy: the datafication of personal information, *The Information Society*, **32** (3), 192–9.

Marciano, R. (2016) *Building a 'Computational Archival Science' Community*, https://saaers.wordpress.com/2016/07.

Marr, B. (2017) *Data Strategy: how to profit from a world of big data, analytics and the Internet of Things*, Kogan Page.

Mayer-Schönberger, V. and Cukier, K. (2013) *Big Data: a revolution that will transform how we live, work and think*, John Murray.

McDonald, J. (1989) Records Management and Data Management: closing the gap, *Records Management Journal*, **1** (1), 4–11.

McDonald, J. and Léveillé, V. (2014) Whither the Retention Schedule in the Era of Big Data and Open Data? *Records Management Journal*, **24** (2), 99–121.

McGann, J. (2013) Using Data Profiling to Mitigate Seven 'Red Flag' Information Risks, *Information Management*, **47** (4), 34–7.

McGonigle, D. and Mastrian, K. (eds) (2012) *Nursing Informatics and the Foundation of Knowledge*, 2nd edn, Jones & Bartlett.

Millar, L. (2017) *Archives: principles and practices*, 2nd edn, Facet Publishing.

Montaña, J. C. (2016) Data Privacy Meets a World of Risk: a landscape in turmoil, *Information Management*, **50** (6), 20–3.

Murphy, C. (2011) How to Get One Version of the Truth, *Information Week*, July, www.informationweek.com/it-leadership/how-to-get-one-version-of-the-truth/d/d-id/1101181.

Naranjo, D., Sánchez, M. and Villalobos, J. (2013) *Connecting the Dots: examining visualization techniques for enterprise architecture model analysis*, http://ceur-ws.org/Vol-1023/paper3.pdf.

Orna, E. (2004) *Information Strategy in Practice*, Gower.

O'Shea, G. (1996) Keeping Electronic Records: issues and strategies, *Provenance*, **1** (2), www.provenance.ca/1995-2000backissues/vol1/no2/features/erecs1a.htm.

Padilla, T. (2016) *On a Collections as Data Imperative*, http://digitalpreservation.gov/meetings/dcs16/tpadilla_OnaCollectionsasDataImperative_final.pdf.

Pal, A. R., and Saha, D. (2015) *Word Sense Disambiguation: a survey*, https://arxiv.org/ftp/arxiv/papers/1508/1508.01346.pdf.

Pechenick, E. A., Danforth, C. M. and Dodds, P. S. (2015) Characterizing the Google Books Corpus: strong limits to inferences of socio-cultural and linguistic evolution, *PLoS ONE*, **10** (10), 1–24.

Poovey, M. (1998) *A History of the Modern Fact: problems of knowledge in the sciences of wealth and society*, University of Chicago Press.

Ranade, S. (2016) *Traces through Time: a probabilistic approach to connected archival data*, http://dcicblog.umd.edu/cas/wp-content/uploads/sites/13/2016/05/2.pdf.

Ratzan, L. (2004) *Understanding Information Systems*, American Library Association.

Reed, B. (2016) *Digital Preservation PERICLES Acting on Change – OAIS*, www.records.com.au/blog/digital-preservation-pericles-acting-on-change-oais.

Research Councils UK (2015) *Traces though Time: prosopography in practice across big data*, http://gtr.rcuk.ac.uk/projects?ref=AH/L010186/1.

Roeder, J., Eppard, P., Underwood, W. and Lauriault, T. P. (2008) Authenticity, Reliability and Accuracy of Digital Records in the Artistic, Scientific and Government Sectors. In Duranti, L. and Preston, R. (eds), *International Research on Permanent Authentic Records in Electronic Systems (InterPARES 2)*, Università di Padova.

Roon, M. (2016) *Blockchains: a new source of truth*, www.linkedin.com/pulse/blockchains-new-source-truth-micha-roon.

Rosenberg, D. (2013) Data before the Fact. In Gitelman, L. (ed.), *'Raw Data'*

Is an Oxymoron, MIT Press.

Rowley, J. (2007) The Wisdom Hierarchy: representations of the DIKW hierarchy, *Journal of Information Science*, **33** (2), 163–80.

Sautter, E. (2011) Conflicts of Laws in Multiple Jurisdictions. In Coleman, L., Lemieux, V. L., Stone, R. and Yeo, G. (eds), *Managing Records in Global Financial Markets*, Facet Publishing.

Scott, J. W. (1999) *Gender and the Politics of History*, 2nd edn, Columbia University Press.

Sewell, W. H. (2005) *Logics of History: social theory and social transformation*, University of Chicago Press.

Shepherd, E. (2017) Right to Information. In MacNeil, H. and Eastwood, T. (eds), *Currents of Archival Thinking*, 2nd edn, Libraries Unlimited.

Shim, J. K. (2000) *Information Systems and Technology for the Noninformation Systems Executive*, CRC Press.

Smit, F. (2017) Records, Hyperobjects and Authenticity. In Smit, F., Glaudemans, A. and Jonker, R. (eds), *Archives in Liquid Times*, Stichting Archiefpublicaties.

Stair, R. M. and Reynolds, G. W. (2016) *Principles of Information Systems*, 12th edn, Cengage.

Thibodeau, K. (2009) The Survival of Records (and Records Management) in the Twenty-First Century. In Tibbo, H. R., Hank, C., Lee, C. A. and Clemens, R. (eds), *Digital Curation: practice, promise and prospects. Proceedings of DigCCurr 2009*, University of North Carolina.

Thomas, D., Fowler, S. and Johnson, V. (2017) *The Silence of the Archive*, Facet Publishing.

Thurston, A. C. (2012) Trustworthy Records and Open Data, *Journal of Community Informatics*, **8** (2), http://ci-journal.net/index.php/ciej/article/view/951/952.

Tuomi, I. (1999–2000) Data Is More than Knowledge: implications of the reversed knowledge hierarchy for knowledge management and organizational memory, *Journal of Management Information Systems*, **16** (3), 103–17.

Van Dijck, J. (2015) Datafication, Dataism and Dataveillance: big data between scientific paradigm and ideology, *Surveillance & Society*, **12** (2), 197–208.

Watson, R. T. (2002) *Data Management*, 3rd edn, John Wiley & Sons.

Wempen, F. (2014) *Computing Fundamentals*, John Wiley & Sons.

Williams, N. and Sjoberg, A. F. (1993) Ethnicity and Gender: the view from above versus the view from below. In Vaughan, T. R., Sjoberg, G. and Reynolds, L. T. (eds), *A Critique of Contemporary American Sociology*, General Hall.

Wilson, M. I., Kellerman, A. and Corey, K. E. (2013) *Global Information Society: technology, knowledge, and mobility*, Rowman & Littlefield.

Yeo, G. (2011) Rising to the Level of a Record? Some thoughts on records and documents, *Records Management Journal*, **21** (1), 8–27.

CHAPTER 6

Representation, performativity and social action: why records are not (just) information

Introduction

Despite the numerous voices proclaiming the value and importance of information and data in the contemporary world, it is far from clear that ideas about information and data can provide an adequate basis for comprehending how records work. This chapter sets out an alternative approach and suggests that records professionals may find it more rewarding to understand records as *representations*. It offers a brief introduction to concepts of representation and explores some of the ways in which representations are deployed in human interaction. It also examines how viewing records as representations can provide a starting-point for investigating their relationships to activities and events, their performative aspects and their varied roles in society. Instead of seeing records as primarily informational, this chapter argues that record-making is always intimately bound to contexts of social action.

Representations

Although concepts of representation have not traditionally played a major part in professional understandings of records, they have been widely discussed in many other disciplines, including art, film and media studies, linguistics, philosophy and psychology. A represent-ation is something that stands, or is believed to stand, for something else. Examples of representations include charts, diagrams, models, statues, pictures, gestures, dramatic performances and musical notations. Language and writing are also often said to be forms of representation.

Commentators have frequently noted that no representation can capture every aspect of the phenomenon it seeks to represent. Representations are always partial.[1] Nevertheless, we encounter them everywhere. Some are primarily aesthetic, but many have practical functions as surrogates for things that would otherwise be absent or inaccessible (Ankersmit, 2001; Cummins, 1996). Representations – and ideas about representation – can help us to comprehend the material and social world in which we live and to make sense of many aspects of human behaviour and experience.

We may find that viewing records as representations is more productive than attempting to view them in informational terms. More specifically, we can see records as representations of *occurrents*. Occurrents are phenomena that have, or are perceived to have, an ending in time. A record stands for an occurrent and remains available after the occurrent has ceased (Yeo, 2007; 2008). The occurrents with which records are most commonly associated are activities and transactions conducted in business or personal life, but it is also possible to have records of statements made, questions asked and feelings expressed, as well as records of 'natural' events unconnected or only loosely connected with human intentionality. Activities, events and similar phenomena do not continue without limit of time; sooner or later, they come to an end, but the records that represent them have an ongoing presence. Records are *persistent* representations because they have the capacity to endure beyond the circumstances that lead to their creation. We cannot suppose that they will be perfect, but we can use them as surrogates for past actions or events that otherwise lie beyond our reach.

We can also have records of what we might call 'states of affairs': records representing how things were at a moment in time. The world around us is constantly changing, and states of affairs cannot be expected to continue unaltered; if we have a record of a state of affairs – of the size, shape, quality or quantity of a particular phenomenon at a particular historical moment – we can recognise it as a representation of an occurrent. In every case, the occurrent lacks persistence, but the record continues to represent it. Over time, understandings of the record and its meanings may evolve and fluctuate, but its representational function survives.

The word 'occurrent' was used in many fields of writing in past centuries, but is now employed chiefly in philosophy. In earlier work, I noted that archivists and records managers often emphasise relationships between records and temporal entities such as functions, activities, transactions and events, but lack a suitable collective term for these entities. I suggested that 'occurrents' – a term philosophers use to refer to temporal phenomena – might be an appropriate collective label (Yeo, 2008, 136). It is sometimes said that an occurrent can be punctual (occurring at a 'point' in time) or non-punctual (extending over a particular time period). Using this terminology, we can affirm that records persist beyond the temporal ending of the occurrents they represent.

Kimberly Anderson (2013) observed that notions of temporal 'endings' are products of western thinking and that many non-western peoples have other understandings of time, including beliefs that the present is not transient and the past is not disconnected from it. She concluded that my approach to characterising records is insufficiently inclusive and needs to be adjusted to take account of ideas about an enduring present. I prefer, however, to take my cue from Kenyan scholar Ali Mazrui, who argued that concepts and practices of record-keeping are unnecessary to those who perceive the past as always present. The dynamic celebratory and commemorative practices of those who understand time in this way should be assessed on their own terms and should not be forced into the alien category of 'records', a move that betrays an intellectual dependency on western criteria of respectability (Mazrui, 1986, 68, 76–7). Records (written or unwritten) only seem necessary in societies that have acquired a notion that actions or events may be subject to endings in time, and are only found in societies that have sought means of transcending those endings through representation.

A record is normally created by a participant in, or an observer of, the occurrent that it represents, either at the time of the occurrent or soon afterwards. Conceptually, it matters little whether the representation is produced by a human or a mechanical device such as a computer; what matters is that the producer of the representation has participated in or directly observed the occurrent in question. In general, we do not understand a representation created by a third party as a record of the activities, events or other occurrents that it describes, although we may construe it as a record of the third party's activity in describing them.

A Victorian painting depicting the battle of Agincourt, an account of the battle written by a modern scholar and Laurence Olivier's film of Shakespeare's *Henry V* are all persistent representations of a notable past event, but because they were not created by participants or observers we are unlikely to consider them *records* of the event concerned. Human participants and observers may not be impartial or objective, but they have first-hand knowledge unavailable to those who did not experience the event: a level of knowledge that seems essential for creating a record.

In proposing a view of records as representations, I rejected notions that records come into existence only when they are captured into formal record-keeping systems (Yeo, 2011). A representational view of records characterises them by examining their relations with occurrents, not in terms of decisions about their management. Although records may cross 'thresholds of formality' (Reed, 2005, 121) during their lives, crossing these thresholds does not determine their status as records. I agree with critics who contend that designation decisions are arbitrary and that records managers need to cast their net more widely than their past practices often permitted, but the wider environment to which records managers must attend is not (as is often now claimed) an environment of information, but a wider environment of records and representations.

Some representations are iconic; they are thought to resemble the things they stand for. The resemblance need not be exact or complete; it merely needs to be sufficient to permit sensitive viewers to recognise it. Photographs seem an obvious example. It is widely accepted that photographs are not as neutral or objective as was once thought, but this acceptance does not diminish our understanding of them as representations of the subjects that photographers select. Photographs are imperfect representations, but insofar as they are understood to represent occurrents in a persistent manner, they can be acknowledged as records. Some are records of activities or events, but others represent states of affairs; we can perceive them as records of 'how things appeared' to the photographer at a particular moment. It has sometimes been claimed that photographs are information (Meyer, 2008–9; Mulvihill, 1990), but most people will probably find this idea unintuitive. It also remains open to dispute whether information can be embedded *within* a photograph. It seems more congruent to argue that information is an affordance offered to us when we examine photographs or other iconic records.

However, not all representations – and not all records – are iconic. Representations can take the form of rituals and ceremonies, and archival scholars have often observed that these sometimes function as a kind of record. Communities may also establish conventions that particular objects, or marks made on objects, serve as representations or records. For thousands of years, humans have accepted that words or other signs can be used to represent external entities. Words can also be combined to make 'texts', and writing systems allow texts to be inscribed for future reference. In almost all societies that have adopted writing, its earliest, or some of its earliest, uses have been in keeping records, and writing systems have disrupted earlier modes of record-keeping. For most people in 21st-century western societies, a prototypical record chiefly comprises written text.

This is not to say that we can create objects that will be universally perceived as representations or records. Objects recognised as records by one community or individual may be perceived differently by others. Photographs, for example, may be acknowledged as records in some contexts of creation, keeping or use, but may be perceived in other contexts as symbolic artefacts or works of art. Web pages can be seen as records but also as publicity mechanisms, computing resources, sales platforms or corporate management tools. Diaries and letters may be viewed as means of communication by their authors, as records by archivists and as literary resources by scholars of literature. All are 'boundary objects' (Star and Griesemer, 1989), entities shared by different communities and comprehended or used in different ways. Nor can we be certain that everyone who encounters a record will be in agreement about its representational aspects. A representation operates only when those who interact with it acknowledge its representational qualities. Writing systems, however, provide conventions that allow representations and records to be interpreted and understood across time and space. In practice, to a large degree, records fulfil their representational function.

A representational view of records is largely focused on actions performed at the time when records are created. While not precluding the likelihood that records will undergo many vicissitudes later in their lives, its primary concern is with the contexts and settings in which a record first comes into being. Although – as we saw in Chapter 2 – many scholars now emphasise the continuing evolution of records through their adventures over time, these later adventures are not distinctive of records. Openness to re-contextualisation, reuse and reinterpretation is not a unique characteristic of the objects we call 'records', but is a feature of all (or almost all) enduring artefacts. Much the same can be said about philosopher Luciano Floridi's claim that definitions of a record should acknowledge the presence of physical signs of damage or deterioration arising from repeated handling (Glaudemans, Jonker and Smit, 2017, 309). When we find such scars, they are part of a record's life-story; as indicators of past use or misuse, they are often significant for practical research purposes; but at a conceptual level they do not help us to distinguish records from other objects we encounter. We can, however, attempt to distinguish records by identifying them as representations of specific occurrents.

Speech acts

Arguably, representation in the form of words and written texts also underlies information scientists' perceptions of data and information. Some information scientists certainly recognise that symbolic representation plays a role in their field. According to László Karvalics (2008, 33), 'systems of information technology operate with information converted into symbols'. To Keith Devlin (1999, 27), information is not *contained* in books or other objects, but is encoded or represented in their markings. Instead of telling us that data *are* facts, some information scientists and computing specialists have affirmed that data *represent* facts (Beynon-Davies, 2009, 94; Dervos and Coleman, 2006, 52). More cautiously, computer scientists Terry Winograd and Fernando Flores (1986, 156) suggested that 'computers . . . manipulate symbolic representations that some person generated on the belief that they corresponded to facts.'

To understand textual records as representations, however, we must probe a little more deeply and examine the theory of speech acts, developed by the philosophers J. L. Austin and John Searle. Speech act theory addresses the ways in which humans use language: how they 'do things with words' (Austin, 1962). It is not widely known in the world of record-keeping, perhaps because the label 'speech acts' has obscured its relevance to a discipline largely focused on written texts. The theory – or, perhaps more correctly, the body of interconnected theories – relates to both speech and writing; some scholars have argued that it is misnamed, but 'speech act theory' remains the label in general use (Yeo, 2010; 2017).

Whether spoken or written, language enables us to state propositions about the world: propositions that we, or our hearers or readers, may choose to regard as informative. However, speech act theory challenges the assumption that the primary or only function of language is to represent or transmit information or (supposed) facts. Austin (1962, 4–7, 151–2) noted that, in speaking or writing, we can also perform an act such as giving an order or committing to an agreement. He observed that performing acts through what he called 'utterances' is characteristic of conveyancing instruments and other legal documents. In a will, for example, the testator writes 'I bequeath my art collection to my daughter', and the bequest is performed by means of the language the testator uses. Archivists acquainted with diplomatic scholarship (the study of documentary authenticity) are familiar with such written 'performative utterances' – as Austin called them – under the guise of dispositive records (cf. Duranti and Preston, 2008, 811). Austin's examples of spoken performative utterances included 'I pronounce you guilty' and 'I name this ship the *Queen Elizabeth*'. Performative utterances that might be either written or spoken include 'I promise' and 'I apologise'. Under the conventions of western societies, to make such an utterance is to perform the act concerned. When we write 'I apologise' in an e-mail to someone we have offended, we do not merely send information about an apology; we perform the act of apologising.

John Langshaw Austin was a British philosopher who specialised in the philosophy of language. His seminal work *How to Do Things with Words*, based on lectures given in 1955, was published posthumously in 1962. After his death, his ideas were taken up by his former pupil John Searle, who became professor of the philosophy of mind and language at the University of California, Berkeley. Searle's work made prevalent the term 'speech act theory' as a label for the thinking of the two philosophers.

Austin's work also led him to investigate the performative nature of stating propositions. At first sight, the performativity of statement-making is not obvious. When we make a statement such as 'The sky is blue', we rarely say or write 'I state that the sky is blue'; this formulation seems overly complex. Nevertheless, simply to say or write 'The sky is blue' (or 'Rome is 200 kilometres from Naples', or 'The sales figures for the third quarter were as follows . . .') is to state the proposition in question. Austin (1962, 133–9) argued that making a statement is just as much an action as bequeathing, apologising or naming a ship.

It follows that we perform speech acts even when we send e-mails, memos or other documents whose role may seem purely informational. Consider, for example, this memo from the Accounts Department:

> I have paid the invoice you asked about.
>
> (signed) Belinda Beancounter.

Like 'The sky is blue', 'I have paid the invoice' may appear to be simply a piece of information, a supposed fact. For our purposes, however, it is more fruitful to view it as a proposition stated by Belinda Beancounter. The transmission of the memo was the performance of an act of stating. Although Belinda did not write 'I hereby state that I have paid the invoice', or even 'I confirm that I have paid the invoice', her signature indicates that she represents herself as stating the proposition that she has paid it.

In the theory of speech acts expounded by Searle (1986; 2002, 143–4), a speech act requires both representation and communication. Belinda's memo represents an act of stating, but a memo of this kind must also be communicated to someone, or to a storage system to which someone has access, if it is to constitute the act of stating that it represents. In this instance, Belinda achieved the act of stating that she had paid the invoice by creating a written representation of this act and sending it to a recipient.

Though often imperfect, representations are key components of speech acts (Yeo, 2010, 100). They depend on acceptance of socially constructed schemes of representation, and are effective only if their creators and recipients share an understanding of a particular scheme, but representational schemes that use spoken or written language facilitate shared understanding and provide powerful tools for interaction. Scholars refer, with varying shades of meaning, to interpretive communities (Fish, 1980), discourse communities (Rafoth, 1988) or speech communities (Gumperz, 2009), whose members have a level of general agreement about the operation of language. Broadly speaking, within such communities, members can perform speech acts using representations that employ the community's accepted scheme.

When a proposition is stated, two layers of representation are employed. Belinda's memo can be seen as offering representations, both of her (earlier) action of paying the invoice and of her (more recent) action of stating that it had been paid. The two layers of representation are entwined; a representation of a proposition is contingent on a representation that performs the act of stating it.

From a record-keeping perspective, Belinda's memo is a record because the representations persist after the act has been performed. Depending on our requirements at a given moment, we can treat the memo as a record of the payment of the invoice, as a record of Belinda's statement that she has paid it, or as both.

Propositions and performativity

Propositions are often said to be testable as to their truth or falsity (Osgood, 1979, 207), and critics have frequently remarked that we cannot always have confidence in the truth of the propositions stated in records. Borrowing a phrase popularised by archival scholar Ciaran Trace (2002), we can aver that what is recorded may not be simply 'what happened'. James O'Toole (2002b) offered an amusing example, noting that his academic diploma described him as an upright youth who had applied himself unceasingly to his studies, although O'Toole felt that this statement was not wholly accurate. We may want to be similarly cautious about Belinda's assertion that she has paid the invoice. Perhaps she has paid it, but perhaps she is lying, or perhaps she genuinely does not know that the payment was not completed and the supplier is threatening legal action.

It has often been observed that the contents of records may be slanted in favour of their creators or the organizations for which their creators work. Consider, for example, the statement of the third-quarter sales figures: the figures might not be wholly fallacious, but can we be sure that no one has massaged them a little, to make the

Sales Department appear in a better light? According to interdisciplinary scholar Geoffrey Bowker (2005, 7), records on navy ships 'are written with an eye to a future legal enquiry should there be a disaster'; scientific records 'tell the story of an ideal past in which all the protocols were duly followed'. To a considerable degree, most organizational records are constructed in ways that attune with organizational cultures or with the prevalent modes of discourse within an organization. Similar tendencies can also be found in personal records; as historian Arthur Schlesinger (1972, 401) noted, 'it may become . . . apparent that A's letters are his own self-serving version of events; that B's diaries are designed . . . to dignify the diarist and discredit his opponents; that C's memoranda are written to improve the record'.

One of the most thorough explorations of the tendentiousness of propositions asserted in records is in a book, provocatively entitled *Boring Records?*, by social worker Katie Prince (1996). Starting from the view – expressed by many of her colleagues – that records are 'boring', Prince set out to investigate the significance of records for the social work profession and the consequences of record-making and record-keeping practices for social workers and their clients. She found that social workers' accounts of clients' circumstances, and of their own interactions with clients, were often influenced by anxieties about confidentiality, by desires to reduce clerical work they perceived as unnecessary and by the shape of the recording forms they were required to use. While rarely aiming at conscious deception, social workers constructed records in ways that would ensure good relations with other stakeholders, help to achieve desired responses, deflect criticism or minimise political strife.

Of course, numerous records are created without any overt intention to manipulate or deceive; many statements by makers of records are sincere attempts to describe actions, events or circumstances as accurately as language permits. A scientist can be expected to acknowledge that the success of the second phase of her research may depend on how well she is able to record the first phase; a social worker can be expected to recognise that the welfare of children or the elderly can be jeopardised unless her records are carefully made. We should not assume that attempts to make reliable records are exceptional or without consequences. However, such attempts are always circumscribed by the contexts in which they are made and the beliefs and assumptions of those who make them; when a human being states a proposition, social and cultural factors always come into play, and no proposition is independent of the world-view of the person making it. Many people whose work requires them to create records by stating propositions about 'what happened' will try to construct their records as conscientiously as possible, but the notion that statements describing activities and events can constitute 'factual and impartial information' of the kind postulated by authors of information management textbooks does not stand up to examination. Following a line of thought developed by Eric Ketelaar (2008, 10), we may conclude that, at best, such records describe 'what the recorder believed or construed to be the truth [or] the reality'.

The concerns that can arise when creators of records make statements about past activities are not simply issues of truth or falsehood. Some record creators – scholars whose grant applications state that their previous research has been world-leading, or politicians whose letters claim that they have put the country's interests before their own – assert propositions that can only be matters of opinion. Statements of supposed facts about the outside world may also need to be treated with caution. Perhaps the sky really is blue, but perhaps it merely appears so to human observers. Perhaps the distance from Rome to Naples depends on the route you take. Perhaps the markets of the world are ready for the development of a new financial product, or consumers are avidly awaiting the launch of a new chocolate bar, but perhaps these are just optimistic projections by members of a marketing team. Although the propositions stated in records are frequently referred to as information, we can recognise that they generally express perceptions of the world rather than empirically verifiable facts; we can also acknowledge that all such statements are subject to variable interpretation by those who read them.

In 2016 and 2017, there was much concern about 'fake news': the dissemination, often through social media, of false – or seemingly false – news stories about prominent individuals or current events. 'Fake news' may be a novel label but it is not a novel phenomenon; as historian Robert Darnton (2017) commented, there are many past examples of the sharing of false news, going back as far as the days of the Roman empire. Nevertheless, the 'fake news' phenomenon attracted particular attention in 2016 and 2017, partly because of an apparent increase in the number of false stories circulating on social media, but also because some politicians and political spin doctors began to use the phrase 'fake news' to describe reports by mainstream news channels of which they disapproved.

Austin's discussion of disputable statements, however, suggests that it may often be easier to identify what is false than to determine what is true. Austin (1962, 143–4) gave the example of someone telling us that 'Lord Raglan won the battle of Alma' during the Crimean War. Raglan was the commander of the British forces, but, Austin said, his orders had little effect on the outcome of the battle, which was arguably won by the initiative shown by soldiers at the front line; it might be appropriate for a school textbook to state that Raglan won the victory, but a military historian might be expected to reach a different conclusion. Suppose, then, that a newspaper reporter sent a despatch from the Crimea asserting that Raglan had won the battle; could this be considered false (or 'fake') news? If we found among the reporter's papers a despatch asserting that the Russians or the little green men from Mars had won the battle, we could rightly condemn it as false, but a despatch stating that the battle was won by Raglan would be much harder to categorise in terms of truth or falsehood.

Even if a reporter's despatches include detailed accounts of the fighting, the havoc it wrought or the suffering it inflicted, we may still be uncertain of their credibility or reliability. As George Orwell noted in *Homage to Catalonia*, his account of the civil war in Spain, readers of his descriptions must be wary of his partisanship, his 'mistakes of fact' and the distortion caused by his 'having seen only one corner of events' (Orwell, 1938, 313). However, there is another aspect to a reporter's despatches where greater levels of certainty seem possible. Let us imagine that, in the course of research in the archives of a newspaper publisher, we find some despatches in which the Crimean reporter made statements about the conflict at Alma. Regardless of whether we believe these statements are true, false or variably interpretable, unless we have grounds for claiming that the despatches have been forged or tampered with we cannot easily deny that the statements were made. The records represent what the reporter said.

We must reach similar conclusions about any other record in which someone makes a statement. Suppose that Donald has sent me a note stating that two cities are 200 kilometres apart. If I feel this is disputable or inaccurate, I may see it as *misinformation* rather than information; but no matter how much I doubt that his proposition can be called information, or how strongly I deny the truth of what he wrote, the note is a record of his stating this proposition, and both he and I will find it difficult to deny that he has stated it. A similar situation arises if, for example, Donald has sent a note to the Defence Ministry stating that our enemy is testing weapons of mass destruction. If his statement differs from other reports, the minister may doubt whether it is to be believed, but because the note is a persistent representation of Donald's statement the ministry is able to preserve a record that Donald cannot easily disown. Nor can the various notes he sent simply be equated with the 'information' that he has made these statements; the notes played intrinsic roles in performing his acts of stating. Like all records, they contributed to the performance of an action at the moment of their issuance. Records resound with a complexity of meaning and performativity, which the simple concept of records as information is not rich enough to encompass.

Data, computers and the making of speech acts

The notion that stating a proposition is the performance of an act is a key insight of Austin's work. Austin's original aim had been to differentiate utterances that are 'sayings' (such as statements or descriptions) from those that are 'actions' (such as orders or promises), labelling the former as 'constative' and the latter as 'performative'. But his exploration of 'constative' utterances led him to discover that making a statement is itself a kind of action. In *How to Do Things with Words*, he collapsed the distinction he had initially proposed; he concluded that 'whenever I "say" anything . . . I shall be performing . . . acts' (Austin, 1962, 133) and that constatives are also performatives. Moreover, we perform an act not only when we write 'I state that task A has been done', but also when we merely write 'task A has been done'; not only when we write 'I assert that the cost of the project is €2000', but also when we write 'project cost = €2000'. Searle (1979, 12) abandoned the label 'constative' and referred to acts of this kind as 'assertive'; they are acts in which propositions about the past, present or future are stated or asserted. In my earlier work discussing records in which a record creator states a proposition (Yeo, 2010, 102–7; 2017), I followed

Searle's terminology and referred to them as 'assertive records'.

Austin's ideas are also relevant when we consider data. As we saw in Chapter 5, data are seldom as uncomplicated as they seem. When we look at a database, no one seems to be making statements; no one is affirming that they can vouch for the data; the apparent absence of signs of authorship gives the impression that the data are uncontroversial and objective. As Winograd and Flores (1986, 156) remarked, 'since the "facts" stored by a computer cannot be readily associated with a commitment by an individual who asserted them, it is easy to be blind to the nature of their origin'. But Austin's insights make us aware that the contents of datasets and databases are not autonomous; they are propositions stated by humans, or computing devices programmed by humans, in particular contexts.

The apparent anonymity of data and the illusion of their factual objectivity have ancient origins. Cultural historian Mary Poovey (1998, 116) has shown how, long before the arrival of computers, the invention of double-entry book-keeping allowed economic transactions to be recorded 'while making the writer seem to disappear'. To a casual observer, the apparent precision of mercantile account books seems to guarantee the unbiased accuracy of their contents, but scholarly investigation has demonstrated that accounting records in the 14th and 15th centuries were not always accurate; they were prone to error and were sometimes 'cooked' (Poovey, 1998, 64; Scott-Warren, 2016, 151–2). In the 19th century, the quest for objective scientific and engineering data led to the development of 'self-recording instruments' that were thought to be free from human intervention or partiality, but the data recorded by these instruments were nonetheless constrained by the standards negotiated by the instrument-makers. A self-recording instrument facilitated data capture, but particular assumptions about what should be recorded and how recording should be done always underlay its design (De Chadarevian, 1993).

More recently, these long-standing tensions and conflicts have been translated into the world of computer technology. In their earliest years, computers were sometimes heralded as emblems of objectivity and truth (Gerovitch, 2002, 354), and this view still enjoys considerable currency. Structured digital data may give every appearance of being rigorously factual, not only because they usually lack indications of authorship, but also because their tightly controlled formats rarely offer space for subtlety or nuance. The rigid field structures of database systems and the terseness of their data may lead us to suppose that the assertions made in these systems are less open to subjectivity than statements rendered in free-flowing narrative form. However, even a single-word entry in a field such as 'Employment status' can remind us that a typical database entry is a contingent statement that someone has made. As occupational scientists Amber Angell and Olga Solomon (2014) suggested, an entry in a healthcare database that describes a patient as 'unemployed' indicates a very different mind-set from an entry that describes her as a 'full-time homemaker'. Elements of data such as 'Sylvie is unemployed' do not represent incontrovertible facts; they represent propositions that a reader may consider true, false or merely equivocal. Viewing them from a perspective informed by speech act theory, we can see that the propositions are represented in the computer system because humans have made acts of assertion: acts inevitably accompanied by possibilities of error, ambiguity and partiality.

Of course, not all data in computer systems are created manually. As volumes of data grow, organizations have sought to reduce or eliminate the need for human operators and increasingly use systems that capture or calculate data without direct human input. Automated systems permit data creation and analysis on a vast scale and at unprecedented speed. However, data captured or calculated automatically are not exempt from human influence; the tools used to produce, format and present them are designed by humans and imbued with human values. Obvious – but by no means the only possible – examples can be found in corporate decision support (or 'business intelligence') systems, which usually offer analytical tools in conjunction with 'dashboards' that display summary data for easy assimilation. Although it is often said that the role of these dashboards is to 'reveal the facts' (Cohen and Kotorov, 2016, 80), the data that such systems present and the mode of their presentation depend on choices made by humans at the point of system design as well as the point of use. In these systems, too, the data presented to users are propositions: for example, the proposition that the call centre is in the top 10% for customer satisfaction; that the number of invoices sent this month is 7250; or that the organization's gross profit is $48,000,000. Whenever computers generate data or statistics in the form of propositions about people, business units, events or other aspects of the world, acts of assertion can be seen to have occurred.

Can computers perform speech acts? For more than two decades, philosophers and philosophically-minded computer scientists have debated how far computers can be seen as 'social actors' and how far, if at all, they can be said to possess intentions or the ability to attach meaning to what they do. Some have framed this debate in terms of whether computers are able to perform speech acts. Jacques Derrida (2002, 74) affirmed that no machine could produce a performative event 'according to the . . . orthodoxy of speech acts', but Robert Demolombe and Vincent Louis (2006) argued that, although it is problematic to assign intentionality to electronic agents, it is appropriate to apply speech act theory when examining how they function.

Much depends on the perspective we adopt. When used for word-processing or sending e-mails, a computer is merely a vehicle for enabling written speech acts to be performed by humans, with a facility for storing the resulting records. But computers are also programmed to give instructions ('Please wait'), ask questions ('Are you sure you want to delete this?') and make statements of their own ('Download is now 50% complete'). Besides these temporary dialogues, computers make statements that are or should be recorded in persistent form. Computer systems state propositions about themselves ('Today's system test detected no errors'), about transactions they were instructed to perform ('Online payment was made on 1st January') or about their users ('User J replied on 31st March'), and they can also employ sensing devices to generate statements about the outside world. All these statements – as well as the statements computers make when data have been processed or analysed – are, or closely resemble, assertive speech acts.

We now appear to be moving into a world where computers and computer-controlled 'smart' or robotic appliances will increasingly communicate among themselves without human intervention and where machines using artificial intelligence will take decisions, conclude contracts and perform many other activities that were once the exclusive domain of humans. A report to the European Parliament has suggested that robotic devices can no longer be considered simply 'tools in the hands of other actors' and that new legal rules will be required to accommodate their ability to act autonomously (European Parliament, Committee on Legal Affairs, 2016).[2] Although the boundary between the computer as tool and the computer as independent agent will remain blurred, developments in artificial intelligence will make it harder for critics to deny that computers can perform speech acts or that speech act theory can usefully be applied to computer data.

Rather than attempting to define records as data, records professionals might prefer to characterise persistent data as records. We have already seen that data in transactional database systems are widely recognised as records, but we could argue that many other kinds of persistent data can also be understood as records. These may include data derived from laboratory procedures or field tests, from observations of natural phenomena or human interactions, or from automated processing or analysis. More specifically, we could argue that persistent data of this kind are *assertive* records: representations of statements or assertions that have been made about people, organizations, places, events, the results of investigations or the state of the world.

Since the era of 19th-century 'self-recording instruments', increasing numbers of systems have been designed to detect such occurrents and make statements about them without overt or immediate human involvement. Today, of course, many systems that make automated statements about occurrents are not built to offer persistence. A speedometer states that a car is travelling at X miles per hour, and a display screen in a bank foyer states that the stock index stands at Y, but the statement is not persistent; within fractions of a second, the system makes a new statement to replace it, as the speed of the car or the level of the index changes. We can expect to see many more systems of this kind in coming years, as the proliferation of sensors and smart devices adds to the flood of data captured for one-time use and then immediately overwritten or deleted. However, as we saw in Chapter 2, the notion that all data in the contemporary world are in constant movement is a fallacy; many systems are – or can be – configured to provide appropriate levels of persistence where these are deemed necessary. Wherever such data persist, we can see them as records of statements or assertions made in particular situations. Although advocates of remixability like to depict digital data as independent objects needing little or no contextualisation, viewing data as records offers a reminder that they have contexts of origin as well as contexts of custody and use. Behind the data, as archivist Hugh Taylor (1987–8, 24) observed, lie the 'act and deed'.

Metadata

We can draw similar conclusions when considering *metadata*. Metadata are data intended to describe a resource or its contexts, enable its preservation or facilitate access to it; they are deemed a vital component of systems for managing records and archives. Although metadata are expected to be closely linked to the records they support, it has often been remarked that they are also records in their own right (Gilliland, 2017, 221; ISO 23081-2: 2009, clause 8.3).

In the light of understandings that take account of speech act theory, we can characterise metadata more precisely as *assertive* records. Indeed, since the beginning of the 21st century, when Clifford Lynch (2000, 34) alluded to metadata as assertions that cluster around an object, professional literature has increasingly recognised their assertive aspect. Although creators of metadata rarely use explicit assertive formulae – such as 'I state that this letter is in John Smith's handwriting' or 'I think that this series was rearranged in the 1960s' – many commentators have noted that metadata (or 'descriptions', if we prefer more traditional language) are 'assertions we make about records' (Ranade, 2016, 2). They are statements about a record and its relationships, made by its custodians, users or other agents at specific moments in its life.

When records are preserved over periods of time, they often acquire links to layers of metadata, in which assertions are made about the records themselves, the circumstances of their creation, the uses and interpretations that have been made of them and the actions or vicissitudes to which they have been subject. British archivists Jon Newman and Len Reilly (2007) implicitly connected humanly generated metadata with acts of assertion when they spoke of a need to reformulate archival descriptions to acknowledge what they called 'suppressed first-person prefixes' such as 'I think that this is . . .' and 'I think the important features of this are . . .'. Such reformulations reflect growing awareness that descriptions are influenced by personal opinion and are often made in situations of uncertainty; they also recognise that different individuals and different communities may want to supply different narratives about records.

Archivists increasingly rely on computer-generated metadata for digital records, and will almost certainly find it necessary to use automated methods of metadata production more widely in the future. However, like other forms of computer-generated data, metadata created in this way are not immune from the risk of software malfunction and remain subordinate to human decisions in system design. Borrowing a phrase from sociologists Bruno Latour and Steve Woolgar (1979, 82), we may say that, all too often, metadata systems are designed to give an impression of presenting facts with 'no modality . . . and no trace of authorship'; but speech act theory prompts us to remember that the 'facts' they present are always statements made by a human or a computer, and no system for presenting them can be isolated from social constraints and human involvement. In practice, however, there is little requirement for the propositions stated by creators of metadata to be perfect or incontrovertible; most metadata merely need to be good enough to fulfil the roles that records professionals and users expect of them.

Doing things with records

While acknowledging that large numbers of speech acts – and large numbers of records – comprise statements of supposed facts, we must also recognise that not all speech acts – and not all records – are of this kind. Searle (1979) offered a taxonomy: he categorised acts that state propositions ('I confirm that I have paid the invoice') as *assertives*, but noted that other acts are *directives*, in which speakers or writers make an enquiry ('Have you paid it yet?') or attempt to get someone else to do something ('Pay it immediately!'), or *commissives*, in which they undertake to do something themselves ('I promise that I will pay it on Friday'). Directive and commissive speech acts vary in strength; giving a command is stronger than making a suggestion or asking a question, and contracts are stronger than casual promises. *Declarative* acts bring about changes in the world, and include utterances that declare war, dismiss an employee or bequeath an art collection.

Acts in all these categories can be performed orally, but may also be performed using writing. Indeed, laws, regulations or societal conventions sometimes insist on writing, especially for acts with legal or quasi-legal consequences, and may even prescribe specific written forms in attempts to render such acts indisputable. Diplomatic scholarship uses the term 'dispositive' to describe written records that effect transactions using legally accepted forms of words. Speech act theorists recognise that many acts, particularly those they label 'declarative', can be associated with legal practice, but they lay little emphasis on formally regulated wording. Because the primary concern of speech act theory is not with law but with the many and varied social acts that can be performed using language, it can offer insights into the role and functionality of written records irrespective of their legal status.

Searle's categorisation of directive, commissive and declarative acts provides a framework for examining how the world of records and record-keeping extends beyond records representing assertions.[3] A directive record, such as a summons to attend court, an invitation to a meeting or a letter asking for financial help, is not a statement of a proposition but an instruction or request. The writer performs the act of instructing or requesting by issuing the record. Similarly, commissive records, such as promissory notes, and declarative records, such as wills, do not merely make statements or send information about promises or bequests; when the note is communicated or the will executed, the writer performs the act of promising or bequeathing, and an obligation or a legacy is generated. The capacity of writing to create obligations and legacies requires more complex conventions than its capacity to convey propositions, but most human societies acknowledge such conventions and accept that many social acts can be effected by communicating or exchanging written documents.[4] A deed of conveyance sells you my house; a letter of dismissal dismisses you from my employment; a will bequeaths you my possessions.

Searle also sought to explain the role of representation in acts of this kind. He noted that some of the words we speak or write are:

> supposed to match an independently existing reality, and . . . we [can] say that they are *true* or *false*. . . . But not all utterances . . . attempt to describe an independently existing reality. . . . Humans have this capacity to create a reality by representing that reality. . . . A representation . . . makes it the case that something exists by representing it as being the case. (Searle, 2012, 29–30)

More specifically:

we can perform an act by saying that we are performing it, i.e. by
representing ourselves as performing it.   (Searle, 1983, 166–7)

Because records are persistent, they are also able to 're-present' – or
present anew – past actions for future inspection, but Searle's account
helps us to see that representations do not merely describe actions that
have taken place at some earlier moment. They can also participate in
an action and help to constitute it. As sociologist and management
scientist Marc Berg (1996, 500) remarked in studying the role of records
in medical practice, 'the creation of the representation . . . is . . .
involved in the very event it represents. . . . Representation and
represented are achieved simultaneously'.

Viewing records from this perspective undermines the claims,
sometimes put forward in writings about record-keeping, that records
are always 'the *consequence* or *product* of an event' (International
Council on Archives, 2008, 9; my italics), or that they merely 'tell
stories' about events or actions that have already occurred. When
records perform directive, commissive or declarative acts, they are not
constructed after the event; records and events emerge together, and
the records are inherent parts of the actions they represent.

Besides offering insights into specialised records such as
summonses, wills or medical case-notes, these observations are equally
relevant to more general forms of record such as letters and
correspondence. When a letter, memo or e-mail message is communicated, it performs an act or (very often) a number of acts. Writers
of letters rarely confine themselves to making statements about events
or states of affairs in the world, but also use their letters to ask
questions or give instructions (directive acts) and to make commitments about their own future actions (commissive acts). Declarative
acts, too, may be performed by means of letters or e-mails; the
purchase of a house or the bequest of an art collection can be expected
to require a formal legal document, but the purchase of a book, the
promotion of an employee or the establishment of a committee can be
performed as part of a chain of correspondence. In each case, the
representation of the action in letters or e-mail messages and the
sending of the messages to their intended recipients achieve the action
concerned.

From speech acts to social acts

Records that perform commissive and declarative acts play important roles in generating rights, responsibilities and obligations. A promise, made in an e-mail, to visit a sick friend creates an obligation on the part of the promisor. A treaty signed by a government creates an obligation that requires the government to act in a particular way in its international relations. The scale of the obligations – and the apparent consequences if they are not honoured – are different, but the principle is the same. Obligations can also be generated by directive records; a summons, for example, obliges its recipient to attend a tribunal. Declarative records can create duties and responsibilities, as well as rights, entitlements, privileges, permissions and authorisations of various kinds. A licence creates a new permission; a patent creates a new monopoly; a deed of conveyance creates a new right of ownership.

At a macro level, declarative records can also create institutional entities such as universities and business corporations; creation of such entities is intertwined with creation of the rights and powers they will exercise and the duties and responsibilities they will have. For example, a royal charter or an act of legislature can establish a university and give it rights to award degrees; the university is then deemed to exist, irrespective of whether it yet has teachers, students or buildings. The university, in turn, can act in a similar way. It can establish institutional entities of its own, such as committees and professorships, and give them rights, duties and responsibilities. Searle (2005, 10–13) observed that 'all institutional structures . . . are matters of rights, duties, obligations, etc.' and that institutional structures and their rights and responsibilities depend on representations that are 'in the broadest sense linguistic': specifically, on the declarative acts whose performance is prerequisite for their existence. In principle, acts of this kind can be performed using spoken language (*speech* acts in the most literal sense); in practice, today, they are performed by issuing written records.

Partnerships, business corporations, government agencies and non-profit institutions can all be created, and acquire and exercise rights and responsibilities, by virtue of declarative records. Moreover, in personal and organizational settings alike, records participate, not only in creating and conferring rights, duties and obligations, but also in sustaining them after the moment of their creation. In Searle's words, 'I promise something on Tuesday, and the act [of making the promise] ceases on Tuesday, but the obligation of the promise continues to exist over Wednesday, Thursday, Friday, etc.'; the obligation endures indefinitely, until it is fulfilled or waived (Smith and Searle, 2003, 305; cf. Smith, 2003). But records also remain in existence after their moments of issuance, and can thus be used to underpin the continuation of obligations, responsibilities, rights and entitlements over time. If Paul has the deed by which Sylvie sold him her house, he can use it to demonstrate that the rights to the house are his. Rights, responsibilities and obligations remain anchored in the records that gave rise to them.

All these phenomena – rights, responsibilities and obligations, and the ability of records to create and sustain them – are social constructions. Rights, obligations and responsibilities can be created because human communities acknowledge the possibility of creating them in particular contexts, and they remain in existence only for as long as communal sanction persists. They are what social scientists Lindsay Prior (2003) and Paul Atkinson and Amanda Coffey (2011) call 'documentary realities': 'organizational features that are created and sustained almost entirely in and through . . . documentation' (Prior, 2003, 60). Nevertheless, rights, responsibilities and obligations, and the ability of records to produce them and demonstrate their continuing existence, are crucial to the functioning of contemporary societies. They are social as well as documentary realities. For Searle, systems of rights, duties, commitments and obligations are 'the glue that holds human societies together' (Searle, 2012, 31); their existence 'makes . . . human civilization possible' (Searle, 2009, 175). Commitments, obligations and responsibilities regulate human behaviour, providing a rationale for conduct that is not driven simply by inclination or self-interest. Our capacity to use records to create rights and obligations and to represent their creation persistently supplies us with a basis for mutual interaction and – according to Peruvian economist Hernando de Soto – an 'invisible infrastructure' for economic success (De Soto, 2000; Smith, 2008, 44–5). It places records at the foundation of social life and activity.

These considerations lead us to frame speech acts as social acts and to situate records in contexts of action. Records usually have multiple and multi-dimensional relationships with action. They participate in actions when they are appraised, selected, arranged or conserved, and when they are consulted, forwarded or copied; they offer us ways to learn about, and make sense of, the actions of other people; and they provide us with templates for future actions of our own. But above all – and this is central to their identity as records – they represent assertive, directive, commissive or declarative acts, which are performed by virtue of a record at the moment of its issuance. Records are 'active agents in episodes of interaction and schemes of social organization' (Prior, 2008, 824; cf. Foscarini, 2013); they are not mere commentaries on action, but are integral to it.

It follows that we must reject notions that records simply contain information about events in the world or that their role in organizations and society is wholly or even primarily informational. Records are not confined to telling us how the world is or was believed to be. The world shapes the form and function of records; at the same time, by co-ordinating human behaviour, establishing rights and responsibilities, or creating social relations, records play a role in shaping the world. They are part of the way we conduct business and live our daily lives. All records – even those in which statements are made and propositions asserted – are representations and instruments of actions performed in particular cultural settings. When a record is inscribed and communicated, what takes place is not a matter of information, but a matter of social action.

The 'information potentials' of records

Where, then, do concepts of information belong in the world of record-keeping? What part, if any, does information play in understanding records as representations of occurrents? How might it fit into a picture of records that emphasises their role in social action?

A fruitful way of answering these questions is to acknowledge that records created in the past offer what German archivist Angelika Menne-Haritz called 'information potentials' to those who later come to use them. Information, Menne-Haritz (2001, 61) wrote, is 'worked out by the users; . . . archives provide information potentials, not the information itself'. As she observed, information is a product of investigation and interpretation, and records can enable their users to undertake such investigation and interpretation. If a record is accessible and users can interpret its representational scheme, they can engage with it to garner information about the actions it represents.

A record can also yield information about other topics. A will, for example, can supply information about what items were bequeathed to whom, but wills can also be used to deduce information about the family connections, charitable impulses and religious convictions of testators, about changing testamentary practices and about the wealth of households in particular regions or time periods. Adopting – or adapting – the terminology proposed by Fernand Braudel, leader of the *Annales* school of French historians, we might say that records of this kind are *événementiels* (they arise from and represent specific actions or events), but researchers can use them to elicit information about *structures de longue durée* (structures of long duration).

The capacity of records to provide later users with information on disparate and often unexpected subjects has been observed by many scholars, including Hilary Jenkinson. Records and archives, Jenkinson (1954, 5) noted, may convey 'incidental information . . . upon an infinite variety of topics which were certainly not in the minds of their compilers'. Magna Carta, for example, has been used by historians and lawyers to make 'deductions which . . . never entered the heads of King John who granted it, the barons who extorted it, or the chancery clerks who copied it' (Jenkinson, 1944, 358). Likewise, admiralty records can yield information about meteorological trends and the location of cargoes for salvage; civic freemen's records can afford information on urban immigration and the political role of trade guilds (Ede, 1968, 190; Stephens, 1981, 89). To one user, a set of e-mail messages might supply information about items of business conducted; to a second, information about social networks; to a third, information about styles of writing. Very often, a record:

> will provide information to an open-ended number of inquiries and inquirers: the historian this morning, the genealogist this afternoon, the lawyer tomorrow, the surveyor next week, another historian with a different topic the week after that. . . . Records and documents always have multiple meanings, . . . whatever the particular question of the moment happen[s] to be.   (O'Toole, 2002a)

These 'information potentials' are implicit in records, but are not explicitly encoded there. As Chapter 4 has suggested, information is not a pre-existing commodity that resides in a record, but a product of human perception or cognition. Using our cognitive faculties, we can gain information by engaging with a record, even if the maker of the record did not set out to 'inform' readers by stating a proposition. When we use records in which specific propositions are asserted, the information we can gain from them is not limited to the propositions that the record-makers put forward. Cognitive faculties also allow a single user to derive different information from the same record in different episodes of use. On other occasions, a single user may elicit very similar information from each of several different records.

Information arises from, and is always dependent on, human agency; it is inextricably connected with people who are, or believe themselves to be, informed. We can view information, not as an autonomous artefact or manipulable object, but as one of the many intangible affordances offered to those who interact with and interpret records.

Information, evidence and other affordances

Records – or interactions with records – have often been said to supply *evidence* as well as information. According to a glossary published by the Society of American Archivists, evidence can be seen both as 'something that is used to support an understanding or argument' and in a more strictly legal sense as proof or disproof of supposed facts (Pearce-Moses, 2005, 152). Some commentators have seen close connections between evidence and information, and some have sought to define evidence as information used to verify hypotheses or draw conclusions. But others have accentuated a difference between the two concepts, and archivists and records managers have often affirmed that information and evidence are distinct goods that a record can offer. The National Archives of Australia adopted this standpoint when it explained that government records provide information for planning and decision-making, and evidence of accountability (Franks, 2013, 60).

A broadly similar notion underlies the appraisal model put forward by Theodore Schellenberg (1956, 139–60), with its emphasis on separate evidential and informational values of records. Schellenberg, however, saw evidential and informational values as stable criteria for deciding which records should be kept; perceiving evidence and information as affordances understands them as variable criteria linked to the ways in which records are used. They are not universal values, but values to particular users in particular contexts. A user's view of what constitutes evidence or information will be determined, not only by the cultural and social practices of an era, but also by the user's own attitudes and preconceptions.

Evidence remains a resilient, if controversial, theme in the published literature about records. Emphasis on evidence is often intended to connect records to the realms of law and corporate governance, but an exclusive focus on evidence does not supply a comprehensive picture of record-making and record-keeping (Yeo, 2007, 343). Some critics have affirmed that a view of records as persistent representations 'relies on an evidentiary paradigm' (Caswell and Punzalan, 2016, 291) or 'reaffirms the prominence of evidence' (Gauld, 2017, 238), but the representational view does not give evidence a privileged status. Viewing records as representations allows us to highlight their performative role in social action at the point of their creation; in their later use, however, evidence is only one among many affordances that records offer, albeit one whose cultural importance has often dominated professional thinking. For users, as historian Markus Friedrich (2015, 471) remarked, records have no 'inherent' function; their affordances are determined by the ways in which users activate them.

Besides information and evidence, affordances of records may include construction or reinforcement of memory and senses of identity and community, as well as generation of emotions, ideas, inspirations and guidance for future action. As we saw in the first two chapters of this book, commentators across many centuries have shared an awareness of records as an underpinning for memory and evidence; explicit recognition of a wider range of affordances is a more recent phenomenon. There are obvious connections between several of these affordances and the 'archival paradigms' proposed by Terry Cook (discussed in Chapter 2), and it could be argued that Cook's 'paradigms' are better understood as affordances that keepers or users of records have accorded particular emphasis at different times. Many affordances of records appear to be intertwined; it is often said, for example, that evidence can confirm memory and that memories, in turn, can help to substantiate senses of identity.

Affordances of records have generally been seen as benefits that accrue to records' *users* rather than their *creators*, but recent scholarship has shown that records can also offer a variety of affordances to those who create them. American historian Geoffrey Koziol has demonstrated how, at the moment of their issuance, early-medieval diplomas could afford their royal creators the capacity to establish or reinforce political friendships and patronage relationships. Such records could also enable their creators to punish or humiliate enemies, avenge perceived wrongs, celebrate victories and advertise political power (Koziol, 2012, 3–4, 39–41). In a different historical context, British archival scholar Andrew Flinn (2011, 154–5) has suggested that records and archives can empower present-day communities, offering benefits and impacts in terms of dialogues about identities and enhanced senses of self-belief and esteem. Some of these affordances may arise from records' artefactual qualities (their form or appearance), rather than their content. Some may be obtained by capturing or collecting records (Flinn, 2011), or even by forging or falsifying them (Koziol, 2012), as well as by using them. Engagement with records is not a uniform experience: although a record may present itself identically to each user, each user may evoke different affordances of meaning, including affordances that the record's creator did not intend. Not all users of records and archives seek information; different users employ or interpret records in different ways.

Endnotes

1 Among scholarly theorists, the notion of representation is often controversial. Some critics excoriate it on the grounds that it seeks to impose single views where many interpretations are possible or assumes the possibility of obtaining exact reproductions of unattainable realities, but others see these understandings as too narrow; acknowledging that representations are imperfect or open to reinterpretation does not oblige us to deny the possibility of any representation at all. Other theorists have argued that representations constitute or shape reality, or that reality can only be viewed through endless networks of representations. For further discussion, see Ankersmit (2001); Coopmans et al. (2014); Dyer (2002).

2 I am grateful to Elizabeth Lomas for drawing this report to my attention.

3 Besides assertive, directive, commissive and declarative speech acts, Searle identified a further category of *expressives* (acts in which speakers or writers express feelings or attitudes). For fuller examinations of these categories, and of connections and disjunctions between speech act theory and the worlds of law and diplomatic scholarship, see Yeo (2010) and (2017).
4 And, increasingly, not only by means of *documents*. In what many commentators see as the coming world of smart contracts and an 'algorithm economy' (Chamber of Digital Commerce, 2016; Cuccuru, 2017), we can expect to see growing numbers of social acts effected by means of software code and exchange of *data*. At the time of writing, this remains breaking news.

References

Anderson, K. (2013) The Footprint and the Stepping Foot: archival records, evidence, and time, *Archival Science*, **13** (4), 349–71.

Angell, A. M. and Solomon, O. (2014) The Social Life of Health Records: understanding families' experiences of autism, *Social Science and Medicine*, **117**, 50–7.

Ankersmit, F. R. (2001) *Historical Representation*, Stanford University Press.

Atkinson, P. and Coffey, A. (2011) Analysing Documentary Realities. In Silverman, D. (ed.), *Qualitative Research*, 3rd edn, Sage.

Austin, J. L. (1962) *How to Do Things with Words*, Clarendon Press.

Berg, M. (1996) Practices of Reading and Writing: the constitutive role of the patient record in medical work, *Sociology of Health and Illness*, **18** (4), 499–524.

Beynon-Davies, P. (2009) *Business Information Systems*, Palgrave Macmillan.

Bowker, G. C. (2005) *Memory Practices in the Sciences*, MIT Press.

Caswell, M. and Punzalan, R. L. (2016) Archives and Human Rights: questioning notions of information and access. In Gorham, U., Taylor, N. G. and Jaeger, P. T. (eds), *Perspectives on Libraries as Institutions of Human Rights and Social Justice*, Emerald.

Chamber of Digital Commerce (2016) *Smart Contracts: 12 use cases for business & beyond*, www.bloq.com/assets/smart-contracts-white-paper.pdf.

Cohen, G. and Kotorov, R. (2016) *Organizational Intelligence: how smart companies use information to become more competitive and profitable*, Information Builders.

Coopmans, C., Vertesi, J., Lynch, M. and Woolgar, S. (eds) (2014) *Representation in Scientific Practice Revisited*, MIT Press.

Cuccuru, P. (2017) Beyond Bitcoin: an early overview on smart contracts, *International Journal of Law and Information Technology*, **25** (3), 179–95.

Cummins, R. (1996) *Representations, Targets, and Attitudes*, MIT Press.

Darnton, R. (2017) The True History of Fake News, *New York Review of Books*, 13 February, www.nybooks.com/daily/2017/02/13/the-true-history-of-fake-news.

De Chadarevian, S. (1993) Graphical Method and Discipline: self-recording instruments in nineteenth-century physiology, *Studies in History and Philosophy of Science*, **24** (2), 267–91.

De Soto, H. (2000) *The Mystery of Capital*, Basic Books.

Demolombe, R. and Louis, V. (2006) Speech Acts with Institutional Effects in Agent Societies, *Lecture Notes in Artificial Intelligence*, **4048**, 101–14.

Derrida, J. (2002) *Without Alibi*, Stanford University Press.

Dervos, D. A. and Coleman, A. (2006) A Common Sense Approach to Defining Data, Information and Metadata. In *Knowledge Organization for a Global Learning Society: proceedings of the Ninth International ISKO Conference*, Ergon.

Devlin, K. (1999) *InfoSense: turning information into knowledge*, W. H. Freeman.

Duranti, L. and Preston, R. (eds) (2008) *International Research on Permanent Authentic Records in Electronic Systems (InterPARES 2)*, Università di Padova.

Dyer, R. (2002) *The Matter of Images: essays on representations*, 2nd edn, Routledge.

Ede, J. R. (1968) The Public Record Office and Its Users, *Archives*, **40**, 185–92.

European Parliament, Committee on Legal Affairs (2016) *Draft Report with Recommendations to the Commission on Civil Law Rules on Robotics*, www.europarl.europa.eu/sides/getDoc.do?pubRef=-//EP//NONSGML%2BCOMPARL%2BPE-582.443%2B01%2BDOC%2BPDF%2BV0//EN.

Fish, S. (1980) *Is There a Text in this Class?* Harvard University Press.

Flinn, A. (2011) The Impact of Independent and Community Archives on Professional Archival Thinking and Practice. In Hill, J. (ed.), *The Future of Archives and Recordkeeping*, Facet Publishing.

Foscarini, F. (2013) Record as Social Action: understanding organizational records through the lens of genre theory, *Information Research*, **18** (3), http://InformationR.net/ir/18-3/colis/paperC08.html.

Franks, P. C. (2013) *Records and Information Management*, American Library Association and Neal-Schuman.

Friedrich, M. (2015) Introduction: new perspectives for the history of archives. In Brendecke, A. (ed.), *Praktiken der Frühen Neuzeit*, Böhlau.

Gauld, C. (2017) Democratising or Privileging: the democratisation of knowledge and the role of the archivist, *Archival Science*, **17** (3), 227–45.

Gerovitch, S. (2002) Love-Hate for Man-Machine Metaphors in Soviet Physiology: from Pavlov to 'physiological cybernetics', *Science in Context*, **15** (2), 339–74.

Gilliland, A. J. (2017) 'The Wink that's Worth a Thousand Words': a contemplation on the nature of metadata and metadata practices in the archival world. In Smit, F., Glaudemans, A. and Jonker, R. (eds), *Archives in Liquid Times*, Stichting Archiefpublicaties.

Glaudemans, A., Jonker, R. and Smit, F. (2017) Documents, Archives and Hyperhistorical Societies: an interview with Luciano Floridi. In Smit, F., Glaudemans, A. and Jonker, R. (eds), *Archives in Liquid Times*, Stichting Archiefpublicaties.

Gumperz, J. J. (2009) The Speech Community. In Duranti, A. (ed.), *Linguistic Anthropology*, 2nd edn, Wiley-Blackwell.

International Council on Archives (2008) *Principles and Functional Requirements for Records in Electronic Office Environments, Module 3: guidelines and functional requirements for records in business systems*, www.adri.gov.au/resources/documents/ICA-M3-BS.pdf.

ISO 23081-2: 2009 *Information and Documentation – Managing Metadata for Records. Part 2: conceptual and implementation issues*, International Organization for Standardization.

Jenkinson, H. (1944) Reflections of an Archivist, *Contemporary Review*, **165**, 355–61.

Jenkinson, H. (1954) *Jewish History and Archives*, Jewish Historical Society of England.

Karvalics, L. Z. (2008) Information Society – What Is It Exactly? The meaning, history and conceptual framework of an expression. In Pintér, R. (ed.), *Information Society: from theory to political practice*, Gondolat.

Ketelaar, E. (2008) Archives as Spaces of Memory, *Journal of the Society of Archivists*, **29** (1), 9–27.

Koziol, G. (2012) *The Politics of Memory and Identity in Carolingian Royal Diplomas*, Brepols.

Latour, B. and Woolgar, S. (1979) *Laboratory Life: the social construction of scientific facts*, Sage.

Lynch, C. (2000) *Authenticity and Integrity in the Digital Environment: an exploratory analysis of the central role of trust*, Council on Library and Information Resources.

Mazrui, A. A. (1986) *The Africans: a triple heritage*, BBC Publications.

Menne-Haritz, A. (2001) Access: the reformulation of an archival paradigm, *Archival Science*, **1** (1), 57–82.

Meyer, C. (2008–9) The FSA Photographs: Information, or Propaganda? *Boston University Arts and Sciences Writing Program Journal*, **1**, www.bu.edu/writingprogram/journal/past-issues/issue-1/the-fsa-photographs-information-or-propaganda.

Mulvihill, M. A. (1990) Visual Data Bases: photographs as information records. In Durance, C. J. (ed.), *Management of Recorded Information: converging disciplines*, K. G. Saur.

Newman, J. and Reilly, L. (2007) *Revisiting Archive Collections: developing a methodology for capturing and incorporating new and hidden information into archive catalogues*, www.ucl.ac.uk/dis/icarus/projects/ARMReN/ARMReN-files/Newman-Reilly-26-06-07-full-1.ppt.

O'Toole, J. M. (2002a) *Comment on 'The Many Meanings of Objects' (Response to Elaine Heumann Gurian)*, https://web.archive.org/web/20041217001959/www.hfmgv.org/research/publications/symposium2002/papers/otoole.asp.

O'Toole, J. M. (2002b) Cortes's Notary: the symbolic power of records, *Archival Science*, **2** (1–2), 45–61.

Orwell, G. (1938) *Homage to Catalonia*, Secker & Warburg.

Osgood, C. E. (1979) What Is a Language? In Aaronson, D. and Rieber, R. W. (eds), *Psycholinguistic Research: implications and applications*, Lawrence Erlbaum.

Pearce-Moses, R. (ed.) (2005) *A Glossary of Archival and Records Terminology*, Society of American Archivists.

Poovey, M. (1998) *A History of the Modern Fact: problems of knowledge in the sciences of wealth and society*, University of Chicago Press.

Prince, K. (1996) *Boring Records? Communication, speech and writing in social work*, Jessica Kingsley.

Prior, L. (2003) *Using Documents in Social Research*, Sage.

Prior, L. (2008) Repositioning Documents in Social Research, *Sociology*, **42** (5), 821–36.

Rafoth, B. A. (1988) Discourse Community: where writers, readers, and texts come together. In Rafoth, B. A. and Rubin, D. L. (eds), *The Social Construction of Written Communication*, Ablex.

Ranade, S. (2016) *Traces through Time: a probabilistic approach to connected archival data*, http://dcicblog.umd.edu/cas/wp-content/uploads/sites/13/2016/05/2.pdf.

Reed, B. (2005) Records. In McKemmish, S., Piggott, M., Reed, B. and Upward, F. (eds), *Archives: recordkeeping in society*, Charles Sturt University.

Schellenberg, T. R. (1956) *Modern Archives: principles and techniques*, F. W. Cheshire.

Schlesinger, A. (1972) The Historian as Participant. In Gilbert, F. and Graubard, S. R. (eds), *Historical Studies Today*, W. W. Norton.

Scott-Warren, J. (2016) Early Modern Bookkeeping and Life-Writing Revisited: accounting for Richard Stonley, *Past and Present*, **230**, supplement 11, 151–70.

Searle, J. R. (1979) *Expression and Meaning: studies in the theory of speech acts*, Cambridge University Press.

Searle, J. R. (1983) *Intentionality: an essay in the philosophy of mind*, Cambridge University Press.

Searle, J. R. (1986) Meaning, Communication, and Representation. In Grandy, R. E. and Warner, R. (eds), *Philosophical Grounds of Rationality*, Clarendon Press.

Searle, J. R. (2002) *Consciousness and Language*, Cambridge University Press.

Searle, J. R. (2005) What Is an Institution? *Journal of Institutional Economics*, **1** (1), 1–22.

Searle, J. R. (2009) What Is Language? Some preliminary remarks, *Etica & Politica/Ethics & Politics*, **11** (1), 173–202.

Searle, J. R. (2012) Human Social Reality and Language, *Phenomenology and Mind*, **2**, 25–33.

Smith, B. (2003) John Searle: from speech acts to social reality. In Smith, B. (ed.), *John Searle*, Cambridge University Press.

Smith, B. (2008) Searle and De Soto: the new ontology of the social world. In Smith, B., Mark, D. M. and Ehrlich, I. (eds), *The Mystery of Capital and the Construction of Social Reality*, Open Court.

Smith, B. and Searle, J. (2003) The Construction of Social Reality: an exchange, *American Journal of Economics and Sociology*, **62** (1), 285–309.

Star, S. L. and Griesemer, J. R. (1989) Institutional Ecology, 'Translations,' and Boundary Objects: amateurs and professionals in Berkeley's Museum of Vertebrate Zoology, *Social Studies of Science*, **19** (3), 387–420.

Stephens, W. B. (1981) *Sources for English Local History*, 2nd edn, Cambridge University Press.

Taylor, H. A. (1987–8) Transformation in the Archives: technological adjustment or paradigm shift? *Archivaria*, **25**, 12–28.

Trace, C. B. (2002) What is Recorded is Never Simply 'What Happened': record keeping in modern organizational culture, *Archival Science*, **2** (1–2), 137–59.

Winograd, T. and Flores, F. (1986) *Understanding Computers and Cognition*, Ablex.

Yeo, G. (2007) Concepts of Record (1): evidence, information, and persistent representations, *American Archivist*, **70** (2), 315–43.

Yeo, G. (2008) Concepts of Record (2): prototypes and boundary objects, *American Archivist*, **71** (1), 118–43.

Yeo, G. (2010) Representing the Act: records and speech act theory, *Journal of the Society of Archivists*, **31** (2), 95–117.

Yeo, G. (2011) Rising to the Level of a Record? Some thoughts on records and documents, *Records Management Journal*, **21** (1), 8–27.

Yeo, G. (2017) Information, Records, and the Philosophy of Speech Acts. In Smit, F., Glaudemans, A. and Jonker, R. (eds), *Archives in Liquid Times*, Stichting Archiefpublicaties.

CHAPTER 7

Managing information or managing records?

Introduction

The view that information is an affordance – an intangible benefit that records or other resources afford to those who use them in particular ways – is not a view likely to be shared by proponents of 'information management'. Influential voices now affirm that, at least in organizational settings, information is an objective commodity, which can and should be controlled, managed and systematised. Other voices, often equally influential, affirm that record-keeping and information management practices have converged and that there is now, or should now be, no effective difference between them. Yet we have seen that, at a conceptual level, our understandings of records and our understandings of information diverge considerably. Records play complex roles in social action, which transcend the capture or supply of information; ideas about information are commonplace in writings about record-keeping, but do not appear to provide an adequate basis for comprehending the complexity of records and their functioning in human society. We seem to have reached a point of critical difficulty, especially if we want to build bridges between conceptual understandings and the field of professional practice.

With this difficulty in mind, this chapter looks more closely at how information and its management are perceived by information managers, and at how the concepts and working practices of 'information management' – as they are commonly understood by information managers and data administrators – relate to concepts and practices of record-keeping. Building on the arguments put forward in earlier chapters, it examines points of contact as well as points of divergence, but concludes that record-keeping has different aims and scope and must therefore remain a distinct practice.

Conceptions and practices of 'information management': information as proposition

Although the term 'information management' is widely used, and its practice widely advocated, in government agencies and commercial businesses in 21st-century western societies, its conceptual framework and operational scope are not always wholly clear. Its proponents rarely agree on precisely what is meant by 'information', and sometimes affirm that each organization needs to define the term in its own way to suit its own needs. The varied understandings and elusive meanings of 'information' – and the seemingly incompatible ways in which different stakeholders use the term – might easily tempt us to agree with Craig Ball's (2011) provocative claim that 'like Nessie and Bigfoot, information management is something many believe exists but no-one has ever shown to be anything but a myth'. In general, however, as we saw in Chapter 4, information management practices rest on a belief that information belongs, not to the realm of the human mind, but to the realm of manageable objects in the physical world. From the viewpoint of an information manager, 'perhaps the most important change that has occurred in the last 50 years is that there is now a perception . . . that information . . . is something to be collected, stored, managed and exploited' (Hill, 2005, 3).

What, then, is this 'something' that organizational information managers believe they can collect, store, manage and exploit? The term 'information management' can be used to refer to the running of a library, providing access to published materials and resources created outside the organization, but increasingly the term is now applied to the management of internal resources. For most information managers with no background in libraries or record-keeping, it seems that 'information management' is not management of information as an affordance, or management of library materials or records, but management of the propositions made in organizational databases and other internal 'information systems'. As we have seen, propositions are more contingent on circumstance and more open to variable interpretation than advocates of information management usually admit. But to many who work in business environments, notions of objective information seem unproblematic, and it appears feasible to manage propositions about the organization, its work, its stakeholders and the environment in which it operates.

The suggestion that information can be identified with propositions has been recognised and discussed – although not always accepted – by a number of writers in the information science field, particularly writers interested in the possibility of defining 'information' (Chapter 4). 'Propositional definitions of information', in which 'a piece of information is considered to be a claim about the world', are one of the seven types of 'conceptions of information' examined by Marcia Bates (2010), and 'information-as-propositional-content' is one of the five definitions of information set out by Jonathan Furner (2015, 364). Broadly similar ideas can sometimes be found in philosophical literature; for philosopher Jeffrey King (2014, 5), propositions 'can . . . be identified with the information content of sentences' and 'play the role of . . . information encoded by sentences'. In information science, Christopher Fox (1983, 85–8) argued that propositions and information have the same, or very similar, characteristics and are ontologically alike. More recently, information scientist Mauricio Almeida (2013, 1689) suggested that 'the information contained in a document' can be identified with 'its propositional content'.

These ideas have remained controversial among scholars of information science – critics have affirmed that 'there is more to . . . information than propositions only' (Dinneen and Brauner, 2015, 385) – but they seem to match the perception of information that most commonly prevails among information management practitioners. Although practitioners almost always refer to 'information' or 'data' and rarely mention propositions explicitly, they often use the term 'information' in much the same way as Fox and Almeida. In practice, information managers' usage combines 'information as proposition' with the conception of 'information as thing' that we met in Chapter 4; a proposition is tacitly equated with the thing that carries it, and it is assumed that the proposition can be managed by managing the thing.

According to Fox (1983, 79), a proposition 'is supposed to represent the world as being a certain way'. But propositions are not limited to those concerned with how the world is, or what is happening in it now; we can also encounter propositions concerned with how the world was, or what happened in it in the past, and propositions concerned with how it is expected to be in the future. Besides propositions such as 'Factory X is capable of producing 200 widgets every day', we may meet with propositions such as 'Factory Y made 60,000 widgets last year' and 'Factory Z will make 80,000 widgets next year'. But information management tends to view propositions concerned with the future – predictions or forecasts of events that have not yet occurred – as marginal to, or beyond, its remit. From an information manager's perspective, propositions about how the world will be tomorrow are 'neither fact nor information, . . . only hope or expectation' (Hill, 2005, 24). Some of the propositions discussed in Chapter 6 ('Scientist A's research is world-leading'; 'Politician B has always put the country's interests before her own') are also matters of opinion or individual judgement, and information management usually shows little concern for them; it prefers to deal with propositions that appear verifiable. The propositions of most interest to information managers are those that can be seen as 'bearers of truth-values, things which are susceptible of truth or falsity' (Fox, 1983, 79).

Like records management, information management is usually encountered as an organizational function. When organizational executives set out to develop their company's products or services, plan advertising campaigns or communicate with customers, they seek to be informed about the current state of affairs – about 'how the world is today' – and their perceived need is for information that is as trustworthy as possible, to provide a basis for planning and decision-making. This need has a high priority in most organizations, and practitioners of information management attempt to respond to it. Their aim is to ensure that executives, and all who work for or with an organization, have access to accurate, reliable and up-to-date propositions, which they refer to as 'information' or 'data'. In general, information management practitioners seek to confirm that the kinds of propositions they believe will be needed have been made and are easily retrievable and sharable within the organization; they also maintain policies and programmes aimed at balancing continuing accessibility and usability with the protection of privacy, confidentiality and security. In addition, they usually try to eradicate what they perceive as redundant duplication and to adjust propositions they deem inadequate or incorrect, in order to meet the organization's perceived requirements for information and data that are up-to-date and accurate.

In attempting to fulfil this mission, they often use the terms 'information' and 'data' more or less interchangeably; some practitioners call themselves data managers or data administrators rather than information managers. A common tactic is to announce 'data quality' initiatives that are intended to evaluate the resources available to organizational executives and staff in terms of criteria such as currency (or 'timeliness'), completeness, accuracy and consistency, and to redress any deficiencies that are found (Batini et al., 2009; Redman, Fox and Levitin, 2012; Tyler, 2017). In writings by – and in textbooks intended for – managers of information or data, the rhetoric of objective truth and factual accuracy is commonplace. According to business information specialists Karim Sidi and Dale Hutchinson (2013, 36), data management aspires 'to identify the single version of the truth'. 'Inaccurate data', we are told, are 'not data at all' (Frické, 2009, 134). It is assumed that 'to be information, a proposition must be true' (Bates, 2010; cf. Dretske, 2008, 276).

Information management and records management: two peas from different pods?

In many respects, the techniques and approaches used by information managers and data administrators are similar to those employed in managing records. For example, the *Code of Practice on the Management of Records* issued in the UK by the Ministry of Justice and The National Archives (2009) advises government agencies to make and keep the records they need; to know where and what these records are; to ensure that they are retrievable and usable, that confidentiality and security are protected and that disposal actions are correctly managed; and to maintain policies and programmes to support the integrity and sustainability of records over time. These are sound recommendations, and very similar advice can be found in other sources of guidance for records managers, including a records management textbook that I co-authored some years ago (Shepherd and Yeo, 2003). Few of these recommended practices, I suggest, look very different from those applied by practitioners of information management or data administration.

Investigation of speech act theory, however, reminds us that the propositions that information managers seek to control do not exist in a vacuum; we encounter them because they have been asserted at specific moments in time. Fox (1983, 83) connected propositions with assertions and noted that 'an important (and perhaps the essential) feature of propositions is that they can be asserted', but information managers and data administrators rarely view propositions in these terms; information management usually ascribes little importance to the contexts in which the propositions in 'information systems' were asserted. Records professionals, however, have traditionally assigned a high priority to contextualisation and have sought to ensure that users can know where, when and by whom resources have been made. Record-keeping is, or should be, concerned not only with propositions, but also with the contextualised acts of assertion that generated them. Some information managers and data administrators are now beginning to take an interest in context (Carata et al., 2014; Missier, 2016; cf. Yeo, 2013), but concerns for contextualisation are generally more characteristic of archives and records management.

The desire to eliminate what is perceived as redundancy, and the seemingly unattainable ambition of guaranteeing accuracy and truth, mark the points where information management and data administration most obviously part company with record-keeping practices and requirements. In distinct contrast to the practice of most information managers, records managers and archivists endeavour to stabilise and preserve propositions asserted in the past, and the records in which the assertions were made, for as long as there are perceived needs for their retention, regardless of whether others made similar assertions or whether they are now believed to be inaccurate or untrue. As David Bearman (1997, 153) observed, information systems (as they are commonly called) are usually designed to deliver information that is timely and non-redundant, whereas records are time-bound and sometimes seem redundant. Faced with the faulty despatch reporting a Russian victory during the Crimean War (Chapter 6), or with some equally questionable assertion made in the context of a modern corporate business, the information manager's instinct will be to correct it; the records professional will want to preserve it as it stands.

This is not to suggest that errors in what I have called 'assertive' records are unimportant or that no care need be exercised when such records are created. In an organizational context, records professionals clearly have a role in encouraging people to create records conscientiously, particularly when the propositions asserted in the records they create can have important consequences for others. In developing countries – and elsewhere – the rights of individuals, as well as the provision of effective government services, can depend on assertions made in records, as many publications of the International Records Management Trust attest (Lowry and Wamukoya, 2014). At government level, when propositions stated in records are untrustworthy, the consequences can include misguided policy initiatives, poor decision-making by state officials and wasteful use of government resources. For individual citizens, unreliable records can lead to loss of employment or pension rights, inadequate health care or conflicts over land ownership.

Perhaps we should take our cue from an insightful comment about George Orwell's writings, made in an essay by political historian Timothy Garton Ash. Orwell, as Chapter 6 noted, warned readers of his *Homage to Catalonia* to 'beware of . . . the distortion . . . caused by my having seen only one corner of events', but Garton Ash (2009, 399) remarked that although Orwell 'got some of his externally verifiable facts wrong . . . we never for a moment doubt that he is trying to tell it exactly as it was'. Like historians and journalists, the creators of assertive records can never fully escape from the partiality of their own viewpoint, but they can – and should – nevertheless try, as far as they are able, to 'tell it as it was'. In this sense, the concerns of records management and information management are not disconnected. But we must also accept that, in practice, record creators sometimes appear to have 'got their facts wrong'; when this has happened, records management insists that it is not simply a matter of rectifying their errors. Even if what was said in the records is thought to have been incorrect, we – and others in the future – can be expected to want to know what was said, who said it and in what circumstances.

Making use of records despite their imperfections

Scholars have long recognised that the makers of records do not always 'tell it exactly as it was'. Considerations of self-interest frequently intervene, and people often choose to report activities and events in ways that seem likely to work to their own advantage, elicit a favourable response or show their conduct in the best possible light; organizational employees may be more concerned with formulating records that meet the expectations of their managers than with attempting precise reporting of events. Many commentators also recognise that, even when record creators have made their best attempts to 'tell it as it was', an assertive record is rarely able to offer multiple perspectives on events or tell its story from every possible angle.

These issues are not confined to records created in our own era. It has not been difficult for critics to discover examples of much older records that appear to display the same weaknesses. Historians Warren Brown (2002) and Sarah Foot (2006) argued that even seemingly neutral and formulaic records such as early medieval charters were constructed with an eye to self-interest. In Anglo-Saxon times, according to Foot, charters were designed to enforce the version of past events that seemed most favourable to those who issued them; there could be many different memories and recollections of what had occurred, but a charter, when drawn up after an event, was intended to impose a single narrative and discourage or prevent the circulation of other versions among contemporaries and later readers. Another historian, Michael Clanchy (1977), described how, at Barnwell Priory in Cambridge, a 13th-century writer (either the prior or a close associate of the prior) composed a register of cases relating to the priory's legal affairs, and interspersed copies of terse and formulaic records from the English law courts with a more expansive commentary explaining what had 'really happened'. Some modern scholars have used the commentary to demonstrate the limitations of the official records of the courts, but it can also be seen as simply another version of events, intended – at least in part – to foreground the role played by the prior and illustrate how he had outwitted his opponents (Clanchy, 1977, 178–80). Instead of, or as well as, using records of this kind to investigate an event that was described, historical researchers can use them to investigate the act of describing it and the motives and circumstances that led to its description.

Scholars have also observed that, although the propositions asserted by record creators may not be impartial, they are far from valueless. They can offer many affordances to users who approach them perceptively. William Sewell (2005, 50) noted that statistical reports, such as the report on Parisian work and industry discussed in Chapter 5, are shaped and distorted by the categorisations adopted by their compilers, but are nonetheless very useful as historical sources. They should be read in the light of an awareness of their limitations, but such awareness does not invalidate their use. Similar conclusions have been reached by scholars who have investigated politicians' pragmatic use of records in bolstering power and maintaining political control. Even if records are imperfect, they can still provide rulers with considerable scope for enforcement of authority. In 17th-century France, for example, Jean-Baptiste Colbert, the chief minister of King Louis XIV, devoted much attention to his record-keeping system; the records did not permit unimpeded control, but they allowed Colbert considerable success in obtaining mastery over the French kingdom (Soll, 2009; Yale, 2015, 343).

In a more benign context, the functional capabilities of records that are less than perfect can also be seen in the world of medicine. In North America in the early 20th century, disquiet about imperfect representational systems was voiced in comments made by doctors about the newly invented technology of X-ray photography. In a report published in 1900 by the American Surgical Association, several doctors expressed concern that X-ray photographs were not infallible; some weaknesses, they said, arose from 'wilfulness or negligence' on the part of camera operators, while others occurred because X-ray technology itself 'has many tricks'. However, as another doctor remarked, 'usefulness and infallibility are not identical' (Daston and Galison, 1992, 110–11). Although it was sometimes erratic in its early days, X-ray technology was widely welcomed and rapidly adopted by the medical profession; X-ray photographic records have continued to provide doctors with highly useful diagnostic tools even while some critics insist that no representation produced by a camera can be perfect. Infallibility is not a precondition for records to supply the affordances that users require of them.

Archival scholars inspired by the scepticism of late-20th-century thinkers such as Jacques Derrida have been among the most insistent voices emphasising that realities are unknowable and that records can offer only the tiniest 'sliver of a window' (Harris, 2002, 64–5) on past situations and events. However, while rejecting foundationalist ideas about accuracy and truth, many of these scholars have also sought to demonstrate that records can frequently 'both replicate and challenge . . . features of injustice' (Wallace, 2017, 275) inflicted by totalitarian governments. In Guatemala, Cambodia, the former East Germany and many other parts of the world that have suffered repression in recent times, it transpires that records once used to maintain the power of tyrants 'can also be used as the basis to restore justice; . . . individuals turn to the archive seeking . . . closure . . . to know, at last, what happened' to the victims of the regime (Yale, 2015, 346). Despite their many inadequacies as windows on the past, records can provide sufficient knowledge of 'what happened' in times of past oppression to meet many of today's calls for healing, closure or social justice. Records – or, more precisely, the propositions asserted in records – are (almost always) imperfect, but (on many occasions) they can do the job that society asks of them. Those who 'turn to the archive' can benefit from records even when the propositions asserted by record creators have been constructed from a position of oppressive power, or when the records appear to tell a single version of a story that could or should be told in other ways.

Knowing 'what was said'

Opinions about the significance or value of an assertive record can be very varied, and do not always depend solely on judgements about the accuracy or impartiality of the propositions that its creator asserted. Indeed, as a recent example demonstrates, questions about the accuracy of a proposition asserted in a record sometimes appear irrelevant to estimates of the record's significance. On his last day in office as Chief Secretary to the Treasury in 2010, in the midst of a financial crisis, British government minister Liam Byrne left on his desk a letter addressed to his successor. In his letter, Byrne made a simple – if dubious – assertion: 'Dear Chief Secretary, I'm afraid there is no money'. Although this proposition was not strictly accurate, The

National Archives has made efforts to secure this letter and has apparently described it as 'an important political document which must be preserved for the nation' (Sandhu, 2016). The letter can be seen as a symbol of 21st-century Britain's severe financial difficulties, but its significance presumably lies in its representation of a wry act of assertion, rather than in the reliability of the proposition that Byrne's sense of humour led him to assert.

In other circumstances, acts of asserting inaccurate propositions can have significance of a very different kind – especially, perhaps, where an organization's business operations are concerned. Suppose, for example, that a bank's interest rate for a particular type of loan is 10% and a letter has been sent to customers erroneously stating that the rate is 5%. The proposition asserted in the letter was incorrect, but the assertion has been made; if a customer acts on the bank's letter, the bank will need a record of 'what was said' to the customer, in order to regularise its relationship with the customer concerned. Similar needs for records of 'what was said' arise if false statements are made as a result of malicious behaviour rather than simple error. If, for example, it is discovered that hackers have infiltrated the bank's computers and have caused damaging statements to appear in internal databases or on corporate websites, the bank will of course need to see that the damage is rectified; at the same time, if there is a possibility that its staff or customers have relied on the false statements, it will also need to know what statements were made and when and where they appeared.

Propositions concerned with expectations for the future – such as the forecast that 'Factory Z will make 80,000 widgets next year' – can provide further examples of an organization's need to discern 'what was said', regardless of whether the forecasts proved correct. At the time they are made, an organization's information manager may view such propositions as unverifiable – and therefore marginal to the core concerns of 'information management' – but the organization is still likely to need records of them. If unwise decisions about the siting or expansion of a factory, the supply of raw materials or the hiring of staff have been based on ill-judged forecasts of the factory's future output, records of those forecasts and of the deliberations that led to them are likely to be in demand. Even when the propositions that people or computers assert are or turn out to be erroneous, they will have consequences if someone else uses them as a basis for decision-making or other action, and records of 'what was said' will be required.

Records can also be invoked to discover what was – or could have been – known to particular individuals or organizations at particular times in the past. In 2014, an official investigation by British charity executive Peter Wanless and lawyer Richard Whittam set out to examine whether it was possible to reconstruct 'what the [British] Home Office knew and did about cases of organised child abuse' between 1979 and 1999. The aim of their investigation was not to ascertain what episodes of abuse had occurred, or 'whether there was . . . abuse that has yet to be fully uncovered', but to 're-establish . . . what was known to the Home Office at the time'; in their report, published in November 2014, the investigators issued a firm reminder that the ability to discern what government officers could have known at given moments is dependent on the quality of record-keeping (Wanless and Whittam, 2014, 2–8).

Two years later, a much larger and more complex inquiry – into British involvement in Iraq between 2001 and 2009 – again highlighted the crucial role of records, not only in establishing what could have been known at the time, but also in seeking to discover whether political leaders had set out to mislead Parliament and the British public in their statements about the Iraqi situation. While recognising that 'the documentary record cannot . . . provide a comprehensive account of all that happened', the Iraq Inquiry relied heavily on records of government business (Iraq Inquiry, 2016, 9). It used records, including minutes of British Cabinet meetings and summaries of exchanges between the British Prime Minister and the President of the USA, not to uncover an actual state of affairs in Iraq, but to try to reveal what politicians knew and what they said about it at the time. Even when what was said about events, actions or situations was tendentious, inaccurate or incomplete, records still have an important role in documenting the statements that were made.

When we examine assertive records, we often find that different statements have been made about the same event. In the USA, a radical professor gave an account of a 1968 civil disturbance that was substantially different from the description provided by the local mayor (Yeo, 2010, 106); in late-20th-century South Africa, a government report on the killing of a motorist and an account of the same episode by an opponent of the apartheid regime provided very different perspectives (Chandler, 2017, 277). A more complex example, discussed by David Thomas, Simon Fowler and Valerie Johnson (2017, 132–4), is the series of statements made by police officers after 96 people died in a fatal crush at Hillsborough football stadium in Sheffield, England, in 1989. Several years later, it became known that many of the officers' statements had been substantially altered before they were submitted to the official inquiry appointed by the British government. The survival of the original statements alongside the rewritten versions has allowed further investigations in the early 21st century to reveal the extent to which the statements made by individual police officers had been altered, to depict the actions of the police at Hillsborough in a more favourable light (Hillsborough Independent Panel, 2012; Thomas, Fowler and Johnson, 2017, 134). Once again, investigators of a critical event have been able to use records to reveal what was said at particular moments in the past: in this instance, to reveal differing statements that the same individuals made, or were instructed to make, at different times. Three decades after the disaster, the records tell as much – or more – about what was asserted by the police as about what actually happened at Hillsborough on that tragic day in 1989. Despite their inability to report an event 'exactly as it was', assertive records allow us to know what was said in the past, by different observers of the event or by the same observers at different times.

Characteristics of records and information

These examples provide some clear demonstrations of differences between record-keeping concepts and the ideas about timeliness and objective truth that flourish in the world of information management and data management. Assertive records can be valuable even when they do not report events with unquestioned accuracy, and approaches to their management need to reflect this distinction. However, these differences have not always been apparent to records professionals and archival institutions in recent years. Particularly in records management literature, claims have sometimes been made that records and data are 'subject to the same management needs' (Chorley, 2017, 150) and that the same management principles apply to both

(Thurston, 2015, 4). As we have seen, there are many points of contact between records management and the management of information and data, but the aims, conceptual frameworks and practical methods of these disciplines are certainly not identical. In organizational settings, both disciplines play important roles, but failure to acknowledge their differences can give rise to much confusion.

In the UK, recent guidance issued to government agencies by The National Archives (TNA) illustrates many of these issues. In the past decade, TNA's website has been expanded to provide ample advice on 'how to manage . . . information'.[1] Much of the area of the website now devoted to the topic of 'information management' takes its intellectual inspiration, not from archival traditions, but from the modes of thinking that prevail in the information management and data management fields. Addressing 'organisations across the public sector', it offers a set of 'information principles', which include the affirmations that 'information is a valued asset' and that it 'must be accurate, valid, reliable, timely, relevant and complete'. TNA's 'information principles' make no mention of records, but other pages on the site use the words 'information' and 'records' more or less interchangeably and sometimes refer to 'records and information management' as a single composite function.[2] Under the rubric of 'planning . . . for good information management', the site points users, not only to the 'information principles' and a companion set of 'knowledge principles', but also to the 2009 *Code of Practice on the Management of Records*, which was briefly discussed earlier in this chapter. In contrast to many of the more recent additions to TNA's suite of advice, the *Code of Practice* was written from a record-keeping standpoint; it stresses that its focus 'is on records and the systems that contain them', but it also affirms that its recommendations 'can be applied . . . to other information' (Ministry of Justice and The National Archives, 2009, 9). Taken as a whole, TNA's current guidance offers a firm impression that perspectives from the information management and record-keeping disciplines are fully transposable. It rightly emphasises that the two traditions share much common ground, but it gives little indication that they also have crucial points of divergence.

When looking for areas of common ground, it is tempting to draw parallels between the lists of qualities such as accuracy, reliability, consistency, timeliness and completeness – often itemised in information management literature as desirable or necessary characteristics of information – and the ostensibly similar lists of record characteristics that feature in many recent writings about records management. Lists of supposedly desirable or necessary characteristics of records have proliferated over the past two decades. In 2001, for example, the authors of the international standard for records management identified four 'characteristics of a record': authenticity, reliability, integrity and usability (ISO 15489-1: 2001, clause 7.2); in the revised version of the standard published in 2016, these same four qualities were described as 'characteristics of *authoritative* records' (ISO 15489-1: 2016, clause 5.2.2; my italics). A 'reliable record', according to both versions of the standard, 'is one whose contents can be trusted as a full and accurate representation'. An earlier records management standard, published in Australia in 1996, had likewise emphasised the need for 'full and accurate records' and proposed that they must be compliant, adequate, complete, meaningful, comprehensive, authentic and inviolate (AS 4390.3-1996, clause 5.3). In North America, the *Generally Accepted Recordkeeping Principles* published by ARMA International (2009) also included affirmations of the need for measures to ensure the integrity, authenticity and reliability of records. Following the models provided by these published standards, it has become commonplace for professional guidelines and organizational records management policies to include similar (though not always identical) lists of the qualities that an organization's records are supposed to possess.

Superficially, requirements that records should possess qualities such as integrity and reliability appear uncontroversial. In organizational settings, reliance on records underpins the conduct of business and fortifies corporate memory; in the wider society, if archives are to fulfil what Michael Moss and David Thomas (2017, 62) called their 'crucial fiduciary role' in supplying evidence by which governments and powerful individuals can be called to account, it would seem essential that the records held in archival institutions are deemed reliable and trustworthy. Even in an age when notions of truth and factuality are increasingly being questioned, the 'road where nothing is trusted . . . leads inexorably to chaos', as Terry Cook (1995) memorably observed. The difficulty is that qualities such as reliability will always be matters of contention. The authors of records management standards and policies almost invariably present them as if they were objective and absolute qualities – as if it would be possible to determine beyond doubt that 'X is a reliable record' – but many critics would argue that they are subjective ('X seems reliable to me') and often graded ('I believe that X is fairly reliable, but I am not sure whether I can rely on it completely'). Users may judge how far they wish to rely on the propositions that record creators assert, but reliability is not a characteristic open to scientific measurement (MacNeil, 2011, 187–8; Yeo, 2013, 224–5). Universal consensus on what can be considered reliable is unlikely to be achieved.

In records management policies and guidelines written over the past two decades, fullness and accuracy have probably been the characteristics most frequently demanded of records. Although the sense in which a record might be considered 'full and accurate' has rarely been spelt out, government records managers and drafters of record-keeping regulations have often insisted that only full and accurate records of all business would meet organizational require-ments, even when government agencies have found it manifestly impossible to comply with such a demand (Horton, 2011, 178). But the prominence assigned to 'authoritative records' in the 2016 version of the international standard may perhaps lead to a new emphasis on 'authoritativeness' as the overarching label for a record's ostensibly desirable qualities. The 2016 version of the standard also affirms that records without appropriate metadata 'lack the characteristics of authoritative records' and that the authoritativeness of records is supported by managing them in systems that are reliable, secure, compliant and comprehensive (ISO 15489-1: 2016, clauses 5.2.3, 5.3.1).

In recent years, many public-sector organizations have published their records management policies on the world wide web. Most of these policies allude to the characteristics that the organization requires, or claims to require, in its records, but the requirements show considerable variation among different organizations, as might be expected. While some policies adopt the language used in the records management standards and refer to a need for the organization's records to possess qualities such as authenticity and integrity, others borrow from information management models and include – for example – aspirations that records should be timely and up-to-date. Some policies or guidance notes go further in incorporating

The notion of 'authoritative' records has featured in several published standards and manuals for records management since 1996 (AS 4390.3-1996, clause 5.3(vii); ISO 23081-1: 2006, clause 4; State Records Authority of New South Wales, 2003, revised 2007), and was briefly discussed in an article in the *Records Management Journal* in 2001 (Healy, 2001, 138–40). Until the 2010s, however, the 'authoritativeness' of records was a minor theme, accorded little emphasis, in the standards and related literature. The term began to be employed more widely in Australia in the mid-2010s, and came to prominence in the 2016 edition of the ISO 15489 standard, whose authors affirmed that records should possess the characteristics of authenticity, reliability, integrity and usability if they are to be considered authoritative (ISO 15489-1: 2016, clause 5.2.1). This affirmation was intended to remove an ambiguity in the previous edition (ISO 15489-1: 2001), where it appeared uncertain whether the standard was presenting these four characteristics as necessary qualities that all records must possess, or merely as desirable qualities that should be aimed at. For the authors of the 2016 edition of the standard, records that are 'poorly structured' (Findlay, 2016, 25) – or are thought to be deficient in terms of authenticity, reliability, integrity or usability – lack 'authoritativeness', but they are still records.

Although ISO 15489-1: 2016 is 'international' in the sense that it has undergone the drafting and approvals processes of, and is published by, the International Organization for Standardization, it bears the stamp of Australian practice and terminology. The InterPARES project, an international research project based in Canada, defined an 'authoritative record' rather differently; it is 'a record that is considered by the creator to be its official record and is usually subject to procedural controls that are not required for other copies. The identification of authoritative records corresponds to the designation of an office of primary responsibility' (Duranti, 2005, 217).

prescriptions or recommendations seemingly derived from the information management field, and suggest that records management programmes have, or should have, a role in eliminating 'out-of-date' or 'superseded' records or in reducing data duplication.[3] Increasing numbers of publicly available policies explicitly claim to embrace both records management and information or data management, and few attempt to make a clear distinction between them.

Anxieties about records being 'out-of-date' have also occasionally surfaced in other professional literature. In 2013, two British commentators on digital archives wrote of the risk that, when archivists take 'electronic snapshots' of datasets, the snapshots might be 'out of date by the time they are downloaded' (Johnson and Thomas, 2013, 459). In the same year, a contributor to the *Bulletin* of the Information and Records Management Society complained that, in his workplace, he routinely saw 'email archives stretching back eight years' in which '98% of the information' was 'almost certainly . . . out of date, inaccurate and inconsistent', and that 'finding 3-, 5-, 7- or even 10-year old information within . . . archives is sadly not uncommon'. His essay proposed that 'anything older than 30 days' should be 'refreshed' (Stafford, 2013, 11–12).

Policy documents and essays such as these show how far ideas derived from data management and information management have begun to influence the thinking of records professionals in recent years. But they fail to recognise some of the most distinctive aspects of record-keeping. The propositions put forward in records are often inconsistent; to some users, their value may lie in their representation of different perspectives from the past. Equally importantly, records do *not* need to be up-to-date. Organizational enquirers, and users more widely, may need to know what an organization's interest rates, prices, terms of employment or inventory levels were (or were said to be) in earlier times, as well as what they are now; affordances such as this are what records provide. An article suggesting the 'refreshing' of 'anything older than 30 days . . . in archives' may be an exceptional case, but it almost certainly would not have been published by a records management professional body in the days before records managers set out to reinvent themselves as information managers. Its author appears to have confused the organization's need for current 'information' with its need for records of what was said and done in the past.

Similar concerns arise with ideas about 'accuracy', a quality often demanded in writings about records management and information management alike. Records in which statements are made about the world will always be accompanied by possibilities of ambiguity, partiality, inadvertent error or deliberate falsehood. However, the significance we can attribute to records of this kind extends beyond our attempts to assess the accuracy of the statements that are made in them. As Randall Jimerson (2009, 6) observed, when records provide accounts of specific events, they 'do not testify to the accuracy or truth of these accounts . . . but rather to the accuracy of how and when the account was created'. When the authors of records management standards or policies speak of a need for accurate records, or when contributors to professional bulletins lament the 'inaccuracies' they have found in organizational records, they almost always overlook the crucial point that Jimerson astutely identified. 'Accuracy' is a more complex and contestable notion than the literature of organizational record-keeping and information management usually suggests.

Assertive records are a means by which propositions – claims about past, present or future actions or situations – are stated. Over time, such records tell us what has been said, and who said it, regardless of whether we now believe it to be true or false, complete or incomplete, unambiguous or a matter of interpretation. From a record-keeping viewpoint, the information manager's act of revising or 'refreshing' a proposition that is thought to be inaccurate or out-of-date entails

'De-duplication' is another area where record-keeping concerns diverge from those of data management or information management. Data managers and information managers often affirm that duplicate data are an unnecessary overhead that can be reduced by undertaking de-duplication exercises, in which duplicate data are identified and removed. Typically, in an exercise of this kind, the contents of blocks of data are compared and duplicate content is then eliminated.

An understanding of records that takes account of speech act theory leads us to a different view of apparent 'duplication'. Suppose that Sylvie and Paul work for the same employer, and that they have both sent reports to their manager setting out identical sales figures. Despite the similarity of their contents, Paul's report does not represent the same act as Sylvie's. Because the sending of the two reports performed two distinct acts of stating, they can be distinguished as separate records. We can draw a similar conclusion if Sylvie has sent apparently identical memos to two different people (or to the same person on two different occasions). Although both were sent by Sylvie and the propositions she stated appear to be the same, the memos represent different acts with different contexts. From a record-keeping perspective, neither memo should be treated as intrinsically superfluous or as a candidate for a routine de-duplication exercise.

This is not to say that de-duplication has no place in the world of record-keeping; especially in digital environments, where numerous seemingly identical copies proliferate on storage media, removal of duplicates often appears a pragmatic necessity. But cautious records professionals will not assume that similarity of content is always a sufficient basis for elimination decisions. Context must also be taken into account; users of assertive records may wish to verify, not only what propositions were stated, but also who stated them, to whom they were addressed, at what dates and in what circumstances.

asserting a new proposition in its place. It thus creates a new record, with its own contexts of origin and its own requirements for retention and access. The creation of this new record does not necessarily render the 'old' record valueless or eliminate the need to keep it for a further period of time. Where retention laws permit, records professionals will seek to preserve the 'old' record alongside the new if – and for as long as – both are thought to be needed.[4] In business settings, where many users will want access only to records that are deemed current, it should be possible to provide systems or interfaces that make current assertive records readily available while hiding older records from users who do not require them. In historically focused archives, where 'older' and 'newer' records may be of equal interest to many users, systems of this kind are unlikely to be necessary.

'Authoritative' records and the scope of record-keeping

If we look for records that can be considered 'authoritative', speech act concepts can again prove useful, not least because they remind us of, and draw our attention to, records that are not assertive. As John Searle (2010, 11) observed, 'there are lots of speech acts that are not in the business of trying to tell us how things are in the world.' At the moment of record-making, many records are not in the business of trying to tell us what has happened in the world; they are in the business of enabling their makers to perform acts of other kinds. A record in which an order is given, a promise made or a set of rights and responsibilities conferred is intimately involved in the act it represents. Looking at such a record from the standpoint of later users, we can see that it is not simply *a* representation – one of many possible representations that could perhaps tell us about the act concerned – but *the* representation that was used to perform the act. When we want records in which we can have the highest level of confidence, these are the records we should call on.

As long ago as the 17th century, German historians and archivists noted that, although records in which an event was *reported* might not be trustworthy representations of the event, a grant of privileges or a ruler's edict was not open to suspicion in the same way (Eskildsen, 2013, 15). At the start of the 21st century, archival scholars Luciana Duranti, Terry Eastwood and Heather MacNeil (2002, 156) put forward a similar argument in the context of digital records, when they observed that 'a dispositive record . . . constitutes the strongest evidence' of an act. Because 'dispositive' records such as grants of privileges – or wills, or letters appointing or promoting employees – are instruments rather than simply reports of actions, we can use them with considerable confidence to discover or corroborate what was done in the past. If we wish to confirm that Sylvie has been appointed as team leader, an entry made after the event in a register or a database will be a useful starting point, but the letter or e-mail message by which her appointment was enacted will always be more authoritative. Because a grant of privileges or a letter of appointment may sometimes be subject to forgery or tampering, later users may still need to make judgements about its authenticity – about whether it is what it professes to be – but if it appears genuine, they are unlikely to be troubled by a need to assess the accuracy of its substantive content.

These arguments can be applied, not only to the kinds of record that diplomatists call 'dispositive' – *declarative* records, in the terminology of speech act theory – but also to *directive* and *commissive* records. When we encounter a record by which a question was asked, an instruction given or a promise made, we do not encounter a mere description of what was done; we encounter the instrument by which the act of questioning, instructing or promising was performed. Our evaluation of a record in which a promise was made is buttressed by the convention of western society that people who write 'I promise' are necessarily committing themselves to an act of promising. We may assess the promise in terms of whether it was kept or broken, sincere or insincere, but unless we have grounds for thinking that the record has been forged, corrupted or tampered with, we need not doubt that the act of promising took place.

An assertive record, too, has a performative aspect, as we have seen. It is an instrument by which an act of assertion is made. Even if later users doubt or dispute the proposition that was asserted, they can have considerably more confidence that the act of assertion took place. We can say much the same about records such as charts, diagrams or drawings, which employ visual rather than written modes of representation; although a later user may dispute or question the contents of these records, the user can be much more certain that a record of this kind represents the graphical 'assertions' that its creator made about its subject-matter. From a perspective that takes account of speech act theory, we might say that the authoritativeness of these records is best sought in their performative aspect.

Recognition of the performativity of records, and of their roles in social action and interaction, should lead us to acknowledge that we cannot hope to understand records or practise record-keeping simply by adopting concepts and methods from information management or data administration. In one sense, the concerns of record-keeping can be seen as more limited than those of information management. As a team of Dutch archivists recently observed, information managers 'focus on . . . the truthfulness of content', but record-keepers 'do not . . . have a particular job in evaluating the factual truth or falsehood' of the propositions put forward in assertive records; generally speaking, such matters are not for records professionals to decide (Glaudemans, Jonker and Smit, 2017, 297, quoting Eric Ketelaar). In other respects, however, the scope of record-keeping is much wider. It is concerned, not only with assertive records that are thought to be factually accurate and up-to-date, but also with records of disputed assertions and those that may no longer be current; with expressions of ideas, opinions or speculative predictions about the future; with records of questions asked and orders or promises given; and with 'declarative' or 'dispositive' records that have made changes in the world by virtue of their issuance. It seeks to ensure that records are adequately contextualised – that statements about the circumstances of record-making and the histories of records' custody and use are securely preserved – and to protect the integrity of records for as long as their retention is deemed necessary. In the digital 'information culture' of the 21st century, record-keeping retains its distinctive aims.

Endnotes

1 See www.nationalarchives.gov.uk/information-management/
   manage-information.
2 At the time of writing, relevant web pages (all undated, but seemingly
   first published c.2014) included 'Information Management',
   www.nationalarchives.gov.uk/information-management, 'How to
   Manage Your Information', www.nationalarchives.gov.uk/information-
   management/manage-information and 'Information Principles',

www.nationalarchives.gov.uk/information-management/
manage-information/planning/information-principles. Similar comments
could be made about the 'Information Management' pages that have
been added in recent years on the website of the National Archives of
Australia, www.naa.gov.au/information-management.

3 Some examples of policies or guidance notes affirming that records need
to be 'up-to-date' include those published by the British Broadcasting
Corporation, www.bbc.co.uk/guidelines/dq/pdf/media/records_
management_policy_v1.4.pdf, City of Wolverhampton,
www.wolverhampton.gov.uk/CHttpHandler.ashx?id=1523,
Skills Development Scotland, www.skillsdevelopmentscotland.co.uk/
media/32868/sds_records_management_policy_v1_0.pdf,
United Nations Archives and Records Management Section,
https://archives.un.org/sites/archives.un.org/files/uploads/files/
Guidance%20Destroying%20Records.pdf, and Manchester University,
http://documents.manchester.ac.uk/display.aspx?DocID=14916. Others
can easily be found on the internet.

4 In some jurisdictions – particularly where European data protection
legislation is in force – laws may mandate the removal of records
deemed erroneous when these relate to named individuals, but when
personal privacy is not at issue there are rarely any legal constraints on
retaining records for as long as their preservation appears affordable and
necessary.

References

Almeida, M. B. (2013) Revisiting Ontologies: a necessary clarification,
Journal of the American Society for Information Science and Technology, **64** (8),
1682–93.

ARMA International (2009) *Generally Accepted Recordkeeping Principles
(GARP)*, ARMA International.

AS 4390.3-1996 *Records Management, Part 3: strategies*, Standards Australia.

Ball, C. (2011) *A Bit about Data Mapping*,
https://ballinyourcourt.wordpress.com/2011/09/23/a-bit-about-data-
mapping.

Bates, M. J. (2010) Information. In Bates, M. J. and Maack, M. N. (eds),
Encyclopedia of Library and Information Sciences, 3rd edn, vol. 3, CRC Press.

Batini, C., Cappiello, C., Francalanci, C. and Maurino, A. (2009)

Methodologies for Data Quality Assessment and Improvement, *ACM Computing Surveys*, **41** (3), 1–52.

Bearman, D. (1997) The Physical Archives and the Virtual Archives, *Archivum*, **43**, 150–67.

Brown, W. (2002) Charters as Weapons: on the role played by early medieval dispute records in the disputes they record, *Journal of Medieval History*, **28** (3), 227–48.

Carata, L., Akoush, S., Balakrishnan, N., Bytheway, T., Sohan, R., Seltzer, M. and Hopper, A. (2014) A Primer on Provenance, *Communications of the ACM*, **57** (5), 52–60.

Chandler, K. S. (2017) Investigating Original Order with Cybernetics and Community Detection Algorithms, *Archival Science*, **17** (3), 267–83.

Chorley, K. M. (2017) The Challenges Presented to Records Management by Open Government Data in the Public Sector in England, *Records Management Journal*, **27** (2), 149–58.

Clanchy, M. (1977) A Medieval Realist: interpreting the rules at Barnwell Priory, Cambridge. In Attwooll, E. (ed.), *Perspectives in Jurisprudence*, University of Glasgow Press.

Cook, T. (1995) Keeping Our Electronic Memory: approaches for securing computer-generated records, *South African Archives Journal*, **37**, 79–95.

Daston, L. and Galison, P. (1992) The Image of Objectivity, *Representations*, **40**, 81–128.

Dinneen, J. D. and Brauner, C. (2015) Practical and Philosophical Considerations for Defining *Information* as Well-Formed, Meaningful Data in the Information Sciences, *Library Trends*, **63** (3), 378–400.

Dretske, F. (2008) The Metaphysics of Information. In Pichler, A. and Hrachovec, H. (eds), *Wittgenstein and the Philosophy of Information*, Ontos.

Duranti, L. (ed.) (2005) *The Long-Term Preservation of Authentic Electronic Records: findings of the InterPARES project*, Archilab.

Duranti, L., Eastwood, T. and MacNeil, H. (2002) *Preservation of the Integrity of Electronic Records*, Kluwer.

Eskildsen, K. R. (2013) Inventing the Archive: testimony and virtue in modern historiography, *History of the Human Sciences*, **26** (4), 8–26.

Findlay, C. (2016) The Revised International Standard on Records Management: a standard fit for the 21st century, *IRMS Bulletin*, **193**, 22–6.

Foot, S. (2006) Reading Anglo-Saxon Charters: memory, record or story? In Tyler, E. M. and Balzaretti, R. (eds), *Narrative and History in the Early Medieval West*, Brepols.

Fox, C. J. (1983) *Information and Misinformation: an investigation of the notions of information, misinformation, informing, and misinforming*, Greenwood Press.

Frické, M. (2009) The Knowledge Pyramid: a critique of the DIKW hierarchy, *Journal of Information Science*, **35** (2), 131–42.

Furner, J. (2015) Information Science Is Neither, *Library Trends*, **63** (3), 362–77.

Garton Ash, T. (2009) *Facts Are Subversive*, Atlantic Books.

Glaudemans, A., Jonker, R. and Smit, F. (2017) Beyond the Traditional Boundaries of Archival Theory: an interview with Eric Ketelaar. In Smit, F., Glaudemans, A. and Jonker, R. (eds), *Archives in Liquid Times*, Stichting Archiefpublicaties.

Harris, V. (2002) The Archival Sliver: power, memory, and archives in South Africa, *Archival Science*, **2** (1–2), 63–82.

Healy, S. (2001) ISO 15489 Records Management: its development and significance, *Records Management Journal*, **11** (3), 133–42.

Hill, M. W. (2005) *The Impact of Information on Society*, 2nd edn, K. G. Saur.

Hillsborough Independent Panel (2012) *Report of the Hillsborough Independent Panel*, http://hillsborough.independent.gov.uk.

Horton, R. (2011) A Cautionary Tale about Laws, Records, and Technology: making a case for electronic records management. In Cook, T. (ed.), *Controlling the Past: documenting society and institutions*, Society of American Archivists.

Iraq Inquiry (2016) *The Report of the Iraq Inquiry: report of a committee of Privy Counsellors*, vol. 1, www.gov.uk/government/uploads/system/uploads/attachment_data/file/535409/The_Report_of_the_Iraq_Inquiry_-_Volume_I.pdf.

ISO 15489-1: 2001, *Information and Documentation – Records Management. Part 1: general*, International Organization for Standardization.

ISO 15489-1: 2016, *Information and Documentation – Records Management. Part 1: concepts and principles*, International Organization for Standardization.

ISO 23081-1: 2006, *Information and Documentation – Records Management Processes – Metadata for Records. Part 1: principles*, International Organization for Standardization.

Jimerson, R. C. (2009) *Archives Power: memory, accountability, and social justice*, Society of American Archivists.

Johnson, V. and Thomas, D. (2013) Digital Information: 'let a hundred flowers bloom . . .'. Is digital a cultural revolution? In Partner, N. and Foot, S. (eds), *The Sage Handbook of Historical Theory*, Sage.

King, J. C. (2014) What Role Do Propositions Play in Our Theories? In King, J. C., Soames, S. and Speaks, J. (eds), *New Thinking about Propositions*, Oxford University Press.

Lowry, J. and Wamukoya, J. (eds) (2014) *Integrity in Government through Records Management: essays in honour of Anne Thurston*, Ashgate.

MacNeil, H. (2011) Trust and Professional Identity: narratives, counter-narratives and lingering ambiguities, *Archival Science*, **11** (3–4), 175–92.

Ministry of Justice and The National Archives [of the UK] (2009) *Lord Chancellor's Code of Practice on the Management of Records Issued under Section 46 of the Freedom of Information Act 2000*, www.nationalarchives.gov.uk/documents/foi-section-46-code-of-practice.pdf.

Missier, P. (2016) The Lifecycle of Provenance Metadata and its Associated Challenges and Opportunities. In Lemieux, V. L. (ed.), *Building Trust in Information: perspectives on the frontiers of provenance*, Springer.

Moss, M. and Thomas, D. (2017) Overlapping Temporalities: the judge, the historian and the citizen, *Archives*, **134**, 51–66.

Redman, T. C., Fox, C. and Levitin, A. (2012) Data and Data Quality. In Bates, M. J. (ed.), *Understanding Information Retrieval Systems: management, types, and standards*, CRC Press.

Sandhu, S. (2016) David Laws: 'no money left' letter is mine until I die, *iNews*, 2 October, https://inews.co.uk/essentials/news/politics/no-money-left-letter-heart-custody-battle-reveals-david-laws.

Searle, J. R. (2010) *Making the Social World*, Oxford University Press.

Sewell, W. H. (2005) *Logics of History: social theory and social transformation*, University of Chicago Press.

Shepherd, E. and Yeo, G. (2003) *Managing Records: a handbook of principles and practice*, Facet Publishing.

Sidi, K. N. and Hutchinson, D. A. (2013) The Trusted Information Payoff: productivity, performance, and profits, *Information Management*, **47** (5), 35–8.

Soll, J. (2009) *The Information Master: Jean-Baptiste Colbert's secret state intelligence system*, University of Michigan Press.

Stafford, D. (2013) Quality, Accuracy, Consistency (What's Happened to Them?), *IRMS Bulletin*, **173**, 7–13.

State Records Authority of New South Wales (2003, revised 2007) *Strategies for Documenting Government Business: the DIRKS manual*, www.records.nsw.gov.au/recordkeeping/advice/dirks/characteristics-functionality.

Thomas, D., Fowler, S. and Johnson, V. (2017) *The Silence of the Archive*, Facet Publishing.

Thurston, A. (2015) *Managing Records and Information for Transparent, Accountable, and Inclusive Governance in the Digital Environment: lessons from Nordic countries*, World Bank.

Tyler, J. E. (2017) Asset Management the Track towards Quality Documentation, *Records Management Journal*, **27** (3), 302–17.

Wallace, D. (2017) Archives and Social Justice. In MacNeil, H. and Eastwood, T. (eds), *Currents of Archival Thinking*, 2nd edn, Libraries Unlimited.

Wanless, P. and Whittam, R. (2014) *An Independent Review of Two Home Office Commissioned Independent Reviews Looking at Information Held in Connection with Child Abuse from 1979–1999*, www.gov.uk/government/uploads/system/uploads/attachment_data/file/372915/Wanless-Whittam_Review_Report.pdf.

Yale, E. (2015) The History of Archives: the state of the discipline, *Book History*, **18**, 332–59.

Yeo, G. (2010) Representing the Act: records and speech act theory, *Journal of the Society of Archivists*, **31** (2), 95–117.

Yeo, G. (2013) Trust and Context in Cyberspace, *Archives and Records: the Journal of the Archives and Records Association*, **34** (2), 214–34.

Concluding thoughts: record-keeping present and future

This book has presented a view of records and information that is substantially different from the views presented in most contemporary textbooks and published guidelines about organizational record-keeping. It has rejected attempts to characterise records simply as containers of information, or as a special kind of information that demands stricter control. Instead, it has offered an understanding of records as persistent representations through which social acts are performed, and an understanding of information as one of the many affordances that records offer to those who engage with them. In proposing these understandings, it has attempted to put forward fuller arguments than are usually found in writings about records and information, where the views that records contain information, or are a category of information, are often asserted but rarely argued in any depth.

Almost certainly, many readers of this book will find its approach controversial. Some may object to its questioning of the 'information paradigm' for records, in which leading players in records management have made so much investment; others may insist that record-keeping is essentially pragmatic and may doubt the relevance of concepts and ideas borrowed or adapted from academic disciplines such as philosophy and psychology. Practitioners of information management or information governance are unlikely to want to see information as an affordance. In early-21st-century writings addressed to businesses and government agencies, information is almost always presented as an organizational 'asset', a measurable entity that can be managed for an organization's benefit and regulated to ensure security and compliance – a view of information that sees it as a material entity and associates it with some of the central concerns long allied with records management. The arguments in this book, however, rest on a belief that robust professional practice should always be grounded in robust professional theory, and on a conviction that professional theories cannot be wholly self-contained but must draw on other fields of knowledge. The book problematises the notion of information assets and suggests that the 'assets' that are the usual focus of information management – at least when that elusive term is used in the sense discussed in Chapter 7 – can best be understood, not as autonomous information, but as contestable propositions asserted at particular times and in particular contexts.

In the closing years of the 20th century, the records management profession dug itself into a corner by defining records very narrowly and by insisting that records management activities were concerned only with records that fell within this narrow definition. When records managers eventually decided that they needed to look for wider horizons, they did not stop to ask whether their earlier perception of records had been unduly restrictive; instead, as we saw in Chapter 3, they tried to jettison the use of the word 'records' and attempted to reinvent their discipline by speaking only, or very largely, about the management or governance of 'information'. In an information culture – a culture or society where the importance and value of information are largely taken for granted – many records managers saw this as self-evidently the correct route to follow. However, in doing so, they not only failed to embrace the richness of broader concepts of records and record-keeping, but also became entangled in ideas about data quality and sources of truth derived from other professions that had already laid claim to large parts of the information management space. Instead of rediscovering wider understandings of records and examining the role of records in social action, they largely tied themselves to a mode of thinking that emphasised facts and the currency of propositions.

This book has attempted to recover and explore some of these wider understandings of records and their place in society. In suggesting that records are representations that their makers employ to perform social actions and in affirming that records offer users a varied range of affordances, it has argued that record-keeping has distinct conceptual bases and emphases, which differentiate the work of records managers and archivists from the work of information managers. It has also argued that, in many ways, record-keeping has a broader remit than the practices commonly known as information management.

Despite these differences, however, record-keeping and information management undoubtedly have close practical connections, not least because the propositions on which information management normally focuses are inseparable from the recorded acts in which they are asserted. Both disciplines have a critical interest in the same materials, although they tend to perceive them in different ways. In organizational settings, the overlapping concerns of records management and information management need to be reflected in an organization's administrative arrangements; it is almost always beneficial for the two functions to be brought together in a single division or business unit. In organizations where records management and information management functions are administratively separate, the closest collaboration between them will be necessary. Whatever the administrative arrangements, unified policies, strategies and procedures will be essential if conflicts are to be avoided.

At the same time, when agreeing a unified policy, the conceptual and practical differences between the disciplines should not be ignored or trivialised. In particular, different approaches to retention and preservation will almost certainly have to be acknowledged and reconciled. As Chapter 7 noted, information management usually emphasises the immediate destruction, or at least the immediate removal, of propositions (or 'information') perceived as inaccurate or out-of-date; records managers – and archivists – generally recognise needs for longer-term retention of many of the records in which such propositions are stated. The perspectives of the different disciplines should be treated with appropriate respect, and careful negotiation will be needed to reconcile them.

Where issues of longer-term retention are concerned, of course, records managers and archivists do not always speak with one voice. Records managers, especially those employed in corporate businesses, generally seek to impose strict time limits on retention and to destroy records as soon as their agreed retention period has expired. Archivists are usually less interested in time-limited retention periods and are likely to argue for the indefinite preservation of selected records identified through formal appraisal exercises. But conducting appraisal exercises and assessing and applying appropriate retention periods have never been easy, and are likely to become increasingly difficult as the volume of digital records continues to grow. It seems likely that, in future years, records professionals will react to these difficulties by seeking practical methods that facilitate the longer-term retention of records in much larger numbers.

The digital deluge

The challenge that records managers and archivists now face is not (as has often been claimed) the assimilation of record-keeping to information management. Record-keeping remains a distinct practice, and records professionals need to maintain their separate professional identity while working collaboratively with other disciplines. But in the digital era there are other major challenges that will demand an effective response. Among the most urgent are the explosive increase in record creation and the consequent need for records professionals to find ways of securing, preserving and providing access to records on an unprecedented scale. Like records managers and archivists, information managers and data administrators have recognised that challenges arise from working in an age of digital profusion; in most organizations, the current propositions on which information management is mainly focused exist in large and increasing quantities. However, records professionals, as this book has shown, are concerned not only with records asserting current propositions, but also with records of propositions asserted in the past; not only with records asserting propositions deemed true, but also with those deemed doubtful or untrue; not only with records asserting supposed facts, but also with those asserting ideas or opinions; and not only with assertive records, but also with records that are directive, commissive or declarative. In addition, records professionals want to ensure that these records are surrounded by appropriate contextual metadata. They see, or should be encouraged to see, these metadata as 'records of assertions about records', rather than as 'data about data'; all metadata are records in their own right, each with distinctive contexts of creation, custody and use, and thus potentially surrounded by contextual metadata of their own. Management of records demands preservation and access solutions on a much larger scale than the management of current 'information'. When the e-mail systems in a government agency may handle 70 million e-mails each month

(Information Governance Initiative, 2015), and when a business corporation such as Walmart logs more than a million new transactions every hour (Kumar, 2017), records professionals must innovate if they are to keep pace with the seemingly limitless growth in the quantity of records.

At a strategic level, the curatorial tasks needed for record-keeping in coming years will not be unfamiliar. We will continue to need measures to support the capture and maintenance of records and their findability, usability and integrity over time. Governance arrangements will still need to be in place to sustain appropriate levels of privacy and confidentiality and to ensure that records and record-keeping systems are secure and compliant. But traditional hand-crafted approaches will no longer be affordable. Responses to the challenge of managing vast numbers of digital records will require us to develop and apply computational techniques, particularly techniques that will assist in contextualising records and providing access to them, while minimising the need for human descriptive effort.

We will not simply require search tools, as information and data managers sometimes suggest; most such tools rest on assumptions that data are largely autonomous and context-free, and records professionals who acknowledge that records are not autonomous will seek tools that can help to provide overviews of complex aggregations, supply context and uncover patterns and interrelationships among records. For much of this capability, we will probably look to analytic tools enhanced by artificial intelligence (Yeo, forthcoming). Tools designed to identify and retrieve references to activities or events are now emerging, and these include experimental tools for automated detection of speech acts in digital texts (De Felice and Deane, 2012; Morales-Ramirez and Perini, 2014; Vosoughi and Roy, 2016). Although these tools are in their infancy and most will need further development if they are to be used for archival purposes, the technology is maturing rapidly; increased reliance on computational approaches will demand cultural adjustment on the part of records professionals, but will enable the management of digital records on a much larger scale by facilitating tasks that would otherwise be impossibly arduous. Preservation processes will also need to be automated, in whole or part. Digital preservation experts have developed tools to automate basic preservation tasks and have begun to explore new automated techniques that will provide greater scalability (Arora, Esteva and Trelogan, 2014; Open Preservation Foundation, 2016). Some experts foresee a more distant time when digital records will largely manage their own preservation and little human intervention will be required.

It may also be possible to use computational methods to automate appraisal and the assessment of retention periods (Harvey and Thompson, 2010; Information Governance Initiative, 2015, 12–13; Issacs, 2013, 24), but experiments in this area have remained problematic, not least because stakeholders are often unwilling to place their trust in disposal decisions based on algorithmic analysis (Lappin, 2014). Moreover, where digital records are concerned, an emphasis on selectivity is largely out of keeping with the spirit of our times. Technologists and computer users increasingly assume that infinitely expandable storage capacities will render the deletion or destruction of digital resources unnecessary. Proponents of 'big data' argue that new analytic tools work best when materials for analysis are kept in vast quantities; instead of seeking to reduce our holdings to what may seem a manageable size, they say, we should embrace retention on a large scale and perhaps even aim to keep everything. Even when total retention appears unaffordable, or when privacy laws impose limits on what can be retained, future archivists and records managers are still likely to keep many more records than their predecessors. If preservation can be automated, retaining records on a large scale will probably be less resource-intensive, and will certainly be less controversial in the eyes of users, than undertaking costly appraisal exercises to underpin selective destruction. When almost all records are created digitally, appraisal, at least in the forms in which it is currently practised, may be obsolescent (Bailey, 2008, 97–108; Gilliland, 2014, 54–5; Yeo, forthcoming). Where selection procedures continue to be applied, decisions about retention should not rely only on assessments of the content of records or the currency of the propositions set out in them, as information management practice often suggests, but should take account of the contexts in which records were created and the social actions that their makers performed.

Records in an information culture

Records professionals must also contend with the challenges that arise from working in a world that accords constant emphasis to information and data: a world where digital records are created and maintained within what are called information systems and where data underpin policy decisions, marketing initiatives, investment strategies and advances in science and medicine. Information governance and (in Europe) data protection now sit high on many corporate agendas. Data and information, we are told, 'have become the most important assets of the 21st century' (Borek et al., 2014, 4); information 'holds an organization's structure and processes together' (Mancini, 2016, 4); 'every business is now a data business' (Marr, 2017, 1). Pronouncements such as these are indicative of what the title of this book calls an information culture: a culture that valorises conceptions of information and data, while apparently paying little heed to records.

Advocacy of record-keeping is often difficult in contemporary workplaces. Managers and employees commonly think of the resources held on their computers as information, not records. Job descriptions and vacancy advertisements, even for positions ostensibly concerned with record-keeping, often stress the information competencies that the organization expects of its employees. In technological circles, the ubiquity of information is taken for granted, and information systems are sometimes seen as 'first-order objects' (Lemieux, Gormly and Rowledge, 2014, 139) whose nature is thought to be self-evident and immune from deconstruction. Information has a glamour that records and archives appear to lack. The perception of records and record-keeping as 'boring', which social worker Katie Prince (1996) found prevalent among her colleagues in the UK, is unfortunately not limited to the social work field.

Prince's study (discussed in Chapter 6) concluded that, far from being boring, records occupy a 'hot seat' in power relations within and beyond the organizations where they are created and used (Prince, 1996, 180); she advised that we ignore the complexities of record-keeping at our peril (Prince, 1996, x). But records managers and archivists have not found it easy to communicate these complexities to others in the places where they work or in the wider society. It need scarcely be said that very few organizational executives will be interested in concepts of affordance, persistent representation or speech acts; complexities such as these are for records professionals to cogitate, and it often seems best to keep the message as simple as possible when record-keeping missions are explained to others within an organization. In recent years, however, records managers – and, to a lesser extent, archivists – have frequently believed that even the use of the word 'records' can be counter-productive when reaching out to other stakeholders. The language that now carries weight in organizations and in the corridors of power is the language of data and information, and many records professionals undoubtedly feel a political imperative to adopt this language when they seek to convince resource allocators or government policy-makers that they can contribute to the 21st-century digital landscape. It often seems easier, and more effective, to talk about information; talking about records rarely appears to have the same resonance.

Nevertheless, this tactic brings risks of its own. It brings the risk of oversimplification: of making record-keeping needs and concerns perhaps appear less demanding than they are. Other dangers may be more insidious. When records managers choose to speak mainly or only about managing information, organizational executives may assume that specialist record-keeping practices and skills are unnecessary and that records management functions can safely be left to information technologists or other players in the information space. All too often, record-keeping comes to be dismissed as irrelevant in a digital era; it is seen as an unwanted legacy of outdated paper-based systems. As Alan Bell (2014, 229) noted, there are also risks that records professionals themselves will be tempted to reject record-keeping concepts as a relic of 'a lost age of ledgers, hanging files and minute books'. These risks should not be underestimated; professional associations and professional leaders need to campaign vigorously to reassert the continuing importance of records and record-keeping in the digital realm. The pervasiveness of the language of information must not lead archivists and records managers to deny or disregard the centrality of the record to their theory and practice.

Many records professionals are employed in settings where definitions of terms such as 'data', 'information' or 'records' are imposed by law or by organizational policy. The definitions used by drafters of laws and policies are not always well chosen, but even if records professionals feel that such definitions are arbitrary or unhelpful, they are often obliged to use – or at least acknowledge – them in their daily work. However, as Trevor Livelton (1996, 4) observed, although many records professionals find legal definitions of records problematic, they 'need not . . . accept them as the sole foundation of their thinking'. Much the same can be said about the vocabulary of data and information. Archivists and records managers should be able to deploy this vocabulary when they believe it is politically necessary, while remaining aware that it offers an inadequate basis for reflective professional thinking about records and record-keeping.

Even in times of technological change, the keeping of records is not identical to managing information. The record-keeping discipline is concerned, not only with what records say, but also with what they do; not only with propositions, but also with the role of records in the performance of action, and with the varied cultural contexts in which they are created, maintained and used. At the moments of their issuance, records are instruments through which social actions are achieved. For their later users, records are often a source of information, but they also offer other affordances: evidence, memory, ideas and inspirations.

References

Arora, R., Esteva, M. and Trelogan, J. (2014) Leveraging High Performance Computing for Managing Large and Evolving Data Collections, *International Journal of Digital Curation*, **9** (2), 17–27.

Bailey, S. (2008) *Managing the Crowd: rethinking records management for the Web 2.0 world*, Facet Publishing.

Bell, A. R. (2014) Participation vs Principle: does technological change marginalize recordkeeping theory? In Brown, C. (ed.), *Archives and Recordkeeping: theory into practice*, Facet Publishing.

Borek, A., Parlikad, A.K., Webb, J. and Woodall, P. (2014) *Total Information Risk Management*, Morgan Kaufmann.

De Felice, R. and Deane, P. (2012) *Identifying Speech Acts in E-Mails*, www.ets.org/Media/Research/pdf/RR-12-16.pdf.

Gilliland, A. J. (2014) Archival Appraisal: practising on shifting sands. In Brown, C. (ed.), *Archives and Recordkeeping: theory into practice*, Facet Publishing.

Harvey, R. and Thompson, D. (2010) Automating the Appraisal of Digital Materials, *Library Hi Tech*, **28** (2), 313–22.

Information Governance Initiative (2015) *Taking Control of Email: what information governance practitioners can learn from the U.S. federal government's Capstone strategy*, www.opentext.de/file_source/OpenText/en_US/PDF/opentext-igi-capstone-wp-2015-03-04-en.pdf.

Issacs, L. (2013) Rolling the Dice with Predictive Coding: leveraging analytics technology for information governance, *Information Management*, **47** (1), 22–5.

Kumar, V. (2017) *Big Data Facts*, https://analyticsweek.com/content/big-data-facts.

Lappin, J. (2014) *Auto-Classification: will cloud vendors get there first?*, http://community.aiim.org/blogs/james-lappin/2014/06/03/auto-classification—-will-cloud-vendors-get-there-first.

Lemieux, V. L., Gormly, B. and Rowledge, L. (2014) Meeting Big Data Challenges with Visual Analytics: the role of records management, *Records Management Journal*, **24** (2), 122–41.

Livelton, T. (1996) *Archival Theory, Records, and the Public*, Scarecrow.

Mancini, J. (2016) *Infonomics: how do you measure the value of information?*, AIIM.

Marr, B. (2017) *Data Strategy: how to profit from a world of big data, analytics and the Internet of Things*, Kogan Page.

Morales-Ramirez, I. and Perini, A. (2014) *Discovering Speech Acts in Online Discussions: a tool-supported method*, http://ceur-ws.org/Vol-1164/PaperDemo01.pdf.

Open Preservation Foundation (2016) *Introducing E-ARK Specifications and the E-ARK Web Platform*, http://openpreservation.org/event/introducing-e-ark-specifications-and-the-e-ark-web-platform.

Prince, K. (1996) *Boring Records? Communication, speech and writing in social work*, Jessica Kingsley.

Vosoughi, S. and Roy, D. (2016) *Tweet Acts: a speech act classifier for Twitter*, https://arxiv.org/pdf/1605.05156.pdf.

Yeo, G. (forthcoming) Can We Keep Everything? The future of appraisal in a world of digital profusion. In Brown, C. (ed.), *Archival Futures*, Facet Publishing.

Index